Marx, Engels, and Marxisms

Series Editors
Marcello Musto, York University, Toronto, ON, Canada
Terrell Carver, University of Bristol, Bristol, UK

The Marx renaissance is underway on a global scale. Wherever the critique of capitalism re-emerges, there is an intellectual and political demand for new, critical engagements with Marxism. The peer-reviewed series Marx, Engels and Marxisms (edited by Marcello Musto & Terrell Carver, with Babak Amini, Francesca Antonini, Paula Rauhala & Kohei Saito as Assistant Editors) publishes monographs, edited volumes, critical editions, reprints of old texts, as well as translations of books already published in other languages. Our volumes come from a wide range of political perspectives, subject matters, academic disciplines and geographical areas, producing an eclectic and informative collection that appeals to a diverse and international audience. Our main areas of focus include: the oeuvre of Marx and Engels, Marxist authors and traditions of the 19th and 20th centuries, labour and social movements, Marxist analyses of contemporary issues, and reception of Marxism in the world.

More information about this series at
http://www.palgrave.com/gp/series/14812

Gustavo Moura de Cavalcanti Mello ·
Henrique Pereira Braga
Editors

Wealth and Poverty in Contemporary Brazilian Capitalism

palgrave
macmillan

Editors
Gustavo Moura de Cavalcanti Mello
Department of Economics
and Post-Graduate Program in Social Policy
Federal University of Espírito Santo
Vitória, Espírito Santo, Brazil

Henrique Pereira Braga
Department of Economics
Federal University of Espírito Santo
Vitória, Espírito Santo, Brazil

ISSN 2524-7123 ISSN 2524-7131 (electronic)
Marx, Engels, and Marxisms
ISBN 978-3-030-82297-2 ISBN 978-3-030-82298-9 (eBook)
https://doi.org/10.1007/978-3-030-82298-9

Cover credit: Ruy Barbosa Pinto/Getty Images

This Palgrave Macmillan imprint is published by the registered company Springer Nature Switzerland AG
The registered company address is: Gewerbestrasse 11, 6330 Cham, Switzerland

Series Editor's Foreword

Titles Published

1. Terrell Carver & Daniel Blank, *A Political History of the Editions of Marx and Engels's "German Ideology" Manuscripts*, 2014.
2. Terrell Carver & Daniel Blank, *Marx and Engels's "German Ideology" Manuscripts: Presentation and Analysis of the "Feuerbach chapter,"* 2014.
3. Alfonso Maurizio Iacono, *The History and Theory of Fetishism*, 2015.
4. Paresh Chattopadhyay, *Marx's Associated Mode of Production: A Critique of Marxism*, 2016.
5. Domenico Losurdo, *Class Struggle: A Political and Philosophical History*, 2016.
6. Frederick Harry Pitts, *Critiquing Capitalism Today: New Ways to Read Marx*, 2017.
7. Ranabir Samaddar, *Karl Marx and the Postcolonial Age*, 2017.
8. George Comninel, *Alienation and Emancipation in the Work of Karl Marx*, 2018.
9. Jean-Numa Ducange & Razmig Keucheyan (Eds.), *The End of the Democratic State: Nicos Poulantzas, a Marxism for the 21st Century*, 2018.
10. Robert X. Ware, *Marx on Emancipation and Socialist Goals: Retrieving Marx for the Future*, 2018.

11. Xavier LaFrance & Charles Post (Eds.), *Case Studies in the Origins of Capitalism*, 2018.
12. John Gregson, *Marxism, Ethics, and Politics: The Work of Alasdair MacIntyre*, 2018.
13. Vladimir Puzone & Luis Felipe Miguel (Eds.), *The Brazilian Left in the 21st Century: Conflict and Conciliation in Peripheral Capitalism*, 2019.
14. James Muldoon & Gaard Kets (Eds.), *The German Revolution and Political Theory*, 2019.
15. Michael Brie, *Rediscovering Lenin: Dialectics of Revolution and Metaphysics of Domination*, 2019.
16. August H. Nimtz, *Marxism versus Liberalism: Comparative Real-Time Political Analysis*, 2019.
17. Gustavo Moura de Cavalcanti Mello and Mauricio de Souza Sabadini (Eds.), *Financial Speculation and Fictitious Profits: A Marxist Analysis*, 2019.
18. Shaibal Gupta, Marcello Musto & Babak Amini (Eds), *Karl Marx's Life, Ideas, and Influences: A Critical Examination on the Bicentenary*, 2019.
19. Igor Shoikhedbrod, *Revisiting Marx's Critique of Liberalism: Rethinking Justice, Legality, and Rights*, 2019.
20. Juan Pablo Rodríguez, *Resisting Neoliberal Capitalism in Chile: The Possibility of Social Critique*, 2019.
21. Kaan Kangal, *Friedrich Engels and the Dialectics of Nature*, 2020.
22. Victor Wallis, *Socialist Practice: Histories and Theories*, 2020.
23. Alfonso Maurizio Iacono, *The Bourgeois and the Savage: A Marxian Critique of the Image of the Isolated Individual in Defoe, Turgot and Smith*, 2020.
24. Terrell Carver, *Engels before Marx*, 2020.
25. Jean-Numa Ducange, *Jules Guesde: The Birth of Socialism and Marxism in France*, 2020.
26. Antonio Oliva, Ivan Novara & Angel Oliva (Eds.), *Marx and Contemporary Critical Theory: The Philosophy of Real Abstraction*, 2020.
27. Francesco Biagi, *Henri Lefebvre's Critical Theory of Space*, 2020.
28. Stefano Petrucciani, *The Ideas of Karl Marx: A Critical Introduction*, 2020.
29. Terrell Carver, *The Life and Thought of Friedrich Engels, 30th Anniversary Edition*, 2020.

30. Giuseppe Vacca, *Alternative Modernities: Antonio Gramsci's Twentieth Century*, 2020.
31. Kevin B. Anderson, Kieran Durkin & Heather Brown (Eds.), *Raya Dunayevskaya's Intersectional Marxism: Race, Gender, and the Dialectics of Liberation*, 2020.
32. Marco Di Maggio, *The Rise and Fall of Communist Parties in France and Italy*, 2020.
33. Ryuji Sasaki, *A New Introduction to Karl Marx: New Materialism, Critique of Political Economy, and the Concept of Metabolism*, 2020.
34. Kohei Saito (Ed.), *Reexamining Engels's Legacy in the 21st Century*, 2021.
35. Paresh Chattopadhyay, *Socialism in Marx's Capital: Towards a Dealienated World*, 2021.
36. Marcello Musto, *Karl Marx's Writings on Alienation*, 2021.
37. Michael Brie & Jörn Schütrumpf, *Rosa Luxemburg: A Revolutionary Marxist at the Limits of Marxism*, 2021.
38. Stefano Petrucciani, *Theodor W. Adorno's Philosophy, Society, and Aesthetics*, 2021.
39. Miguel Vedda, *Siegfried Kracauer, or, The Allegories of Improvisation: Critical Studies*, 2021.
40. Ronaldo Munck, *Rethinking Development: Marxist Perspectives*, 2021.
41. Jean-Numa Ducange & Elisa Marcobelli (Eds.), *Selected Writings of Jean Jaurès: On Socialism, Pacifism and Marxism*, 2021.
42. Elisa Marcobelli, *Internationalism Toward Diplomatic Crisis: The Second International and French, German and Italian Socialists*, 2021.
43. James Steinhoff, *Automation and Autonomy: Labour, Capital and Machines in the Artificial Intelligence Industry*, 2021.
44. Juan Dal Maso, *Hegemony and Class Struggle: Trotsky, Gramsci and Marxism*, 2021.

Titles Forthcoming

Adriana Petra, *Intellectuals and Communist Culture: Itineraries, Problems and Debates in Post-war Argentina*

Agon Hamza, *Slavoj Žižek and the Reconstruction of Marxism*

Alexandros Chrysis, *The Marx of Communism: Setting Limits in the Realm of Communism*
Alexis Cukier, *Democratic Work: Radical Democracy and the Future of Labour*
Attila Melegh, *Anti-Migrant Populism in Eastern Europe and Hungary: A Marxist Analysis*
Bertel Nygaard, *Marxism, Labor Movements, and Historiography*
Christoph Henning, *Theories of Alienation: From Rousseau to the Present*
Daniel Egan, *Capitalism, War, and Revolution: A Marxist Analysis*
David Norman Smith, *Self-Emancipation: Marx's Unfinished Theory of the Working Class*
Dong-Min Rieu, *A Mathematical Approach to Marxian Value Theory: Time, Money, and Labor Productivity*
Emanuela Conversano, *Capital from Afar: Anthropology and Critique of Political Economy in the Late Marx*
Éric Aunoble, *French Views on the Russian Revolution*
Fabio Perocco (Ed.), *Racism in and for the Welfare State*
Francesca Antonini, *Reassessing Marx's Eighteenth Brumaire: Dictatorship, State, and Revolution*
Genevieve Ritchie, Sara Carpenter & Shahrzad Mojab (Eds.), *Marxism and Migration*
George C. Comninel, *The Feudal Foundations of Modern Europe*
Gianfranco Ragona & Monica Quirico, *Frontier Socialism: Self-organisation and Anti-capitalism*
Jeong Seongjin, *Korean Capitalism in the 21st Century: Marxist Analysis and Alternatives*
João Antonio de Paula, Huga da Gama Cerqueira, Eduardo da Motta e Albuquer & Leonardo de Deus, *Marxian Economics for the 21st Century: Revaluating Marx's Critique of Political Economy*
Joe Collins, *Applying Marx's Capital to the 21st century*
José Ricardo Villanueva Lira, *Marxism and the Origins of International Relations*
Kei Ehara (Ed.), *Japanese Discourse on the Marxian Theory of Finance*
Kolja Lindner, *Marx, Marxism and the Question of Eurocentrism*
Lelio Demichelis, *Marx, Alienation and Techno-capitalism*
Levy del Aguila Marchena, *Communism, Political Power and Personal Freedom in Marx*
Marcello Mustè, *Marxism and Philosophy of Praxis: An Italian Perspective from Labriola to Gramsci*

Marcello Musto, *Rethinking Alternatives with Marx*
Marcelo Badaró, *The Working Class from Marx to Our Times*
Marcos Del Roio, *Gramsci and the Emancipation of the Subaltern Classes*
Marie-Cecile Bouju, *A Political History of the Publishing Houses of the French Communist Party*
Martin Cortés, *Marxism, Time and Politics: On the Autonomy of the Political*
Mauro Buccheri, *Radical Humanism for the Left: The Quest for Meaning in Late Capitalism*
Paolo Favilli, *Historiography and Marxism: Innovations in Mid-Century Italy*
Patrizia Dogliani, *A Political History of the International Union of Socialist Youth*
Paul Raekstad, *Karl Marx's Realist Critique of Capitalism: Freedom, Alienation, and Socialism*
Peter McMylor, Graeme Kirkpatrick & Simin Fadaee (Eds.), *Marxism, Religion, and Emancipatory Politics*
Rémy Herrera, *Confronting Mainstream Economics to Overcome Capitalism*
Salvatore Prinzi, *Representation, Expression, and Institution: The Philosophy of Merleau-Ponty and Castoriadis*
Satoshi Matsui, *Normative Theories of Liberalism and Socialism: Marxist Analysis of Values*
Shannon Brincat, *Dialectical Dialogues in Contemporary World Politics: A Meeting of Traditions in Global Comparative Philosophy*
Spencer A. Leonard, *Marx, the India Question, and the Crisis of Cosmopolitanism*
Stephen Maher, *Corporate Capitalism and the Integral State: General Electric and a Century of American Power*
Tamás Krausz, Eszter Bartha (Eds.), *Socialist Experiences in Eastern Europe: A Hungarian Perspective*
Terrell Carver, Smail Rapic (Eds.), *Friedrich Engels for the 21st Century: Perspectives and Problems*
Thomas Kemple, *Capital after Classical Sociology: The Faustian Lives of Social Theory*
Tomonaga Tairako, *A New Perspective on Marx's Philosophy and Political Economy*
Tsuyoshi Yuki, *Socialism, Markets and the Critique of Money: The Theory of "Labour Note"*

V Geetha, *Bhimrao Ramji Ambedkar and the Question of Socialism in India*
Vesa Oittinen, *Marx's Russian Moment*
Vincenzo Mele, *City and Modernity in George Simmel and Walter Benjamin: Fragments of Metropolis*
Xavier Vigna, *A Political History of Factories in France: The Workers' Insubordination of 1968*
Zhi Li, *The Concept of the Individual in the Thought of Karl Marx*

Foreword: Agenda for "Emerging" Countries

The book *Wealth and Poverty in Contemporary Brazilian Capitalism* offers an excellent Marxist analysis of facets of contemporary capitalism based on the Brazilian reality of increasing polarization and impoverization in the era of neo-liberalism and dictation of social and economic policies by the far right in the government. This analysis shares many insights with a collaborative research project that started in 2011 between Brazil and China.

Since 2011, from China, our research team has closely collaborated with a research team in Brazil when we initiated a comparative study of seven emerging countries (E7), which included Brazil, China, India, Indonesia, South Africa, Turkey and Venezuela. The seven countries were chosen because they were at the time portrayed by mainstream media as moving from the periphery to the core. Scholar activists from the seven countries set up national research teams. Prof Paulo Nakatani was leader of the Brazilian research team, with members including Prof Rogerio Naques Faleiros, Prof Neide César Vargas, Dr Paula Nabuco, Prof Renata Couto Moreira, Prof Helder Gomes and Prof Adriana Ilha da Silva. The first phase of the comparative study ended in 2012 with a report and an academic conference in Beijing. The research output of the second phase was a 458-page book *Globalization and National Competitions: A Comparative Study of Seven Emerging Countries* (in Chinese) published in January 2021. Over 75,000 copies were sold in the first five months. This is an indication of the interest among Chinese readership in an intellectual position that interrogates neo-liberalism and capitalism, and assumes a position for the subaltern and the Global South.

The cooperation among E7 research teams, particularly between Brazilian and Chinese researchers, has continued in the last ten years, not only in producing research output, but also in exchange programmes such as a series of field trips in Brazil and China, visiting scholar programmes, CAPES-PRINT research projects and South-South Forums on Sustainability (2011- the present). Based largely on a Marxist critique of colonialism and financial capitalism, we endeavour to explore alternative thoughts and theorize practices on the ground.

In their being thrust into the "modern" times, China and Brazil were both invaded and plundered by the imperialist powers. Transformation into a modern state for China was, however, facilitated by a bureaucratic structure and a cultural identification since its unification under the Qin Dynasty in 221 b.c. With some extent of historical continuity and a continental scale, the 1949 revolution introduced reforms, the most prominent being the land reform. Despite all the ups and downs as elaborated in Wen Tiejun's *Ten Crises: The Political Economy of China's Development (1949–2020)*,[1] China has had the material and human conditions to develop its economy. Its "rise" cannot be tolerated by the imperialist powers and it is now suffering from sanctions by the USA, economic downturn, financialization trap and ecological degradation, though it has so far had the COVID-19 pandemic under control.

Like Brazil and countries on the periphery, China has taken the path of development and for a decade in the 1960s, China was effectively excluded from the two major camps: the Soviet camp and the US camp. During this period, China was obliged to seek industrialization within its own borders and had somehow been compelled to *delinking*, as Samir Amin called it. After the normalization of foreign relations in the early 1970s, China once again brought in foreign capital, and by the late 1990s, China had by and large been integrated into globalization, importing raw materials, exporting manufactured goods and services, joining financialization and beginning to extend its industrial and services production

[1] Wen Tiejun's *Ten Crises: The Political Economy of China's Development (1949–2020)*, Palgrave McMillian, June 2021. Also see Wen Tiejun's E-Lectures produced by the Global University for Sustainability, https://our-global-u.org/oguorg/en/series-no-5-chinas-real-experiences-professor-wen-tiejun-on-ten-cyclical-economic-crises-in-china-1949-2016/.

capacities through the Belt and Road Initiative. After China became explicitly targeted by the USA as the primary economic and technological rival, coupled with the global crises of the pandemic, even though China may not be prone to seeking delinking (which is for the most part forced on China rather than being a consciously pursued strategy), the situation may warrant moves towards delinking and searching for alternatives.

China's trajectory is an example of the plight and struggles of the Global South. On the one hand, 500 years of global history of plunder and genocide have today continued in a mutated form. The contemporary neo-fascist trend of financial capitalism is reliant on military aggression. We have witnessed a cataclysmic shift of the structure of the global debt crisis at the turn of the millennium. Bad debt has now shifted from peripheral countries comprising 80% of the world population to core countries with 20% of the world population. Indeed, we have come to see that the more modernized a core country, the higher its total public and private debts. The so-called modernization as modelled after the Global North is not the model template to be copied by humanity. The elites of the indebted core countries of the twenty-first century are rejecting the very institutions and schemes that the Global North, as creditors in the late twentieth century, had imposed on countries of the Global South. This follows the Global North elites' financial-sector bailouts, which created the vast bulk of their countries' public debts. Instead of overhauling the system and reducing debts, governments in the Global North have excessively increased their monetary base and issued government bonds which run the risk of aggravating global inflation, thus further externalizing the cost of the crisis to the Global South.

The current global financial crisis is in essence a consequence of the transition throughout the 1990s from the Cold War bipolar geo-politics between USA and USSR, to a unipolar hegemony of the USA, with the ensuing new global geopolitical strategy based on currency supremacy and its regional circulation aimed at further advancing the hegemonic bloc's economic interests. The current deadlock is further aggravated by the bankruptcy of the ethical and cultural foundation that has guided this advancement, the failure of education as cultural medium and degeneration of the intellectuals as agents for local cultural heritage. Speculative and exploitative financial practices, buttressed by rampant greed, insatiable desire for power and control, vanity and arrogance, individualism and selfishness, consumerism and materialism, have resulted not only in the destruction of livelihoods and environments, but also the deterioration of the values that bind one people to other peoples, one community to other communities: defending the commons, and respect and love for fellow human beings. Thus, what the governments and corporations of the Global North have presented to the rest of the world as a financial crisis, taken in its totality, is de facto a crisis of civilization.

For resource countries like Brazil, Venezuela and South Africa, which mainly rely on the export of raw materials for their fiscal revenues and social welfare policies, momentary prosperity is difficult to sustain in the long term. On the one hand, the core countries and transnational corporations that have appropriated the resources would not give up their privileges, and even leftist parties in the periphery countries, when in power, fail to implement radical land reform and nationalization of key resource sectors.

However, under extreme hardship, the people of the Global South have not given up their dignity by submitting to the world order defended by the 1% elite. We see the people organizing themselves, rebuilding their communities and from bottom up establishing people's sovereignty over land, industry and livelihood. In India and Indonesia, countries with a large population and a majority of peasants, the people have risen in struggles. Whereas from 1995 to 2015, 310,000 farmers committed suicide in India, there has been a turn for collective action: despite the pandemic, from 26 November 2020, over 300,000 farmers have organized and marched into the capital New Delhi in farm vehicles and tractors to protest against the government's adoption of three agricultural laws that favour big business. The protest has persisted for over six months. In October 2020, Indonesian labourers took to the streets to protest against the government's passing of laws which allowed capitalist oppression of the working class. Similar people's mobilizations have been taking place in Brazil to protest the neo-liberal policies of the Bolsonaro government. A wave of resistance is sweeping across the Global South.

In the same vein, in China, since 2000, we have been engaged in the new rural reconstruction movement to organize training courses on ecological agriculture and cooperatives for peasants, facilitate university students in supporting and learning from rural communities, promote literature and art of migrant workers, mobilize urban people to go to the countryside, urge for urban-rural integration and initiate cultural movements for loving and returning to home villages.

As we believe it is paramount for social movements to be learning from each other, since 2011, we have organized the South South Forum on Sustainability (SSFS). Taking note of the consequences and effects on nature and on peoples from the Global South in this implosion of capitalism, the SSFS has brought together feminists, scholars, peace activists, community workers, food producers and rural regeneration promoters to review, articulate and debate theories and practices in transformative and collective actions called forth by the crisis of capitalism affecting the ecological, the social, the political and the economic. Drawing upon the experiences of community governance in Asia, Africa and Latin America, SSFS is a platform for dialogues and exchanges among the grassroots on resistance practices in the production, dissemination and use of knowledge as instruments of problematization and self-organization, as well as interactions among thinkers in search of paradigms for peace, justice and a new socialism.

The E7 comparative study and the SSFSs set out to build South-South understanding and collaboration and promote sustainable practices and diverse ecological civilizations. One of the mottos we work on is the "Three Ss for Sustainability" based on sovereignty, solidarity and security. Globally, massive numbers of grassroots movements, people's organizations, indigenous peoples, women, ethnic minorities and marginalized groups in the Global South have dared to resist domination and exploitation and create livelihood alternatives and self-managed social systems in their own contexts. There is much to learn from localized, sustainable practices in people's daily lives.

Promoting a critical perspective from the Global South, the book *Wealth and Poverty in Contemporary Brazilian Capitalism*, edited by Prof Gustavo Moura de Cavalcanti Mello and Prof Henrique Pereira Braga, is an important contribution to a Marxist critique of how barbaric finance capital has impacted on Brazilian society and nature. On the basis of this critique, movements for people's sovereignty, solidarity and security can be defined and pursued. As the motto of the World Social Forum goes,

Another World is Possible, and it is with hope and audacity that the battles for another possible world are fought.

Lau Kin Chi
Global University for Sustainability
Lingnan University
Hong Kong, China

Acknowledgements

"This study was written by some members of the Capes-PRINT Internationalization Project from UFES University, and was financed in part by the Coordination for the Improvement of Higher Education Personnel—Brazil (CAPES)—Finance Code 001".

About this Book

This book seeks to contribute to the debate of the current tendencies of capital accumulation at the global scale. Starting from the fact that, in the early twenty-first century, humanity is facing an unusual situation. It has broadened its "control" over nature and, through these advances, built a society whose output can guarantee a dignified life for all human beings. This would be a laudable achievement if it were not for the accompanying demerits. For instance: the growth of all kinds of violence; the persistence of hunger; the debasement of work.

Departing from Brazil as conceived as a symbiotic part of global capitalism, the first three chapters of this book theorize these three phenomena by relating them with capital accumulation. In the last three ones, the authors deal with the tendencies associated with the reproduction of wealth: financialization, digital currencies and the structural crises of capital.

Contents

Editors and Contributors

About the Editors

Mello, Gustavo Moura de Cavalcanti has a Ph.D. and M.Sc. in Sociology at the School of Philosophy, Literature, and Human Sciences at the University of São Paulo (USP), Brazil. He also has BSc Economics from the Economics and Business Administration School at the University of São Paulo (USP). He was a Post-doctorate Research Fellow within the Department of Sociology of IFCHUnicamp, University of Campinas. He was a Visiting Fellow at Goldsmiths College, University of London, in 2020. Currently, he is an Assistant Professor in the Department of Economics and member of the post-graduate program in Social Policy at the Federal University of Espirito Santo, Brazil. He was also Director of the Brazilian Society of Economic Policy (SEP) from 2018 to 2020 and Editor of Journal from Brazilian Society of Political Economy since june 2020. He is a member of the working group "Crises and the World Economy" of the Latin-American and Caribbean Social Science Council (CLACSO) and "Studies on World Money and Financialization" at the Federal University of Espirito Santo. His research is mainly focused on contemporary capitalism, financial crises, state theory and political economy.

Henrique Pereira Braga is an Adjunct Professor of Economics Department at Federal University of Espirito Santo (UFES). He has Bachelor's at Economics from Fluminense Federal University (2008), Master's at Economics from State University of Campinas (2011) and Ph.D.'s at Economics from State University of Campinas (2016). He was Former Editor of Journal from Brazilian Society of Political Economy (Revista da SEP) from May 2019 to August 2020. He is Director of Brazilian Society of Political Economy from 2020 to 2022. He is a member of the working group "Studies in Economic Thought and Social Theories" at the Federal University of Espirito Santo and Associate Member of the working group "Interdisciplinary Center for Studies and Research on Marx and Marxism" at the Fluminense Federal University.His research is mainly focused on economic theories, social theories and contemporary capitalism.

Contributors

Henrique Pereira Braga Department of Economics, Federal University of Espírito Santo, Vitória, Brazil

Ana Paula Colombi Department of Economics and Post-Graduate Program in Social Policy, Federal University of Espírito Santo, Vitória, Brazil

Mauricio de Souza Sabadini Department of Economics and Post-Graduate Program in Social Policy, Federal University of Espírito Santo, Vitória, Brazil

Helder Gomes SCM, Vitória, Brazil

Gustavo Moura de Cavalcanti Mello Department of Economics and Post-Graduate Program in Social Policy, Federal University of Espírito Santo, Vitória, Brazil

Lívia de Cássia Godoi Moraes Department of Social Science and Post-Graduate Program in Social Policy, Federal University of Espírito Santo, Vitória, Brazil

Paulo Nakatani Department of Economics and Post-Graduate Program in Social Policy, Federal University of Espírito Santo, Vitória, Brazil

Adriano Lopes Almeida Teixeira Department of Economics and Post-Graduate Program in Social Policy, University of Espírito Santo, Vitória, Brazil

Erebus Wong Lingnan University, Hong Kong, China

List of Figures

List of Tables

CHAPTER 1

Introduction

Gustavo Moura de Cavalcanti Mello and Henrique Pereira Braga

For decades authors of different critical theoretical persuasions, and especially those in the field of Marxian criticism of political economy, have been analysing and found that the dynamics of capital accumulation at the global scale have become increasingly extreme. In recent years, Wolfgang Strobeck, Shoshana Zuboff, Saskia Sassen, Giorgio Agamben, Achille Mbembe, etc. have produced widely circulated works on themes such as the absolute limits of capitalism, the capitalism of security, the capitalism of exclusion and expulsion, states of exception, necropolitics and the production of world civil war. In the more properly Marxist camp, the propositions of Marx's, Engels, Rosa Luxemburg, Henry Grosmann, Paul Matick, Ernest Mandel, among others, have been invoked amid debates on the collapse of capitalism, which mobilises notions such as: "obsolete

G. M. de C. Mello (✉) · H. P. Braga
Department of Economics, Federal University of Espírito Santo, Vitória, Brazil
e-mail: gustavo.m.mello@ufes.br

H. P. Braga
e-mail: henrique.p.braga@ufes.br

G. M. de C. Mello and H. P. Braga (eds.), *Wealth and Poverty in Contemporary Brazilian Capitalism*, Marx, Engels, and Marxisms,
https://doi.org/10.1007/978-3-030-82298-9_1

capitalism" (Samir Amin); the "crisis of value" (Robert Kurz); the "structural crisis of capital" (István Mészaros); the "civilizing crisis" (François Chesnais); "zombie capitalism" (Chris Harman); to name just a few.

"Wealth and Poverty in Contemporary Brazilian Capitalism" seeks to contribute to this debate by starting from the fact that, in the early twenty-first century, humanity is facing an unusual situation. It has broadened its "control" over nature and, through these advances, built a society whose output is capable of guaranteeing a dignified life for all human beings, as it produces an abundance of material and cultural accumulation. This would be a laudable achievement if it were not for the accompanying demerits: the growth of all kinds of violence; the persistence of hunger; the proliferation of slums and poor housing; the debasement of work and increased exploitation and dispossession; environmental degradation; a pandemic of psychological disorders; wars; large numbers of refugees and prisoners; racism, misogyny, xenophobia, intolerance; political and religious fanaticism; decline in the provision of public services etc. The growth and affirmation of fascist or neo-fascist tendencies across a variety of diverse countries is an index of this process and introduces perverse perspectives that require exhaustive consideration, and that must be fought with all effort, including at the theoretical level.

To confront this challenge, the book brings together a group of researchers versed in economics and in branches of the social sciences, all intertwined through collaboration within the Internationalisation Programme, "Urban Environment for Today and Tomorrow" organised by the University of Espírito Santo and financed by CAPES—Coordenação de Aperfeiçoamento de Pessoal de Nível Superior. Although intended to deepen the comprehensive critical understanding of contemporary capitalism, the different chapters will have the Brazilian reality at their centre. Capitalism is, after all, a fragmentary and contradictory totality, which has the world market as its stage, and which is organised in a hierarchical and complex manner, based on reciprocal conditioning between its components. The chapters have Brazil as their point of departure, but they are not restricted to this *locus* as if it were some exotic episode of global capitalism, we acknowledge that this *locus* is a symbiotic part of global capitalism.

Starting from the critique of political economy as social theory, and from the analysis of the specific form of wealth in this society, we understand that, far from being a detour or aberration, the current tendency toward the brutalisation of social relations is inherent in Sisyphus's capital form and value appreciation. An historic turning point within the proposed analysis was the stagflation crisis of the 1970's, an expression of post-World War II capital over-accumulation, which has been repeated since then in new configurations and in multiplying crises. The contemporary forms of manifestation of the over-accumulation of capital will serve as the fulcrum for a set of analyses that will run through the book, within which it is worth mentioning: (1) investigation into the prominence and dominance acquired by the fictitious and rentier forms of capital; (2) study of the transformations of, and the role assumed by, the State in recent decades as it has become increasingly active while simultaneously becoming more subordinate to the dictates of highly centralised and trans-national economic conglomerates; (3) investigation into the impact of the financialisation of capital accumulation within the "world of work".

Throughout, we maintain the Brazilian reality as a fundamental empirical reference point because, despite many promises of "progress" and "development" and changes in the way it inserts itself into the world market (from being a primary-exporting colony to that of a country subject to different relationships of dependency, characterised by the submission of a significant portion of its population to brutal relations of exploitation and plunder), Brazil stands out as one of the largest and most unequal economies on the planet, exhibiting both ostentation and poverty in a context of chronic civil (class) war that has been intensifying over recent years.

Considering, as did Marx, that the peripheral countries of the capitalist system reveal the hidden truths of the central countries, then this makes Brazil a rich source of knowledge for this research. Another point of interest should be mentioned: history shows that certain economic and social management experiments carried out in peripheral countries have a potential for generalisation. In this sense, the unusual link between ultraliberalism and the far right, which materialised with the election of Jair Bolsonaro, must be carefully considered.

This reflection on global capitalism from the Brazilian perspective begins with the Chapter 2, which demonstrates that the Marxian concept of barbarism—in short, the use of direct and indirect violence as a foundation of social relations contemporary—is related to the increasing reduction of people and the environment to mere means of realising the relentless drive for capital accumulation. To illustrate the argument, recent Brazilian phenomena are considered, which, in the wake of the 2014 economic crisis, point to the expansion of the militarised control of urban territories by paramilitary forces (militia), mass incarceration and the acceleration of the expulsion of indigenous populations to allow mineral extraction, agriculture and land speculation.

In Chapter 3, the author proposes to destabilise the usual concepts of wealth and poverty that guide debates on income inequality and wealth. Inspired by Marx, it argues that wealth and poverty are, in capitalism, two faces of the same coin, so that the process of production and reproduction of capitalist wealth engenders the impoverishment of human beings, by reinforcing heteronomous forms of relationship. In this regard, the Brazilian case is enlightening: its alarming statistics on the distribution of income and wealth, and despite their wild underestimation, capture a picture of material abundance amid heteronomy. The latter is also expressed in the autocratic form of organisation of its institutions, whose resilience in perpetuating poverty is envied by the global ruling classes.

In addition to the distribution of income and wealth, work and gender relations are also illustrative of heteronomy. This is the theme of the Chapter 4, which approaches the issue of how the institutionalisation of fiscal austerity and the attacks on the hard-won historical rights of Brazilian workers, are the manifestation the universal movement of the capitalist mode of production at the periphery. This accumulation of capital through violence has shades of marked barbarism toward women.

An examination of the financialisation process, which runs through the social processes of income and wealth distribution, and through work and gender relations, is developed in Chapter 5, on the category of "fictitious profits". For the authors, this category is a conceptual contribution capable of characterising contemporary capitalism, explaining its "survival" after the 1970 crisis and reinforcing increasingly vile relations between human beings. In this regard, the Brazilian case is illustrative of how the financialisation process, which been taking place since the last decades of the last century, has contributed to making Brazil a profitable space for accumulation, even allowing for its deindustrialisation and the expansion of extraction and agricultural activities.

The development of the money form is fundamental to understanding the financialisation process as it is one of the abstractions central to the functioning of the regime of capitalist domination. This subject is addressed in Chapter 6. Inspired by the debate around new digital currencies and their relationship to fictitious accumulation, the long decline of the dollar as world currency and the accelerated growth of China, the authors analyse some aspects of the disputes for hegemony in the interstate system and the place played by Brazil in this context.

To close the reflections on global capitalism from the Brazilian perspective, Chapter 7, revisits the historical processes that have, since the 1970s, resulted in the unique trajectory of the Brazilian economy, captured, as it is, in an organised global speculative trap. This approach considers the structural consequences of this subordination process as an inheritance of the Old Colonial System in at least four basic dimensions: (1) land ownership structure, as a founding element of the decolonisation movement; (2) the late, incomplete, technologically discontinuous and specialised inclusion of domestic production into the imperialist industrialisation process; (3) the requirement for a diversified set of production relations which combine the expansion of wage control with the maintenance, on a large scale, of archaic forms of domination; (4) the reproduction of an extremely authoritarian police regime as a requirement for the continuation of the subaltern logic of transferring wealth abroad, which, in addition to disputes over the marginal portions of wealth left by the imperialist forces, now shifts the focus to the task to participating internationally in the generation of fictitious wealth, particularly through public debt management.

With this set of critical reflections of contemporary capitalism, with Brazil as its starting point, the readings presented here endorse and update the Marxian analysis of the nature of civic-barbarity proper to capitalist development, in which human beings are nothing but disposable cogs in the capital accumulation process. If such readings are correct, the analysis of contemporary Brazilian capitalism allows us to understand the current trend for the radicalisation of the predatory and excessive character of capital accumulation, which are tending to become universal, from a more properly economic and political perspective. If the realities at the periphery shed light on how the world is becoming more barbaric, they also illuminate the possible forms of resistance and the construction of alternative social relations, which can only emerge from a denial of the totalitarian domination of the capital form.

CHAPTER 2

In the Bowels of Capital: On Modern Barbarism

Gustavo Moura de Cavalcanti Mello

Introduction: The Apologetics of Unilateralism and Dualism

Over recent decades, iron, fire, and a large dose of media narcotisation have spread the perception, to a greater or lesser degree consciously, that the capitalist mode of production is the ultimate destiny of human existence. At the ideological level, two opposing attitudes have emerged which deserve highlighting: the triumphalism that arose from the collapse of the Soviet bloc, and a fatalism proper to the self-fulfilling prophecy of Margaret Thatcher, and many others, that, "there is no alternative". Those who praise the recent achievements of "human ingenuity" are looking forward to a bright future for humanity, which, after its many successes, is surely on the verge of extirpating poverty from the world.[1] Those against, only have ears for the trumpets of the apocalypse,

G. M. de C. Mello (✉)
Department of Economics and Post-Graduate Program in Social Policy, Federal University of Espírito Santo, Vitória, Brazil
e-mail: gustavo.m.mello@ufes.br

G. M. de C. Mello and H. P. Braga (eds.), *Wealth and Poverty in Contemporary Brazilian Capitalism*, Marx, Engels, and Marxisms,
https://doi.org/10.1007/978-3-030-82298-9_2

and they identify the "signs of the times"—environmental catastrophes, economic crises, intensification of social antagonism, wars, and the advent of "artificial intelligence"—as indications that humanity is approaching the ultimate conflict between good and evil, and, according to a wide spectrum of preaching motivated by all kinds of faith,[2] the subsequent salvation of the elect. In acute cases of these psychoses, the enthusiasts for capitalism are preparing for this apocalypse; these are the lunatic bunker builders, extreme manifestations of the "survivalist" logic (Lasch, 1984), who are investing not only in their underground refuges, but also in their place in heaven, or more precisely in would-be Martian colonies or some similar refuge. This is the logic with which many of the top managers of Silicon Valley, between various acts of proselytism in defence of the establishment, are engaged—the noble task of ensuring the survival of the species in the face of the impending cataclysm.[3]

These positions, with their crude contradictions, tend to hide real contradictions that a fuller understanding, alongside formal logic, is unable to support. At stake here, are issues related to the conception of history and the concept—or rather, the ideology—of progress, which are confused by a teleological, or even eschatological, perspective. These are, in a sense, reactions to a form of social reproduction marked by an increasing technological and technical potential, which, according to the "Anthropocene" or "Capitalocene" theorists (cf. Danowski & Castro, 2014), have elevated modern societies to the promising condition of a geophysical force. This opens up unprecedented theoretical possibilities for transforming reality—including emancipatory reality—which, far from preventing them, may in fact catalyse catastrophes, social ills, and the direst forms of violence and suffering. Taken to the extreme, they may initiate a trend towards the self-annihilation of humanity.

Even among relevant thinkers, a chronic inability to link these distinct dimensions of modernity is common, and they often fall into unilateral or dualist positions. It is convenient to briefly illustrate these positions based on the propositions of several economists and to pay some attention to their apologist stance. We should recall that, in his mature critique of political economy, Marx had already demonstrated that the clarification of the mythical "social contract", which has passed through many versions of Robinson Crusoe, been reproduced to exhaustion by political economy, and eventually arrived at Darwinism and its projection of capitalist competition onto the animal and vegetable kingdoms,[4] is, in the final analysis, a device to represent the present as the culmination of a long evolutionary process. Its fundamental determinations go back to a primeval stage, which, despite occasional mishaps and deviations, conditions this trajectory; and it is thus that modern societies are naturalised and perpetuated (cf. Marx, 1982).

Different attitudes emerged. Take, for example, the folly of John Maynard Keynes, when he predicted, in 1930, that over a period of one hundred years the standard of living in "progressive" countries would rise by at least four or eight times and humanity would be rid of the "economic problem" for the first time in history (Keynes, 1963: 364–365), and that a new dilemma would then emerge, as all people, without exception, would tremble at the dawn of this, "era of pleasure and abundance" (ibid.: 368). The great dilemma of humanity would then be the need to satisfy the "old Adam" who had been introjected over the centuries, which Keynes projected would be achieved with 15 h of work per week (ibid.: 369). Keynes ignores both the contradiction between the material and abstract dimensions of social wealth, with its antagonistic and unequal nature founded on exploitation and plunder, and the social determination of technology and technique subsumed to capital. We observe that he projects the suffering of the bourgeois parasites onto all humanity, which with its predatory form of insertion into the world, and unconcerned with even the most basic dimensions of existence, dies of boredom while contemplating its own existential misery.

In the process of consolidating the capitalist mode of production and among the fierce clashes between truly bourgeois forces, popular forces, and those of the Old Regime, the apologetic perspective failed to stifle a genuine impetus to understand the emerging contexts, the fine operating mechanisms of modern societies and their fundamental tendencies. The profound thinker Adam Smith, appealed to Divine Providence in supporting his thesis that the mercantile order was natural and spontaneous—and unknowable, given the multiplicity and complexity of economic interactions—and beneficial for the societal group, according to the anthological image of the "invisible hand". So, "without intending it, without knowing it", says Smith, the rich, "advance the interest of the society, and afford means to the multiplication of the species. When Providence divided the earth among a few lordly masters, it neither forgot nor abandoned those who seemed to have been left out in the partition." (Smith, 1982: 206). Nevertheless, Smith recognised a whole set of inequities and ailments typical of modern societies, starting with its structurally unequal character, concluding that, "wherever there is great property there is great inequality", and that, "the affluence of the few supposes the indigence of the many" (Smith, 1977: 947). Likewise, he vigorously denounced the antisocial arrivism of the business community, "an order of men whose interest is never exactly the same with that of the public, who have generally an interest to deceive and even to oppress the public, and who accordingly have, upon many occasions, both deceived and oppressed it" (ibid.: 349). He was also aware of the deleterious effects of the technical division of labour on the individual imprisoned in repetitive and unfair tasks, through which he, "becomes as stupid and ignorant as it is possible for a human creature to become" (ibid.: 1040), and of the classist nature of the modern State, devoted to the interests of owners, and concludes that, "civil government, so far as it is instituted for the security of property, is in reality instituted for the defence of the rich against the poor, or of those who have some property against those who have none at all" (ibid.: 953).

It would not be long before this intellectual integrity disappeared from economists' circles almost without a trace, supplanted by a more sophisticated sleight of hand, which sought to conceal the violence that structures modern societies beneath the effusive and cynical blanket of progress. Soon, haunted by popular radicalisation, Carey would be brave enough to denounce Ricardo's *Principles of Political Economy*, as, "the true manual of the demagogue who wants to conquer power through agrarianism, war and pillaging" (Carey, 1848: 74), countering it with the "law of universal harmony", "one in virtue of which there is established a perfect harmony of real and true interests among the various classes of mankind" (Carey, 1865: 113). The era of crude economics had arrived, whose fundamental traits would cut across most of the subsequent currents of economic thought. Decades later, authors like Ludwig von Mises would unilaterally invoke Smith's legacy, converting entrepreneurs into servants of society, exploited by the, "Non-progressive majority" (Mises, 2010: 36). In a more sophisticated way, Friedrich von Hayek would sing the praises of the individual heteronomy imposed by market mechanisms. After all, for Hayek (1990), "it was submission to the impersonal forces of the market that made the progress of a civilization possible, and that, without it, would not have developed. It is, therefore, by submitting ourselves that we help day by day to build something whose magnitude surpasses our understanding" (p. 186). More importantly, these authors radicalise the unilateral, oppressive, and agonistic concept of freedom already manifest in the Universal Declaration of Human Rights, which, "[…] makes every man see in other men not the realisation of his own freedom, but the barrier to it" (Marx, 1975a: 166) as an external and restrictive limit. Inverting the classic contractualist logic, these Austrian economists take economic freedom, freedom of market competition, as the source of all freedom. After all, markets should be a boon that, regardless of individual or collective intentions, emerge spontaneously as the only means of exchanging information and interaction that can, under the driving force of competition, generate new productive methods, invent new products, and refine their requirements, and through a complex and adaptive price system, be aware of relative scarcities and the demand for inputs and final products. All social progress, even the most elementary subsistence in complex societies such as modern ones, would depend on markets, which would, nevertheless, be under heavy fire from collectivism. In this war of life and death, all weapons are valid, and this explains Hayek's support for a bloody Chilean dictatorship. In this case, Hayek, without considering the nonsense of the disjunctive, did not hesitate to embrace an authoritarian "liberal" government over a democratic "interventionist" one, arguing that "in certain historical circumstances personal freedom" can be "better protected under an authoritarian government than under a democratic one" (Hayek apud Caldwell & Montes, 2014). Along a similar line is Mises' praise of fascism, which, according to him, would be forever praised as the saviour of, "European civilization" (Mises, 1978: 51). Here is a small sample of the base neoliberal conception of freedom, shamelessly and cynically used to legitimise agency and direct violence, just two of the characteristics that emerge as intrinsic components of mercantile logic. But we are getting ahead of ourselves.

In the mid-nineteenth century, both within and outside the field of socialism, there was a strong tradition that recognised and criticised the social ills inherent in evolving capitalism and which emphasised its obstinate character. To escape the complexities of dualism, it is necessary to mobilise the weapons of Marxian dialectics, through which Marx bequeathed ineluctable contributions to the proper conceptual understanding of this process, with repercussions that go beyond his historical horizon, as we intend to demonstrate. Here it is necessary to raise a shortcoming of our analysis; the critique of political economy, while prohibiting moralistic perspectives and requiring total immersion in the depths of social reality, highlights the fault-lines of "order", i.e., the points at which domination is weakened and social powers repressed, as well as the elements and social relationships that resist submitting to the demands of capital. This important and distinctive dimension of the Marxian intellectual experiment will be secondary here, for reasons of lack of space, in favour of conceptual reflection on the barbaric character of the capital form.

The Progress of Barbarism and in Barbarism

There is no univocal understanding of the links between barbarism and modernity in Marxian works, and we do not intend to trace a genealogy of Marxian propositions on the subject, which sometime conflict with each other. Nonetheless, it is convenient to gather together and comment on a set of passages, from different works, to abstract from them a concept of barbarism proper. Bear in mind, beforehand, that this concept seeks to understand the irrational, violent, and disruptive core of modern societies, which, anchored in the ideology of progress, represent the peak of human development, the era of Enlightenment. This effort to demystify runs through Marxian intellectual output and is present in the first works published by Marx—it is in his essays *On the Jewish question* and *Critique of Hegel's Philosophy of Right: Introduction*, in the *Franco-Prussian Annals*, in *The Holy Family*, written together with Engels, and in the Marginal Glosses to the article *The King of Prussia and Social Reform.* In them, under the influence of Feuerbach, Marx conceives of religion, German idealism, politics (and the State), as well as money and private property as alienated, autonomous social forms, which are the fruit of human action, but which have escaped from their control, becoming a kind of second nature. With this, a universal condition of subordination and heteronomy emerges, in which the individual becomes, "the slave of labour for gain and of his own as well as other men's selfish need" (Marx & Engels, 1975a: 113). So,

> The slavery of civil society is in appearance the greatest freedom because it is in appearance the fully developed independence of the individual, who considers as his own freedom the uncurbed movement, no longer bound by a common bond or by man, of the estranged elements of his life, such as property, industry, religion, etc., whereas actually this is his fully developed slavery and inhumanity. (Marx & Engels, 1975a: 116)

More specifically, overcoming various forms of domination of a personal, religious, and patriarchal nature results not in true emancipation but in the advent of an impersonal and universal domination, attributed here to the deification of money. So, it is the persistence of religious alienation in secular forms, proper to the production of a fantastic and strange reality in which the individual, "can be active practically, and produce objects in practice, only by putting his products, and his activity, under the domination of an alien being, and bestowing the significance of an alien entity—money—on them" (Marx, 1975a: 174).[5] Consequently, the same society that produces a complex system of universal interdependence, reduces social nexuses to the abstract mediation of money and individuals to a state of competition and indifference towards other social actors. However, such a state appears to these individuals as the realisation of freedom, formalised in law. This establishes the limits of that freedom as being, those that do not restrict the freedom of others, "just as the boundary between two fields is determined by a boundary post. It is a question of the liberty of man as an isolated monad, withdrawn into himself" (Marx, 1975a: 162), which does not connect, but separates people from each other, effectively isolating them. The analogy between the law and a fence is not by chance, after all, "the practical application of man's right to liberty is man's right to private property" (ibid.: 49). As a corollary, this agonistic conception of freedom has as a counterpart the elevation of the notion of "security" as, "the highest social concept of civil society, the concept of police, expressing the fact that the whole of society exists only to guarantee to each of its members the preservation of his person, his rights, and his property" (Marx, 1975a: 163).

Modern thinking enthrones the "rational" individual as a demiurge of the real, and sees him as something reified and submitted to the condition of a Kantian "minority", but from the perspective of social criticism, it is about understanding the irrational nucleus that lies at the heart of modernity, and its structure, through a critical effort that reaches its apogee in the Marxian analysis of the fetishism of merchandise, money, and capital. Ultimately, by defining the process of the subjectification of capital and its various forms as fetishism, whose counterpart is the reification of individuals reduced to the condition of supports of these forms, Marx ironically denounces the "totemic" pivot of modern societies—not only as a persistence of the myth of the Enlightenment, which boasts of having overcome it, but as a constituent element of a set of modern social practices in the different dimensions of social life.

In his *Economic-Philosophical Manuscripts*, Marx emphasises the relevance of civilization and barbarism in modernity. For example, when considering the terrible housing conditions of most of the working population at the time, Marx (1975b) laments that,

> Even the need for fresh air ceases to be a need for the worker. Man returns to a cave dwelling, which is now, however, contaminated with the pestilential breath of civilisation, and which he continues to occupy only precariously, it being for him an alien habitation which can be withdrawn from him any day—a place from which, if he does not pay, he can be thrown out any day. (p. 307)

Engulfed by the technical and social division of labour, physically and mentally mutilated by their shackling to the machine and to a mechanical existence,[6] and forced to adapt to the most demeaning situations, individuals have a predatory, instrumental, and superficial relationship with the objects of consumption and towards other individuals. In this way, "private property has made us so stupid and one-sided", says Marx, "that an object is only ours when we have it — when it exists for us as capital, or when it is directly possessed, eaten, drunk, worn, inhabited, etc.—in short, when it is used by us" (Marx, 1975b: 300). The complex and varied forms of experimentation, fruition, and generation of reality are degraded and made unilateral; so that, "in the place of all physical and mental senses there has therefore come the sheer estrangement of all these senses, the sense of having" (ibid.: 300).[7] Taking advantage of this new form of existential misery, an entire tautological economic dynamic has been structured, which is simultaneously a form of social control, since, as Marx (1975b) reflects, "industry speculates on the refinement of needs, it speculates however just as much on their crudeness, but on their artificially produced crudeness, whose true enjoyment, therefore, is self-stupefaction— this illusory satisfaction of need - this civilization contained within the crude barbarism of need." (p. 311). In this way, even in periods when the material living conditions of parts of the working population are improved and after the ephemeral consumerist numbness has passed, individuals are condemned to be repeatedly frustrated by the promises of satisfaction that the goods whisper in their shiny windows.

From the outset, one can see the recurrent analysis of the progress of capital accumulation and social regression in Marxian work as two sides of the same coin. In his speech delivered in April 1856, at a "People's Paper" anniversary party, Marx (1980a) returned to the theme:

> In our days, everything seems pregnant with its contrary. Machinery, gifted with the wonderful power of shortening and fructifying human labour, we behold starving and overworking it. The new-fangled sources of wealth, by some strange, weird spell, are turned into sources of want. The victories of art seem bought by the loss of character. At the same pace that mankind masters nature, man seems to become enslaved to other men or to his own infamy. Even the pure light of science seems unable to shine but on the dark background of ignorance. All our invention and progress seem to result in endowing material forces with intellectual life, and in stultifying human life into a material force. This antagonism between modern industry and science on the one hand, modern misery and dissolution on the other hand; this antagonism between the productive powers and the social relations of our epoch is a fact, palpable, overwhelming, and not to be controverted. (pp. 665–666)[8]

There has been technical-material progress, which corresponds to both the advance of the real subsumption of labour to capital, under the aegis of extracting the relative surplus value, and to the subordination of the different spheres of social life to the blind, automatic, excessive, and insatiable movement of capital accumulation, and their reduction to moments of the fragmented and contradictory totality that is the capitalist mode of production.[9] At the same time, social life loses depth, is impoverished in meaning, and the individual languishes, spending himself. Denying both the nostalgic, idyllic view of the past and that which hypostatises the present as the "end of history", Marx proposed a critical look at the set of social formations that have emerged, each in their distinct periods. In this way, the present sheds light on the past and vice versa, producing knowledge that, in turn, feeds the struggle necessary for producing the "new", for overcoming human "prehistory" and for overcoming class divisions and the fetishism of capital. In his words,

> In earlier stages of development, the single individual seems to be developed more fully, because he has not yet worked out his relationships in their fullness or erected them as independent social powers and relations opposite himself. It is as ridiculous to yearn for a return to that original fullness as it is to believe that with this complete emptiness history has come to a standstill. (Marx, 1993: 162)

In this system of universal reification, dominated by the "automatic subject"—the "contradiction in process"—formal freedom and equality are the (legal) forms of manifestation, in the sphere of circulation, of the coercion and inequality inherent to the process of extraction of surplus value in the sphere of production (Grespan, 2002). Individuals become supports for the capital form—variable capital, in the case of workers as personifications of capital, and capital-money, in the case of the owners of the means of production—in such a way that his will resides in things, his freedom is that which emanates from the commodity and, in the end, this formal freedom is the mystified form of the emergence of modern economic enslavement. Their equality lies in reducing individuals to the condition of fungible goods, and this is the mystified form of the inequality between workers and capitalists. As already noted in *The Poverty of Philosophy*,

> There came a time when everything that men had considered as inalienable became an object of exchange, of traffic and could be alienated. This is the time when the very things which till then had been communicated, but never exchanged; given, but never sold; acquired, but never bought—virtue, love, conviction, knowledge, conscience, etc.—when everything finally passed into commerce. It is the time of general corruption, of universal venality, or, to speak in terms of political economy, the time when everything, moral or physical, having become a marketable value, is brought to the market to be assessed at its truest value." (Marx, 1980b: 140)[10]

The defence of private property emerged as a prerequisite for the generalisation of competition as a pillar of modern sociability, and as a means of preserving class divisions exacerbated by capitalist development, conditioned by the development of exploitation. This is because, as Marx points out, "No antagonism, no progress. This is the law that civilization has followed up to our days. Until now, the productive forces have developed by virtue of this system of class antagonisms" (Marx 1980b: 159). This is one of the main functions of the modern State, the political form of capital, a theme that Marx returns to often throughout his intellectual journey, having found that,

> At the same pace at which the progress of modern industry developed, widened, intensified the class antagonism between capital and labour, the State power assumed more and more the character of the national power of capital over labour, of a public force organised for social enslavement, of an engine of class despotism. (Marx, 1980c: 360).

These relationships become even more evident when one considers the origins of private property and waged workers ("as free as a bird") as prerequisites for capital accumulation. In those States that would eventually form the central capitalist countries, within the scope of the unequal world market, these prerequisites emerged from the, "idyllic methods of primitive accumulation." (Marx, 1990: 895), such as enclosures and the expropriation of common land and the means of production; the violent uprooting of vast population groups, forced to migrate to urban centres; and the theft of ecclesiastic and state property. To these terrorist mechanisms of expropriation, one can add compulsory labour, incarceration, and torture—including branding, flogging, mutilation and even execution—always supported by "grotesque laws", aimed at acclimatising the dispossessed masses to the modern and brutal conditions of production (Marx, 1990: 899). Colonialism was equally important, under which the populations that fell under the metropolitan yoke were massacred, plundered, and enslaved, and which soon became the most profitable and relevant commercial enterprise of the time, a source of capital that flooded the metropolises and eventually financed the Industrial Revolution (Marx, 1990: 922). Under colonialism, and considering the inconceivability of universal private property, two factors developed. The freedom to sell the labour force, which emerged as the form of economic coercion to which the working population is subjected, and the generalisation of free wage labour took, which is the historical counterpart to the institution of modern slavery in the colonies. Slavery, wrote the young Marx,, "is just as much the pivot of bourgeois industry as machinery, credits, etc. Without slavery you have no cotton; without cotton you have no modern industry" (Marx 1980b: 194), an idea that he would take up in *Capital*, in which he concludes that, "the veiled; slavery of the wage labourers in Europe needed the unqualified slavery of the New World as its pedestal" (Marx, 1990: 925).

All of this is to mention just a few aspects of the barbarism that gave birth to the specifically capitalist mode of production. Private property emerged from brutal plunder, free wage labour, modern slavery and the most bloodthirsty and excessive methods of exploitation and discipline, with the management of the productive space as the fundamental locus.[11] In both the *Economic and Philosophical Manuscripts of 1844* and the conference on *Wage Labour and Capital*, Marx denounced the reintroduction, in factories and in prisons, in central capitalist countries, of a technique of punishment and torture employed in classical antiquity, a kind of mill powered by human traction. He concludes, "barbarism reappears, but created in the lap of civilization itself and belonging to it; hence leprous barbarism, barbarism as leprosy of civilization" (Marx, 1987a: 434).[12]

In no way did the abolition of these instruments of torture eliminate the demeaning nature of labour subordinated to capital. In manufacturing, founded on the technical and social division of labour, direct producers were eliminated by the bringing together of increasing specialisation of labour activities, the intensification of work, the extension of the working day and the usuary of their "sweat". What became established was a productive dynamic that, in a properly despotic organisational form (Marx, 1990: 450), emerged as, "a more refined and civilised means of exploitation" (Marx, 1990: 478), which "converts the worker into a crippled monstrosity by furthering his particular skill as in a forcing-house, through the suppression of a whole world of productive drives and inclinations, just as in the states of La Plata they butcher a whole beast for the sake of his hide or his tallow" (Marx, 1990: 481). In large-scale industry, when capital finds a technical base suited to being included in an automatic machine system, the subsumption of labour to capital reduces workers to being an appendage to the production process, its extirpates their job satisfaction and is as far as can be imagined from being an emancipation from repetitive work and the cultivation of versatility, let alone a substantial reduction in working hours. The machine system, this "animated monster", "exhausts the nervous system to the uttermost; at the same time, it does away with the many-sided play of the muscles, and confiscates every atom of freedom, both in bodily and in intellectual activity" (Marx, 1990: 548) and becomes a new "means of torture" and slavery for workers (Marx, 1990: 548). Under the aegis of the combined extraction of relative and absolute surplus value, there is an increase in objectification, intensification of work, the extension of working hours, as well as a stratified relative overpopulation, including the most impoverished workers and the ranks of paupers. In Marx's words, capital obliges workers, "systematically to work to form an industrial reserve force that shall be ready at a moment's notice; during one part of the year, he decimates this force by the most inhuman toil, during the other part he lets it starve for lack of work." (Marx, 1990: 608). As an aside, this relationship of predation on the workforce was also linked with nature, in such a way that, "all progress in capitalist agriculture is a progress in the art, not only of robbing the worker, but of robbing the soil", and that, "capitalist production, therefore, only develops the techniques and the degree of combination of the social process of production by simultaneously undermining the original sources of all wealth - the soil and the worker" (Marx, 1990: 638).

Still regarding large-scale industry, because of concentration and centralisation and the creation of immense productive structures that are very fixed capital intensive, the home-based system (*the putting-out, or piecework system*), the "external department of the factory", is re-emerging, "Which has in its under-payment and over-work its methodical means of 'producing redundancy'", after all, the "unlimited exploitation of cheap labour-power is the sole foundation of their ability to compete." (Marx, 1990: 605). A regime of wages for piecework exists which is, "the form of wage most appropriate to the capitalist mode of production" (Marx, 1990: 698) since it lends itself to intensifying competition among workers, to internalising the discipline of work as "self-discipline", and it becomes "the most fruitful source of reductions in wages, and of frauds committed by the capitalists" (Marx, 1990: 694).

Colonial brutality was not limited to the early stages of capitalist development. Most of those atrocities had been thoroughly analysed by Marx during his lifetime, having been scarred, at the beginning of his career as a journalist and editor of *A Gazeta Renana*, by the repression of the population who had been prohibited from collecting firewood from lands that had, until the previous day, been communal, a practice that had for generations been essential for withstanding the severe German winter (Marx, 1975c). It is also worth recalling, on the same theme, the experience of India, the subject of controversial articles by Marx published in the *New York Daily Tribune*. In his notorious piece *"The future results of British rule in India"*, of July 1853, Marx denounced that "the profound hypocrisy and inherent barbarism of bourgeois civilization lies unveiled before our eyes, turning from its home, where it assumes respectable forms, to the colonies, where it goes naked" (Marx, 2007: 224). He then enumerated the vast plunder of land and other state assets, extortion, censorship, and religious persecution, and even the creation of an industry of "prostitution" and "organised crimes in the temple of Juggernaut" (ibid.: 224). He emphasised that it was not something fortuitous or episodic, but the "organic results of the whole system of production as it is now constituted. That production rests on the supreme rule of capital." (ibid.: 225).[13] It was in the same article that he evoked the image of "human progress" as "that hideous, pagan idol, who would not drink the nectar but from the skulls of the slain" (ibid.: 297).

Despite his critical and vigorous denunciation of British atrocities, in this article Marx characterises Indian society as rigid and static and questions the role of capital as a liberator of potential revolutionaries who would eventually liberate India from this whole ordeal.[14] These propositions served to feed the unfortunate "stagist" perspective of history, initially promoted by the Soviet *nomenclature* and replicated by political organisations around the world. This echoes the infamous philosophy of Hegelian history, seen as the long triumphal march of the Absolute Spirit, fusing theology with teleology.[15] Fortunately, this would not be Marx's last word on the subject. Quite the contrary, through his critique of the capital-form a different, more open, conception of history emerges, which declines any kind of "finalism", as can be seen, for example, in the refusal to embrace a general historical-philosophical theory, and his reminder that, "notably analogous events, but taking place in different historical circumstances, lead to totally different results" (Marx & Engels, 1965: 313). After all, confronted by a totalitarian social form, the only way of overcoming its internal barriers is through the association of freely socialised individuals, who collectively, in a conscious and planned way, organise the process of the material and spiritual reproduction of their lives, and can then avoid their own annihilation resulting from the environmental destruction and social degradation demanded by the endless nature of the appreciation of value. For the rest of his life, Marx was increasingly attracted to studying the plurality of forms of relationship with the land and of social organisation in different social formations, and therefore of the history of peoples and their struggles, including considering the possibility of some of them taking part in a process of international and universal emancipation, avoiding passing through the hardships imposed by the full subsumption of the capital form (cf. Marx & Engels, 2004).[16]

It only remains to revisit the intimate relationship between the capital form and militarism. In the Early Middle Ages, the increasingly technological and expensive dynamics of war, with weapons of high cost and complexity—particularly the invention of firearms and, especially, cannons—began to demand the maintenance of increasingly expensive permanent, specialised, and salaried armies (Kurz, 2014, Chapter 6). This drove the establishment of increasingly comprehensive tax systems, as well as the universalisation of money as an indispensable social nexus. All these factors reinforced the trend towards political centralisation, which then immediately became a source of pressure for the expansion of military spending, the tax system, and the "monetisation" of social life. Added to this, at the heart of modern credit systems based on public debt, is the financing of military ventures. War, with its spoils and the yoke placed on the defeated populations, soon proved to be a lucrative business, based, in a sense, on a *racket* logic, which established a dynamic of plundering, in which the representatives of the time offered producers, traders, financiers and the general population protection against a threat that they often themselves represented. This dynamic was validated and legitimised through a legal system imposed by those same representatives (Tilly, 1989). So, war, expansionism, and territorial control could be said to be one of the midwives of modernity and is the base of the constitution of nation-states and the potential antagonisms between them.[17] Over the subsequent years, the dynamics of accumulation have only become autonomous in relation to military enterprises to a limited extent, as the scale of the military-industrial complex in central capitalist countries testifies.

Furthermore, some characteristic elements of modern industry originated in the armed forces and weapons industry, including, among other things, the wage system, the intensive use of machinery, the modern technical division of labour, and the system of despotic and hierarchical organisation of work which engendered a, "barrack-like discipline, which is elaborated into a complete system in the factory" (Marx, 1990: 549). There is a personal note by Marx in the final part of the unfinished 1858 *Introduction to the Grundrisse*, which should be mentioned for its synthetic character,

> War developed earlier than peace; the way in which certain economic relations such as wage labour, machinery etc. develop earlier, owing to war and in the armies etc., than in the interior of bourgeois society. The relation of productive force and relations of exchange also especially vivid in the army. (Marx 1993: 109)

In the same vein, in a letter to Engels on September 25th 1857, Marx maintained that, "more graphically than anything else the history of the army demonstrates the tightness of our views as to the connection between the productive forces and social relations" (Marx & Engels,

1987b: 186), and in addition to reiterating the aforementioned innovations developed within the armed forces and which later served the capitalist mode of production, he wrote to Engels, "even the special value of metals and their USE as money would seem to have been based originally — as soon as Grimm's Stone Age was over — on their significance in war." (ibid.: 186).

Finally, it is worth mentioning the passages in which Marx associates the state of barbarism with the economic crises immanent to the dynamics of capital accumulation. In these situations, "society suddenly finds itself put back into a state of momentary barbarism; it appears as if a famine, a universal war of devastation had cut off the supply of every means of subsistence; industry and commerce seem to be destroyed; and why? Because there is too much civilization, too much means of subsistence, too much industry, too much commerce" (Marx & Engels, 1987a: 490). It is the emergence of barbarism as hubris, as excessive, as excess, and therefore as a phenomenon inherent to modern social formations. Notwithstanding that this phenomenon is periodical, Marx again emphasises its necessity, which he does not consider aberrant or deviant.[18]

On the contrary, it is rooted in determinations and tendencies inherent to capitalist social formations, among which it is important to emphasise the "general law of capital accumulation", the "law that maintains relative overpopulation", and that,

> Accumulation of wealth at one pole is, therefore, at the same time accumulation of misery, the torment of labour, slavery, ignorance, brutalisation and moral degradation at the opposite pole, i.e., on the side of the class that produces its own product as capital. (Marx, 1990: 799)

In summary, more than being a set of sporadic or contingent phenomena, according to Ruy Fausto's synthesis, "the idea of progress-regression can be summarised by saying 'barbarism is … civilization', adding, however, 'as barbarism' (or 'barbarism becomes civilization, but as barbarism')" (Fausto, 2002: 123). Or even, "barbarism is civilised as barbarism, it means that there is progress *of* barbarism and *in* barbarism (this is at least one of the meanings of the judgment)" (Fausto, 2002: 123).

And the Rubble of Progress Accumulates …

From this analysis, it is possible to extract a set of elements that aid the understanding of the present. These include the need to recognise the intimate nature of capital and overcome the apparent manifestation of the phenomena; that limited historical situations are impossible to generalise, bearing in mind the "uneven and combined" character of capitalist development globally; and the mistake of presenting the State and the Law, and their fake omnipotence and universality, as widows of the welfare state. Moreover, several contemporary social phenomena can be recognised in these brief considerations on the barbaric nature of capital. The same tendencies that, in Marx's time, condemned one portion of the working population to long and exhausting working hours, and the other portion to the ranks of the industrial reserve army and poverty, have, over recent decades produced a "scorched earth", over which the voraciousness of capital has spread without hinderance. Once capital was free of the checks and balances represented by labour organisations and the spectre of communist revolution and had reinforced its mobility and performance on a truly transnational scale, it started to dynamise labour legislation and impoverish and privatise social policy, opening up vast fields of action in, among others, health, education, and social security systems. Among other consequences, such capital achievements make the guarantee of the reproduction of the workforce more uncertain and arbitrary, and they compete to extend working hours, often presented as being more "flexible", as is the case of "zero-hours contract" in the United Kingdom, or the "intermittent journey", in Brazil, but are intended to lower costs, and intensify work and competition between workers (cf. Chapter 4 of this book).[19] Such trends are reinforced by the generalisation of personal indebtedness, which sometimes becomes a common and necessary component of the survival dynamics of the working population, and which acts as a kind of "secondary exploitation" of workers and as a means of hoarding added value in the form of interest (Marx, 1991: 754; cf. Chapter 5 of this book).

In its worldwide offensive, capital has made use of the innumerable technological innovations introduced over recent decades. The characteristic fields of the so-called third and fourth industrial revolutions—microelectronics, telematics, nanotechnology, biotechnology, robotics, information technology, artificial intelligence, etc.—some of which were still at an early stage of development, have led to the extension of the real subsumption of labour to capital into areas and activities that once resisted it. Capital has also developed techniques for managing and controlling work, often remotely, and by imposing standards that are then internalised by workers and monitored in real time by customers. In addition to driving the concentration and centralisation of capital, as a strategy for appropriating surplus value through different forms of income (Paulani, 2016), many of these technologies have, in their own way, accelerated the *putting-out system* and expanded *piecework*. This has instituted hybrid forms of exploitation, such as those in which the workers advance a good part of the means of production (excluding the algorithms that support these "platforms") and which gives the holders of the respective patents the right to appropriate a good part of the surplus produced under increasingly harsh working conditions. Michael Perelman (2013) noted some years ago that, alongside traditional forms of plunder, the commodification of knowledge has gained prominence as a contemporary manifestation of the "enclosures" characteristic of early accumulation.

Furthermore, many of these technologies are labour-saving, even doing away with several specialties, which increases so-called technological unemployment and further intensifies competition between workers (cf. Kurz, 2014). Marx's observed that, in producing technological and technical conditions that might lead to, "the reduction of society's necessary work to a minimum" (Marx, 1993: 706), capital places, "…working time as the only measure and source of wealth", and that its thirst for surplus value only intensifies. It imprisons, "the gigantic social forces […] within the limits required to maintain the value already created as a value" (p. 706), preventing the achievement of the, "free development of individualities". Partly because of technological development under the aegis of the capital form, many countries have relative overpopulations. The number of people considered superfluous, surplus, or even unemployable, has reached unprecedented levels. Faced with the antagonisms provoked by such a situation, these groups have found themselves the target of focussed social policies—with low cost and a strong commercial bias, which are intended to resolve the "inefficiency" of universal social policies—and of policies of repression, which are two sides of the same coin. Mass incarceration, ghettoisation, the militarisation of social life and militia control of territories, genocide, terror, and policies of extermination, both state and parastatal, have become part of daily urban life in some countries (cf. Mbembe, 2018). Incidentally, a particularly strategic role is played here by algorithmic social control and surveillance technologies, driven by *big data* and artificial intelligence, which have started to permeate every pore of social life. Security cameras, smartphones, laptops, and household goods are fed 24 h a day, by choice or otherwise, with data that allows them to gather information regarding an individual's lifestyle, and based on that information bombard individuals with advertisements, news, and directives that both mobilise and condition actions, insofar as they hinder access to any experience that transcends this hermetic universe and especially those that might confront the dictatorship of capital. The tools of work and leisure are themselves tools of surveillance and conditioning, competing to blur the boundaries between one another, and creating a type of social control that is both total and insidious, since it is naturalised and relies on the active participation of individuals to sustain itself.

This is another dimension of the plundering process inherent to the relationship between capital and labour, a truly subjective plundering. As we have seen, intimacy, feelings, values, desires, and taste are all captured, shaped, and conditioned by the tautological movement of accumulation, in such a way that the process of subsuming labour to capital includes the psychological structure itself and the forming of patterns of suffering. This is one of the main functions of the culture industry, which understands this and extrapolates the moulding of workers en masse, through "education, tradition and custom", who then come to accept the demands of the capitalist mode of production as, "evident natural laws" (Marx 1990: 358). According to Adorno and Horkheimer (2014), there is a psychological expropriation that in a sense relieves the individual of the, "painful internal dialectic of moral conscience, self-preservation and impulses", since their decisions become the prerogative of corporate bureaucratic structures and the State, or, on a personal level, "a mass culture scheme, which expropriates from its forced consumers their last internal impulses" (ibid.: 166–167).[20] This process is reinforced by the advent of social networks and information technologies, through which, "the power of technology and capital becomes opaque and intangible, while the intimacy of each individual is shown with the helpless transparency of a drop of dew." (Bucci, 2020). With this, the totalitarian nature of capital is confirmed, Eugênio Bucci (2020) continues, "what is totalitarianism if not the state in which power is opaque and privacy is transparent?". In this sense, and according to the reflections of João Bernardo (2014), a paradox arises from our frantic engagement with selfies, posts, and memes, on the Instagrams, Facebooks, Tiktoks and Whatsapps of life, "an unprecedented visual exacerbation of the self", which, by "being made public in real time, implies the destruction of privacy, which until now has happened exclusively in totalitarian regimes and in the slums" (p. 73). This destruction is even more relentless because it is voluntarily operated by the individual himself. So,

> While society is ideologically disrupted by encouraging the person to concentrate on himself, the individual's protective boundaries are eliminated because he publicly exposes all his gestures to all eyes. The practical realisation of this paradox is one of the greatest ideological triumphs of capitalism, which begins an era of undisputed domination. (ibid.: 73)

By creating this narcissistic and hyper-exposed universe, Bernardo continues, individuals manage to satisfy both the chimera of free will, proposed by the "economic ideology of the market" and "by the political ideology of citizenship", and the effective injunctions of the market and politics, namely, those that condition them to "destroy the social by concentrating on the individual and to dilute the boundaries of the individual by suppressing privacy." (ibid.: 73).[21] These mechanisms for exploitation, disciplining, capturing subjectivity, conditioning behaviour, and consumption patterns, and maybe even counterinsurgency, form an inextricable web.

It is not necessary to remind ourselves that many of these technologies were created by the military, and their current uses revive their original flaws. The use of nascent computer technology in the Second World War is widely known, from the efforts to decrypt German Enigma messages, in ballistic calculations, and in enabling and increasing the efficiency of the Nazi slave-labour enterprise and the extermination of the Jews. There is also the development of the Internet by the US defence department during the Cold War. It is imperative to mention a milestone in this process, the immense repercussions of which are being felt today: the creation of the atomic bomb, a major achievement of capitalist progress, which made the threat of the "End of Times" a reality and inaugurated the "Time of the End", an era marked by the possibility of humanity's imminent annihilation (Anders, 2013). Without bearing this in mind, the wave of the military colonisation of state management structures after the Second World War, which have made capitalist democracies more formal, remains incomprehensible (Bernardo, 2018: 1349–1353). After all, how can we, given the prospect of nuclear apocalypse, democratically decide whether to push the button or not?

The two World Wars created a virtual indistinction between the military and civilian population, the latter having been overwhelmed by the effort of *total war*, even becoming a *strategic target*, and the subsequent military colonisation of the State made this indistinction permanent. With it, the boundaries that discriminate between internal and external enemies have become blurred, as have those between a state of peace and war—which have begun to dispense with formal declarations. Taken to the extreme, a state of permanent war exists, or a state of permanent political exception (Agamben, 2004), which have culminated, according to Agamben, in a "world civil war", or, according to Paul Virilio (2008), in a "War against civilians" (p. 12). Riding the neoliberal wave, these two trends have been reinforced: the tendency towards the privatisation of sovereignty has deepened, as Eric Hobsbawm (2002) observed at the beginning of the new millennium in a text that begins, "the twentieth century was the most murderous in recorded history" (s/p). It is, "a world in which armed operations are essentially no longer in the hands of governments or their authorised agents and in which the disputing parties have no common characteristics, status or objectives, except the willingness to use violence." (ibid). This trend has advanced alongside the production of "war machines", by means of which exploitation, plunder, population control and extermination policies have merged under the aegis of direct violence (Mbembe, 2018).

Furthermore, on the most conventional geopolitical level, an arms race is underway, which is reflected in the growth of global military spending over the last five years, which has returned to the level previously attained in 1988,[22] and in warmongering rhetoric which has returned to the centre of the scene, which includes the exchange of nuclear threats between great powers.[23] This runs parallel to the commercial and technological war between the United States and China, which is also a dispute over the maintenance of the dollar as world money, over the control of infrastructure and access to world markets, and over political, economic, and cultural influence.

Another factor that has acquired greater relevance over recent decades is environmental destruction and the predatory use of renewable and non-renewable natural resources. Without entering the arguments surrounding global warming, and to consider Brazil alone, there is a growing offensive against indigenous and quilombola peoples as well as small-scale producers—a secular genocide that has taken on a new form in the context of the COVID-19 pandemic[24] to make their lands available for exploitation by landowners, mining companies and the like.[25] The same goes for the increasing number of fires in the Amazon and the Pantanal and deforestation, which have grown exponentially (Aragão et al., 2020). These same trends are behind more dramatic episodes, such as the crimes in Mariana and Brumadinho, where the arrivism of the Samarco and Vale companies took the lives of hundreds of people, devastated vast areas, contaminated rivers, seas and agricultural areas and deprived countless families of their livelihoods (Freitas et al., 2019), or the oil spill on the northeast coast of Brazil which was criminally neglected by the Brazilian federal government (Pena et al., 2020).

It is worth noting that the combined effect of the triad formed by unemployment and the economic collapse of several countries, by conflicts, and by environmental catastrophes has caused waves of migration that have broken all historic levels for refugees, which has surpassed that established during the Second World War. According to the latest figures from the United Nations High Commission for Refugees,[26] globally, almost 80 million people have been forced to leave their homes, with more than 26 million becoming refugees.

The final dimension of contemporary barbarism to be considered here is that related to economic crises, of which there have been hundreds worldwide since 1970. If we were to consider them carefully, it would be possible to identify patterns and nexuses within a succession of events ranging from stagflation crises and oil and interest shocks to the currency crises that rippled around the world in the 1990s and early 2000s (and which have gained strength again in recent years), and that they extend from the debt crisis in peripheral capitalist countries that followed the interest rate shock in 1979, to the sovereign debt crisis in the first half of 2010. This includes the crash of Continental Illinois in 1985, the New York Stock Exchange in 1987, Savings and Loans, in the first half of the 1990s, and Long-Term Capital Management, in 1998 and is also expressed in episodes such as the "dot.com crisis" in 2001 and the "market subprime crisis", triggered in 2007, to which we must now add the crisis triggered by the COVID-19 pandemic. Even a superficial analysis of this turbulent series reveals the establishment, in the current phase of the development of the capitalist mode of production, of a state of permanent economic exception resulting from a chronic overaccumulation of capital, and in which these crises and the threat of crisis have authorised the free exercise of capital's predatory character, faithful to the slogan "*après moi le Déluge*" (Marx, 1990: 381). Beyond the terrible social consequences, which involve a sharp increase in inequality and the production of waves of unemployment, indebtedness, evictions, poverty, etc., in general these crises have led to the strengthening of large transnational conglomerates, which phagocytisethecapital of lesser economic powers and ruthlessly capture State structures and devices. All of this has taken place through policies such as "too big to fail" and "quantitative easing", which tend to reinforce the spiral of State indebtedness, and through the imposition of austerity and privatisation policies. In short, despite the brevity of these considerations regarding the horrors that it continues to produce, we see that the current stage of capitalism owes nothing to its precedents.

Final Considerations

This set of phenomena, which challenges the ideology of progress, did not emerge by chance. At a high level of abstraction, the preceding analysis seeks to demonstrate that they are manifestations that correspond to the very concept of capital, whose commandment is the conversion of all the time available to society into time for overwork, no matter the cost. The bill for this perverse logic never ceases to arrive or to grow, in the form of all kinds of unspeakable violence, subjection and plunder, especially against those who do not have the means of production and against the environment. Countering these apologist arguments, in the mid-1940s Adorno and Horkheimer found that,

> …adapting to the power of progress involves the progress of power, always leading back to those recessive formations that show that it is not the failure of progress, but exactly successful progress, which is guilty of its own opposite. The curse of unstoppable progress is unstoppable regression. (Adorno e Horkheimer, 2014: 46)

Contrary to the idyllic ideology of progress, there seems to be a kind of law, "by virtue of which, in the future, there will be, and can be, nothing but violence, corruption and barbarism on the bourgeois' agenda" (Cesaire, 1977: 56). While it prohibits moralistic perspectives and requires immersion in the depths of social reality, the critique of political economy reveals the fissures in the order, the points where domination is weakened, social powers repressed, and the elements and social relations that resist submitting to the demands of capital exist. After all, there is no way out: "whether scarcity and oppression continue - both are the same thing - will depend exclusively on the avoidance of catastrophe through the rational organisation of total society, as humanity" (Adorno, 1995: 38). The task of revolutionising society from top to bottom and breaking with the social antagonisms and the fetishism of that structure would be chimeric if there were no potential emancipators at its core. To understand this, within Marxian works, a dimension of social life acquires special relevance: that of the organisation and struggle of workers, organised by class, which it will not be possible to analyse here.

It bears repeating, that the survival of the capital form requires that barbarism be produced on an expanded scale, and that the powers of social emancipation are stifled. The despotism of capital and its totalitarian character acquire an insane character, in a permanent effort to prevent counter-revolution. The elimination of the barriers that were once erected by organised workers to contain capitalist voracity, the intensification of social suffering, and the insolubility of the contradictions that intensify the vicissitudes of capital accumulation, may indicate that capitalist production has entered its senile stage (Amin, 2002). Time is running out, after all, as Walter Benjamin (2012) warned,

> History knows nothing of the bad infinity in the image of the two combatants eternally fighting [...]. And if the elimination of the bourgeoisie has not been carried out until an almost calculable moment in economic and technical development (inflation and the gas war indicate this), all is lost. Before the spark reaches dynamite, the burning wick must be cut. (p. 46)

Notes

1. "Progress is a historical fact. The numbers show that over the past seven decades humans have become (on average) longer-lived, healthier, safer, richer, freer, fairer, happier and smarter, not just in the West but worldwide" (Pinker, 2019). For a discussion on Pinker's figures, cf. Hickel (2019).
2. "The present cosmic cycle is coming to its end [...]. The virus is a signal of the end of times" (Teitelbaum, 2020).

3. The case of Elon Musk is exemplary, because while he intends to save the billionaires with his Space-X spaceships, he sells low-cost flamethrowers, the basic element of any self-respecting anti-zombie survival kit. (cf. https://www.theguardian.com/technology/2018/feb/01/elon-musk-sells-out-boring-company-flamethrowers-fire). He still has time to defend coup d'état against governments that create obstacles to his ventures. Questioned on his interest in the overthrow of Evo Morales, he replied: "We are going to hit [coup d'état] on whoever we want! Deal with it"(https://noticias.r7.com/internacional/citando-bolivia-elon-musk-defende-patrocinio-a-golpes-de-estado-27072020).
4. In a letter to Engels in mid-June 1862, Marx remarks ironically: "It is remarkable how Darwin rediscovers, among the beasts and plants, the society of England with its division of labour, competition, opening up of new markets, 'inventions' and Malthusian 'struggle for existence'. It is Hobbes' bellum omnium contra omnes and is reminiscent of Hegel's Phenomenology, in which civil society figures as an 'intellectual animal kingdom', whereas, in Darwin, the animal kingdom figures as civil society." (Marx e Engels, 1987a: 381).
5. This motto reappears in a famous passage from the *Communist Party Manifesto*, in which Marx and Engels find that the bourgeoisie "Has pitilessly torn asunder the motley feudal ties that bound man to his "natural superiors" and has left remaining no other nexus between man and man than naked self-interest, than callous "cash payment". [...] It has resolved personal worth into exchange value, and in place of the numberless indefeasible chartered freedoms, has set up that single, unconscionable freedom— Free Trade. In one word, for exploitation, veiled by religious and political illusions, it has substituted naked, shameless, direct, brutal exploitation" (Marx & Engels, 1975b: 486–487). Furthermore, "Modern bourgeois society with its relations of production, of exchange and of property, a society that has conjured up such gigantic means of production and of exchange, is like the sorcerer, who is no longer able to control the powers of the nether world whom he has called up by his spells" (Marx & Engels, 1975b: 489).
6. "The machine accommodates itself to the weakness of the human being in order to make the weak human being into a machine" (Marx 1975b: 308).
7. According to Guy Debord (2005: 7 and 13), this degradation of "being" to "having" should be followed by the degradation of "having" to "appearing", as Feuerbach had already suggested.
8. In *The Misery of Philosophy*, we read: "in existing society, in industry based on individual exchange, anarchy of production, which is the source of so much misery, is at the same time the source of all progress" (Marx 1980b: 164). For his part, right at the beginning of *Herr Vogt*, Marx asserts that

"civilisation, according to Fourier, is distinguished from barbarism by the fact that in it lies simple are replaced by lies composite." (Marx 1987b: 38).

9. "All earlier forms of property condemn the greater part of humanity, the slaves, to be pure instruments of labour. Historical development, political development, art, science, etc. take place in higher circles over their heads. But only capital has subjugated historical progress to the service of wealth" (Marx 1993: 589–590).
10. According to two well-known passages of *Capital*, "things which in and for themselves are not commodities, things such as conscience, honour, etc. can be offered for sale by their holders, and thus acquire the form of commodities through their price (Marx 1990: 187). In summary, "everything becomes saleable and purchasable. Circulation becomes the great social retort into which everything is thrown, to come out again as the money crystal. Nothing is immune from this alchemy, the bones of the saints cannot withstand it, let alone more delicate *res sacrosanctae, extra commercium hominum*" (Marx, 1990: 229).
11. Marx recalled an anonymous pamphlet from 1765 that advocated the creation of work-houses, which should be "Houses of Terror", in which inmates would be required to work 12-h workdays. This institution was not only created but became widespread: "it was called the factory. And this time the ideal was a pale shadow compared with the reality" (Marx, 1990: 389).
12. "The crudest methods (and instruments) of human labour are coming back: the treadmill of the Roman slaves, for instance, is the means of production, the means of existence, of many English workers" (Marx 1975b: 308).
13. In the same sense, in his "*TheRevoltinthe IndianArmy*", of September 1857, Marx finds that in that system of domination "torture formed the organic institution of its financial policy" (Marx 2007: 234).
14. "It is quite true that, in carrying out a social revolution in Hindustan, England acted on the impulse of the most petty interests, giving evidence of real stupidity in the way of imposing its interests. But this is not the case. What it is about is whether humanity can fulfil its mission without a real deep revolution in the social state of Asia. If not, then, and despite all its crimes, England was the unconscious instrument of history when carrying out this revolution." (Marx, 2007: 291). Marx snaps: "in this case, however painful for our personal feelings is the spectacle of an old world that breaks down, from the point of view of history we have full right to exclaim like Goethe: 'Who regrets the damage / if the fruits they are pleasures / Tamerlane in his reign / did he not crush thousands of beings?'." (ibid.: 291).

15. The truth of this process, which emerged post festum—fly well, old owl of Minerva—that is, the achievement of full freedom, "under the auspices of an omniscient providence" (Marx, 1990: 280), would have redeemed the countless and unspeakable atrocities that had accumulated along the way. From this perspective, "the negative element [in the story] disappears as something subordinate and defeated. This is possible, on the one hand, through the awareness of the true fundamental objective of the world and, on the other hand, in the awareness of the fact that this objective has been achieved in the world and that evil cannot finally prevail beyond it." (Hegel, 2001: 60).
16. At the end of the 1850s and throughout the 1860s, the peoples' struggles that came to be seen as passive and without history, were seen by Marx as crucial for the communist revolution. He goes so far as to argue that the emancipation of English workers would be conditioned by that of Irish workers, and that of white North American workers by that of enslaved ones, and the same scheme would be present in analyses of China, Spain, Turkey, among others. But it was mainly in the 1870s that even this somewhat instrumental perspective would be overtaken, as evidenced, among other works, by his *Ethnological Notebooks* (cf. Marx 1974; Tible, 2014). His political activities within the International Workers' Association probably contributed considerably to these changes in perspective.
17. "Since Hobbes, the leviathan's task of guaranteeing ownership by contractual law and domesticating competition in the countryside is completed by its summary power abroad, that is, against other states. Patriarchal monsters of the 'general will' must continue to face each other mainly in the non-contractual 'state of nature'. The violent shock is inevitable and natural, since the 'general will' must multiply with the multiplication of States; like capital, states also exist only in the plural" (Kurz, 2010).
18. "The conditions of bourgeois society are too narrow to comprise the wealth created by them. And how does the bourgeoisie get over these crises? On the one hand by enforced destruction of a mass of productive forces; on the other, by the conquest of new markets, and by the more thorough exploitation of the old ones. That is to say, by paving the way for more extensive and more destructive crises, and by diminishing the means whereby crises are prevented" (Marx & Engels, 1975b: 490).
19. Trends barely concealed by the ideology of entrepreneurship, which embraces widespread competition as the dominant—or even unique—pattern of behaviour, and which cultivates social indifference and atomisation. Far from elevating everyone to the status of bosses or at least increasing social mobility, there is a process of precariousness. It should not be surprising, therefore, that there are those who associate this type of employment of the labour force with the old slave-earning regime,

which spread mainly in the nineteenth century, in Brazilian urban centres, into which slaves were forced to launch themselves daily. the search for paid occupations in order to periodically pay a certain amount to their owner and still guarantee their own sustenance, which in general required intensive performance of the most diverse activities (Passa Palavra, 2020).

20. Perhaps due to this expression of barbarism in the production of subjectivity, Freud sees that "we are living in an especially remarkable period. We discovered, to our amazement, that progress was allied to barbarism" (Freud, 1996: 71). Or even more broadly, "… whatever the way in which we define the concept of civilization, it is an indisputable fact that all the things we seek in order to protect ourselves against threats from the sources of suffering are part of that same civilization" (Freud, 1997: 38).
21. And the author snaps: "This paradox has a name - futility. The result of the exacerbation of capitalist social relations thanks to electronic technology and especially to information technology is the generalisation of futility. Seconding everything before the image of the self and, simultaneously, destroying the value of the self by trivialising its gestures and paths has two consequences: on the one hand, the frivolity with which the prodigies of nature and human ingenuity are considered when, in photographs and films, they are placed behind the person's image; on the other hand, the reduction of the person to the status of trifle when everything he thinks and does is exposed to the eyes of others. I do not believe that futility can be better defined than by the combination of frivolity and insignificance" (Bernardo, 2014: 73–74). Finally, he sardonically laments, "bringing together so many technological potentials to achieve this! Imagine that if, in its time, the invention of the wheel had excited the crowds mainly because it allowed them to play with the yo-yo".
22. Cf. https://www.sipri.org/publications/2020/sipri-fact-sheets/trends-world-military-expenditure-2019.
23. For example, in April 2020, after the US government announced it had equipped submarines with low-powered nuclear warheads, the Russian government threatened to retaliate with a massive nuclear attack on any firing from any submarine (cf. https://www1.folha.uol.com.br/mundo/2020/04/russia-ameaca-eua-com-ataque-nuclear-por-causa-de-nova-arma-de-trump.shtml).
24. Cf. https://acervo.socioambiental.org/acervo/publicacoes-isa/impacts-pandemic-yanomami-indigenous-territory-minersoutcovidout.
25. Cf. https://deolhonosruralistas.com.br/, and https://cimi.org.br/.
26. Cf. https://www.unhcr.org/figures-at-a-glance.html.

References

Adorno, T. (1995). *Modelos críticos 2*. Vozes.

Adorno, T., & Horkheimer, M. (2014). *Dialética do Esclarecimento* [Electronic Resource]. Zahar.

Agamben, G. (2004). *Estado de Exceção*. Boitempo.

Amin, S. (2002). Capitalismo Senil. *Revista da SEP*, n.11, 79–102.

Anders, G. (2013). Teses para a Era Atômica. *Sopro*, n.87. Disponível em: http://culturaebarbarie.org/sopro/outros/anders.html#.XyWskOdv_IU. Acesso em August 5 2020.

Aragão, L. E. O. C. et al. (2020). O desafio do Brasil para conter o desmatamento e as queimadas na Amazônia durante a pandemia por COVID-19 em 2020: implicações ambientais, sociais e sua governança. *SEI/INPE*.

Benjamin, W. (2012). *Rua de mão única*. Brasiliense.

Bernardo, J. (2014). A complexa arquitetura da futilidade. In: R. H. Tavares, & S. S. Gomes (orgs.). *Sociedade, educação e redes: desafios à formação crítica* (pp. 57–77). Junqueira & Marin.

Bernardo, J. (2018). *Labirintos do Fascismo* [Electronic Resource]. Disponível em: https://vosstanie.blogspot.com/2018/02/labirintos-do-fascismo-3-versao-joao.html. Acesso em August 7, 2020.

Bucci, E. (2020). O convite ao fascismo. *A Terra é Redonda*. Disponível em: https://aterraeredonda.com.br/o-convite-ao-fascismo/. Acesso em August 8, 2020.

Caldwell, B., & Montes, L. (2014). Friedrich Hayek and his visits to Chile. *CHOPE Working Paper*, No. 2014–12. Duke University, Center for the History of Political Economy (CHOPE).

Carey, H. B. (1848). *The past, the present and the future*. Carey & Hart.

Carey, H. B. (1865). *Principles of social science* (Vol. III). J.B. Lippincott & C.O.

Cesaire, A. (1977). *Discurso sobre o colonialismo*. Sá da Costa Editores.

Danowski, D., & Castro, E. V. (2014). *Há mundo por vir? Ensaio sobre os medos e os fins*. Instituto Socioambiental.

Debord, G. (2005). *A Sociedade do Espetáculo*. Edições Antipáticas.

Fausto, R. (2002). *Marx: Lógica e Política – Investigações para uma Reconstituição do Sentido da Dialética*. Tomo III. Editora 34.

Freitas, C. M. et al. (2019). Da Samarco em Mariana à Vale em Brumadinho: desastres em barragens de mineração e Saúde Coletiva. *Cadernos de Saúde Pública*, v.35(5).

Freud, S. (1996). *Moisés e o Monoteísmo*. In: *Obras completas de Sigmund Freud* (Vol. 28). Imago.

Freud, S. (1997).*O Mal-Estar na Civilização*. In: *Obras completas de Sigmund Freud* (Vol. 21). Imago.

Grespan, J. L. (2002). A Dialética Do Avesso. *Crítica Marxista, 14*, 26–47.

Hayek, F. V. (1990). *O caminho da servidão*. Instituto Liberal.

Hegel, F. W. (2001). *A Razão na História*. Centauro.
Hickel, J. (2019). A letter to Steven Pinker (and Bill Gates, for that matter) about global poverty. Disponível: https://www.jasonhickel.org/blog/2019/2/3/pinker-and-global-poverty. Acesso em August 3, 2020.
Hobsbawm, E. (2002). War and peace in the 20th century. *London Review of Books*. Disponível em: https://www.lrb.co.uk/the-paper/v24/n04/eric-hobsbawm/war-and-peace-in-the-20th-century. Acesso em August 10, 2020.
Keynes, J. M. (1963). Economic possibilities for our grandchildren. In*Essays in Persuasion*. W. W. Norton & Cia.
Kurz, R. (2010). Não há Leviatã que nos salve. Disponível em: http://www.obeco-online.org/rkurz390.htm. Acesso em August 5, 2020.
Kurz, R. (2014). *Dinheiro sem valor: linhas gerais para uma transformação da crítica da economia política*. Antígona.
Lasch, C. (1984). *The minimal self: Survival in troubled times*. Norton & Company.
Marx, K. (1974). *The ethnological notebooks: Studies of Morgan, Phear, Maine, Lubbock*. Van Gorcum & Comp. B. V.
Marx, K. (1975a). On the Jewish question. In*Collected works* (Vol. 3). Lawrence and Wishart.
Marx, K. (1975b). Economic and Philosophical Manuscripts. In*Collected works* (Vol. 3). Lawrence and Wishart.
Marx, K. (1975c). Proceedings of the Sixth Rhine Province Assembly. Debates on the law on thefts of wood. In *Collected works* (Vol. 1). Lawrence and Wishart.
Marx, K. (1980a). Speech at the anniversary of the people's paper. In K. Marx (Eds.),*Collected works* (Vol. 14). International Publishers.
Marx, K. (1980b). Poverty of philosophy. In K. Marx (Eds.), *Collected works* (Vol. 6). International Publishers.
Marx, K. (1980c) Civil war in France. In K. Marx (Eds.), *Collected works* (Vol. 22). International Publishers.
Marx, K. (1982). Introdução de 1857. In *Para a Crítica da Economia Política*. Abril Cultural.
Marx, K. (1987a). Wage labor and capital. In *Collected works* (Vol. 6). Lawrence and Wishart.
Marx, K. (1987b). Herr Vogt. In: *Collected works* (Vol. 17). Lawrence and Wishart.
Marx, K. (1990). *Capital: Critique of political economy* (Vol. I). Penguin Books.
Marx, K. (1991). *Capital: Critique of political economy* (Vol. III). Penguin Books.
Marx, K. (1993). *Grundrisse: Foundations of the critique of political economy*. Penguin Books/New Left Review.

Marx, K. (2007). *Dispatches for New York Daily Tribune: Selected journalism of Karl Marx*. Penguin Books.
Marx, K., & Engels, F. (1965). *Selected correspondence*. Progress Publishers.
Marx, K., & Engels, F. (1975a). The holy family. In *Collected works* (Vol. 3). Lawrence and Wishart.
Marx, K., & Engels, F. (1975b). The communist manifesto. In *Collected works* (Vol. 6). Lawrence and Wishart.
Marx, K., & Engels, F. (1987a). Letter to Friedrich Engels in 18/06/1862. In *Collected works* (Vol. 41). Lawrence and Wishart.
Marx, K., & Engels, F. (1987b). Letter to Friedrich Engels in 25/09/1858. In *Collected works* (Vol. 40). Lawrence and Wishart.
Marx, K., & Engels, F. (2004). Preface to the Russian Edition of 1882. In *The communist manifesto*. Penguin Classics.
Mbembe, A. (2018). *Necropolítica: biopoder, soberania, estado de exceção, política da morte*. N-1 Edições.
Mises, L. (1978). *Liberalism: A socio-economic exposition*. Institute for Humane Studies.
Mises, L. (2010). *A Mentalidade Anticapitalista*. Instituto Ludwig von Mises Brasil.
Passa Palavra. (2020). Empreendendo a lavagem cerebral. Disponível em: https://passapalavra.info/2020/08/133528/. Acesso em August 10, 2020.
Paulani, L. M. (2016). Acumulação e rentismo: Resgatando a teoria da renda de Marx para pensar o capitalismo contemporâneo. *Revista De Economia Política, 36*(3), 514–535.
Pena, G. L., Northcross, A., Lima, M. A., & Rêgo, R. C. (2020). The crude oil spill on the Brazilian coast in 2019: The question of public health emergency. *Cadernos de Saúde Pública, 36*(2).
Perelman, M. (2013). Intellectual property rights and the commodity form: New dimensions in the legislated transfer of surplus value. *Review of Radical Political Economics, 35*(3), 304–311.
Pinker, S. (2019). What can we expect from the 2020s? *Financial Times*. Available at: https://www.ft.com/content/e448f4ae-224e-11ea-92da-f0c92e957a96.
Smith, A. (1977). *An inquiry into the nature and causes of the wealth of nations* [Electronic Resource]. University of Chicago Press.
Smith, A. (1982). *The theory of moral sentiments*. Liberty Fund.
Teitelbaum, B. (2020). COVID-19: A crise que os "Tradicionalistas" radicais esperavam 2020. Disponível em: https://aterraeredonda.com.br/covid-19-a-crise-que-os-tradicionalistas-radicais esperavam/. Acesso em August 3, 2020.
Tible, J. (2014). Marx e os Outros. *Lua Nova, 91*, 199–228.
Tilly, C. (1989). *Coercion, capital, and European states, AD 990—1990. Ma: Coercion, capital, and European States, AD 990–1990*. Blackwell.
Virilio. (2008). *Pure war*. MIT Press.

CHAPTER 3

Rethinking Wealth and Poverty in Capitalist Society

Henrique Pereira Braga

Over the last two decades, Brazilian society has undergone considerable transformations. The 2000s began with the rise to power of the Workers' Party (PT), a party seen by many as representing the popular classes desire

This work is a result, and contains parts, of the doctoral thesis in economic sciences, defended in January 2016 at the Unicamp Institute of Economics, under the guidance of Professor Plínio de Arruda Sampaio Jr., who undertook an overseas sandwich PhD year at the University of Chicago under the supervision of Professor Moishe Postone (both studies were funded by CAPES), as reflected in the subsequent research, published in Braga (2016; 2018) and Braga and Zanatta (2021). Finally, I would like to thank sociologist Caroline Tresoldi for her careful reading, reference suggestions and critical comments, as well as sociologist Gustavo Mello for further comments.

H. P. Braga (✉)
Department of Economics, Federal University of Espírito Santo, Vitória, Brazil
e-mail: henrique.p.braga@ufes.br

G. M. de C. Mello and H. P. Braga (eds.), *Wealth and Poverty in Contemporary Brazilian Capitalism*, Marx, Engels, and Marxisms,
https://doi.org/10.1007/978-3-030-82298-9_3

for a more dignified life—from access to a minimum income, to education, to lighting, to potable water, even a university education, opening up the possibility of social improvement. Until the end of the 2000s, this dream seemed possible, as the country was showing economic indicators that suggested it was consolidating its economic role in Latin America, which even led to a belief in a global role, joining China, Russia, South Africa and India in the BRICS economic bloc, and capable of rivalling OECD countries.

When the lights went out in the 2010s, another Brazil was revealed. The economic crisis that the country has faced since 2015 has had serious effects on the lives of the population. The last few years have recorded some of the worst economic indicators in the country's recent history (Sampaio, 2017; Carvalho, 2018). The end of the decade marked the arrival of a political figure representing the extreme right popular movement, a manifestation of autocracy as a way of organising power,[1] and the hopes of the beginning of the new century seem to have given way to hatred and resentment (Pinheiro-Machado & Scalco, 2020). Whether these negative effects were fuelled, for a part of Brazilian society, by unrealised dreams in recent years, or by the frustration of some regarding dreams achieved by those who should not have even dared to dream, or by a combination of both, is a question still only partially answered.

In any case, the theme of income inequality and the concentration of wealth have been central to discussions on the transformations in Brazilian society over recent decades. By way of comparison, the Gini Index of Brazilian income distribution, calculated by the World Bank through household survey data, was 58.4 in 2001, while in 2018 it had fallen to 53.9, the lowest point being 51.2 in 2015. When compared to Russia, one of the few BRICS countries with data available at the World Bank, the size of the discrepancy is evident: the former Soviet republic went from 36.9 to 37.5 in the same period (World Bank Group, 2020). This data shows a considerable difference in the Gini Index between the two countries, with Brazil being a more unequal country. It also shows a drop in the index in Brazil and a slight increase in income inequality in Russia.[2]

Despite the extremely high income inequality in Brazil, the analysis of data from household survey data, carried out by the Brazilian statistician Rodolfo Hoffmann (2017, 2019; Hoffmann et al., 2018), indicates that this inequality declined sharply between 2001 and 2014, and that since 2015 the decline has ceased. The decline was interrupted, according to Hoffmann, by the economic crisis that worsened the job market—for example, the average unemployment rate stood at 4.8% in 2014, while the following year the average unemployment rate was 9.6%—and contributed to the decline in income of part of the population and to the increase in the proportion of income dedicated to paying debts. This is because the Brazilian economic growth that occurred from 2004—with a brief interruption during the 2008 financial crisis—was, according to Hoffmann, based on the expansion of consumption, resulting from the increase in income and the availability of credit. This growth can be explained by increases in the minimum wage and the greater guarantees provided by formal contracted employment (Baltar, 2015).

When combining Brazil's household survey data with detailed information on income tax declarations for the period 2001–2015, Irish economist Mark Morgan (2017: 1) suggests that the change in the distribution of Brazilian income occurred in a different way: a greater concentration at the top (1% richest and 10% richest) and a slight improvement in the income of the lowest 50%, while the remaining 40% saw a decline in their share of national income. In his argument, this data provides clues as to where the concentration of income has remained over the last two decades, changing the position of the middle band in the set of this distribution. This band started to move towards the lowest 50%, which, Morgan observes, has an, "extremely low command of income". In summary, at the beginning of the twenty-first century, the country appeared to have experienced a fall in income inequality when, in fact, there was a process of maintaining the concentration of income within the wealthiest.

Analysing the annual data on Personal Income Tax for the period 1926 to 2013 and looking closely at the income of the richest in Brazil, Brazilian sociologist Pedro Souza (2018) demonstrates the stability of the income of the rich. To define rich in this instance, the author includes those whose income is between "0.01% and 15% of the top" of the national income distribution. This portion of the population took between 20 and 25% of national income, which shows where the concentration of income lies (Souza, 2018: 369–370). This study draws attention to an important point regarding political changes and the distribution of income at the top: at the moment when the income of the wealthiest had fallen to its lowest proportion, there were major political and institutional upheavals and, in subsequent years, the proportion of national income going to the richest rose again (Souza, 2018: 370–371). This is an indication that the Brazilian elite, with broad support from the middle classes, continues to control the processes of social change so as not to damage the interests of this strata of society so accustomed to stability (Fernandes, 1975).

In studies by Morgan (2017) and Souza (2018), a change in the interpretation of the distribution of Brazilian income is noticeable, when compared to Hoffmann's interpretation (2017, 2019; Hoffmann et al., 2018), a change that can be attributed to a methodology that began to be adopted and applied to newly released income tax data.[3] Instead of considering only data from "per household" sample surveys, which is largely declaratory data and, therefore, an underestimate for the highest earners (Hoffmann, 2019: 7; Souza, 2018: 372), researchers have also been analysing income data, national income data and annual income tax returns made by the families closest to the top of the distribution pyramid. This new methodological-statistical approach has led to greater precision regarding how unequal the distribution of Brazilian income is and its relationship to the distribution of wealth, and it is possible to observe which social strata have most lost its purchasing power over the last two decades.

As it better shows the complexity of the distribution of income within a given society, the methodological change represents a considerable analytical advance, which then poses a set of questions for theoretical and broader public debate. One question concerns the understanding of "wealth" and "poverty" that accompanies this view of the problem of income inequality. Considering only the statistical debate, the concept of wealth (or poverty), from which the formulation of the indicators starts, raises the problem of which sources of income are captured by the estimates and which go unnoticed. This forms the first of many limitations to our understanding of income inequality. In sample research, for example, you can declare less than you truly earn, and while this declaration can be adjusted using the Income Tax data, it does not allow for accounting manoeuvres or tax evasion[4] and it leaves aside companies, assuming that the national income is distributed among individuals. This suggests that, in the Brazilian case, inequality is underestimated and that the concentration of income is even greater than that visible.

Despite its shortcomings, the empirical results obtained from this methodological-statistical change have had an important impact on the debate, the book *Capital in the twenty-first century*, by the French economist Thomas Piketty (2014)[5] being central to the discussion. In it, the author describes the behaviour of income and wealth inequality in the twentieth century, analysing data from some more developed European countries and the United States, and points out some trends at the beginning of the twenty-first century, such as the general increase in income inequality. Broadly speaking, Piketty argues that inequality has grown because the return on wealth accumulated in the past has, since the 1970s, been growing faster than current production and income, turning entrepreneurs into rentiers who are increasingly dominant over those who just hold a job. For Piketty (2014: 571–572), this situation compromises social cohesion.

Without going into the merits of this controversial conclusion, it is important to note that at the beginning of his book Piketty (2014: 48) defines the concept of wealth from which his analysis of the distribution of income and wealth starts: "I use the words 'capital' and 'wealth' interchangeably, as if they were perfectly synonymous". So, it is worth asking: what does Piketty conceptualise as capital? According to him,

> [...] capital is defined as the sum total of nonhuman assets that can be owned and exchanged on some market. Capital includes all forms of real property including residential real estate as well as financial and professional capital (plants, infrastructure, machinery, patents, and so on) used by firms and government agencies. (Piketty, 2014: 46)

If capital is ownership over commodities that can be traded and generate income for its owners, we can conclude that inequality of wealth lies in discrepancies in the ownership of these tradable assets in the market. It is not by chance that Piketty proposes the taxation of capital or wealth as a means to curb recent increases in income inequality (Piketty, 2014: 496–497). In his most recent book, *Capital and Ideology*, Piketty (2020: 967) formulates an even bolder proposal: to institute non-permanent private property. Meaning, in a nutshell, a distribution of property that would cause a recurring generational start, so that only those with productive merits would have "wealth" and the inherent inequality of each human and their efforts would be the determining attributes of income and wealth inequality, not inherited wealth.

This way of conceptualising wealth is also present in global studies of wealth and income inequality, as Branco Milanovic (2012), a well-known economist who worked for years at the World Bank, explains:

> When we think of income inequality, our first reaction is to think of it within the borders of a country [...] However, in the era of globalisation another way to look at inequality between individuals is to go beyond the confines of a nation-state, and to look at inequality between all individuals in the world. (Milanovic, 2012: 3)

Milanovic, along with Christoph Lakner, formulated a global distribution of interpersonal income through the combination of household survey data in several countries, concluding that, between 1988 and 2018, interpersonal income inequality increased. The authors justify their research not only on the basis of globalisation, as indicated by Milanovic in the passage cited above, but also in the "equal" treatment of people around the globe: "[…] Our interest in global interpersonal inequality is founded upon a concern for individual well-being, which treats persons the same irrespective of their country of residence […]" (Lakner & Milanovic, 2013: 204).

Although they claim to know the "philosophical" problems associated with this "cosmopolitan" approach, their central objective is to register the need to consider a global solution to confront this problem. The work of the British economist Anthony Atkinson (2015) follows a similar line, for him growing inequality originates from systematic tax relief for the richest and from labour and financial deregulation that have, over the last few decades, provided an environment in which individual differences are combined with the perpetuation of pre-established inequalities due to differences in inherited wealth, resulting in growing income inequality between families.

In summary, Atkinson suggests that the origin of growing inequality lies in "wealth", accumulated by a given family, passing from generation to generation without the heirs having contributed its formation. From the point of view of individual effort, the permanence of the ownership of this wealth, which results in an income not related to their work, cannot be justified. In his words:

> Inheritance is typically seen as one of the mechanisms by which the wealthy are able to preserve their position at the top of the distribution, but there is nothing intrinsically wrong with inheritance. The problem is that inheritance is highly unequal. If everyone inherited the same amount, the playing field would be level. A step in this direction is to ensure that everyone receives a minimum inheritance; hence the following proposal: Proposal 6:

> There should be a capital endowment (minimum inheritance) paid to all at adulthood. (Atkinson, 2015: 170)

To circumvent the problem of the perpetuation of inheritance and the income it generates, Atkinson indicates that taxation is necessary to equalise wealth and allow each person's efforts—considering their family difficulties and their rise, independent of their family ties—to be the guarantee of their enrichment—i.e. their access to a higher consumption pattern (Atkinson, 2015: 179–185). This is not about judging Atkinson's (2015) conclusion, or his political proposal. Rather, we draw attention to the understanding of wealth from which the field of study of income inequality began.

So far, these studies have defined wealth as the stock of goods and services, measured in terms of money and tradable assets, necessary for a diversity of ways of living. It is not by chance that the discussion has been centred on the best way for a group of individuals to efficiently manage this accumulated stock so as to increase its returns, including in monetary terms, in a way that it enables increased purchasing power and consumption capacity and, as a result, the well-being of the population as a whole.

In these approaches to the problem of inequality, the theme of poverty does not appear, except by means of alluding to it via the naming of a certain stratum of income distribution, for example, the Bottom 50%. It forms another field of study, in which the "income insufficient" to achieve a certain minimum of well-being has been established as a metric for measuring the evolution of poverty over time. The international body responsible for leading these studies is the World Bank, whose summary document of the poverty indicator defines it in the following terms:

> The World Bank uses an international poverty line based on the national thresholds of some of the poorest countries. To account for changes in relative prices across countries over time, the 2011 PPP was adopted in 2015 as the standard. This involved an upward adjustment of the international poverty line to US$1.90 a day in income or consumption expenditure so as to preserve the real value of the US$1.25-a-day line in 2005 PPP that was the previous international line. (World Bank Group, 2016: 24)

Without pursuing the issue of the underestimation of the number of people in poverty caused by the US$ 1.90 per day level,[6] it is worth noting that poverty is measured strictly from income, with no relation to wealth and its production. The predominant understanding is that this is a problem caused by the poor themselves (e.g. Piketty, 2020: 1–2) or that, when trying to mitigate poverty, it arises from the degrading living conditions of the poor which impede their participation in the production of goods (e.g. World Bank Group, 2016: 129–149).

Among the various questions that can be asked regarding the concept of wealth and poverty summarised here, it is interesting to understand how these concepts feature the human condition within these societies. To question the human condition in a certain society is, after all, to question the form of the human being and ask oneself about its specificity within a given complex of relationships (Lukács, 1969, 1980). That is, it is to consider the assumptions by which a certain way of producing social life is reproduced. This also helps in understanding the way in which the heteronomy of people is configured in a certain society, and how the forms of social distinction between individuals are founded. Although these assumptions are not the premise of any specific theory, they are indispensable for the proper understanding of the analysed object, as they are present independent of the researcher's theoretical proclivities.[7]

Although, at first glance, these issues seem commonplace in the debate, they have the analytical potential to expose the ways in which a society differentiates its singularities, forms rifts and normalises life horizons. Namely: *being* rich or *being* poor raises the question of how one comes to be one or the other and, from a political point of view, what it is possible to do about the latter. In such thinking, the rich or poor person is distinguished by their level of "income", the meaning of which can be summed up as the power to command and dispose of *things*, i.e. ones *purchasing power*. The best known way to exercise this power is through money, so that *being rich* or *being poor* is measured by the amount of money we carry in our pockets or on our credit card limits.

The presumption of this form of distinguishing human beings is the social process through which people reproduce their lives. In its contemporary form, this mode of production of life is called, "capitalism". Scholars of income inequality make their analyses from the perspective of capitalism, but they do not seem to ground their explanations of the phenomenon of persistent income inequality in capitalism. In other words, they start from a certain social structure, but do not consider the very specificity of this structure, the way it conditions human production, and which makes the commodity form imperative.[8]

Perhaps it is the specifics of contemporary social structure that establishes the persistent inequality of income and wealth. This raises the hypothesis that differences between countries are explained more by their place in the, "modern commodity production system" (Kurz, 1993: 161), than by their institutional arrangements. In this argument, it is not a question of ignoring institutional differences between countries, but of emphasising the global framework of countries and, thus, the overarching dynamic that has existed since the formation and consolidation of the world market at the end of the eighteenth century.

In raising these questions, this chapter's contribution to the debate is, so to speak, meta-theoretical: it exposes a reading of the structures that shape contemporary social relations, showing their contribution to explaining the persistence of inequality, including income inequality, in contemporary society. The theoretical thrust is to present Karl Marx's understanding of wealth and poverty (1818–1883), highlighting how he explains the structures that shape contemporary social relations. The key argument is that the critical social theory formulated by Marx both blames the phenomenon of persistent income and wealth inequality on capitalism, which has been empirically verified by several scholars, of which the Brazilian case is among the most expressive; and indicates how capitalism itself provides the material conditions to *overcome* (*Aufhebung*) this phenomenon.[9]

To achieve this proposed objective, some of Marx's main writings dedicated to the critique of political economy are revisited. His discoveries and publications, and their wide circulation after World War II, decisively impacted the interpretation of his critical theory of society. It is worth asking, however, why go back to the writings of Marx, a German intellectual formed by a rigorous reading of classical German philosophy together with extensive reading of works on political economy, to reflect on the problem of wealth and poverty in capitalist society?

In his critique of political economy, Marx developed an understanding of capitalist society that understands its causal nexus, showing us how its component parts form an irreducible set, either of the parts or of the whole, and which, for the society under examination, forms a contradictory movement presented in social practices, which both reproduces this structure of practices and, simultaneously, engenders the objective and subjective conditions for overcoming it.[10]

This contradictory movement is expressed in the daily characteristics of capitalist society, one of which is material abundance concentrated in a few hands, alongside the difficulties of many in gaining a minimum standard of living—i.e. nutritious food, clothing, housing, literacy and health care. This contradiction struck Marx in his first writing critiquing political economy, the *Economic-Philosophical Manuscripts of 1844* (hereafter *Manuscripts*), in which he begins by showing how political economy portrays the so-called three sources of "national income": labour, capital and land ownership. The highlight of this initial excerpt from the *Manuscripts* is his portrayal of the demeaning condition of workers, although "labour" is praised by political economists as the primary source of wealth (Marx, 1975: 235–246).

The fundamental starting point in the *Manuscripts* is Marx's observation (idem: 270–271) that political economy does not precisely explain the ultimate social condition for the existence of wage labour and private property, the sources of wealth. Marx calls such a condition, estrangement or alienation.[11] Claiming that this is the foundation of bourgeois society, Marx then spends the rest of the work arguing that this foundation results from the relationships between people, as opposed to being the result of divine relations, so that in overcoming them they go through a transformation of social relations so that estrangement ceases to be their foundation. He suggests that estrangement is present in all class societies. While making his *overcoming* proposition, Marx reinforces his arguments, takes up points and presents important aspects for the understanding of estrangement.

In synthesis, this foundation can be explained as follows: the divide between humans of social classes—in which we have, on the one hand, the owners of the means of production and, on the other, humans as workers—is based on the estrangement of the owners, the workers—regarding the results of their activity and the act of carrying out this activity—the human race and each human being. In this scenario, people view others and nature as external and strange objects—i.e. only as a means for the achievement of a given purpose, but whose mode of execution and meaning escapes them—so that their activity, or the appropriation of the results of the activity, does not contribute to developing their mastery (which is not an end in itself), but only to their wear and tear, with the objective of producing objects for the immediate enjoyment of another (idem: 235–237, 271–275, 277–280, 281–282).

In a society where private property takes the form of property that can be bought and sold (idem: 266–267) and work takes the form of waged labour—i.e. buying and selling one's labour capacity as a way of life—then, according to Marx, estrangement develops to its maximum. This is because the degradation of humans as salaried workers, and the contrast of this deterioration with the social wealth produced by them, would be of such a magnitude that the worker's life would become *living to labour*. This social position explains, for Marx, why by political economy positions labour as the primary source of all wealth, where it is necessary, according to economists, that workers receive only enough to subsist (idem: 235, 274–275).

Their counterpart, the private owners, are the owners of this accumulated wealth, which they enjoy in the form of *having* and not in the form of *being*.[12] They do not, however, enrich themselves, because that is a set of external objectivities, but they enrich their social power, in the form of money that can buy them anything and everything (idem: 299–300).[13]

Importantly, the abolition of estrangement does not mean the generalisation of the ownership of external, or estranged (alienated), material abundance, which Marx calls, "material wealth". On the contrary, overcoming estrangement requires the appropriation of this wealth through the enrichment of all humans. The production process itself (or the activities involved in that production) must be configured to expand the mastery of humans, so that the objectivities, although always external, will not be estranged because they are carried out through their internalisation by people. So, appropriation is not the socialisation of the results of production, or the control of the means of production by the State, since, in both cases, estrangement becomes universal.[14]

Overcoming this degrading social reality, degrading because either peoples' lives are transformed into labour, or because their only horizon is the enrichment of the objective world expressed through the power of money, requires that estrangement is overcome through the appropriation of the social force of production arising from this deterioration of social relations. For Marx, this force becomes "capital" (idem: 272).

From a synthesis of the *Manuscripts*, Marx makes explicit that the process of producing material abundance is degrading to humans, and that the growth of this wealth constitutes the core of the impoverishment of social life. With the development of the concept of capital, in the *Foundations of the Critique of Political Economy (Grundrisse)*, wrote between 1857 and 1858, he goes on to qualify that the estrangement that occurs in bourgeois society comes from a specific social relationship, understood through the concept of "capital". This signifies that the means for overcoming estrangement assume the need to achieve a different way of life, in which the development of human individuality is the foundation of wealth, and that this requires the abolition of capital.

From this interpretation of Marx's thoughts, the sketches gathered in the *Grundrisse* provide material for the understanding of the relationship between the *Manuscripts* and *Capital*, as they explain both the changes and continuities in the authors' thinking in his criticism of political economy. At least two aspects of Marx's criticism can be highlighted as points of contact between these writings, showing a certain unity of the author's thoughts, regardless of their inevitable incompleteness and changes over time. This is Marx's advance in criticising the concept of "capital", as formulated by political economy, and, therefore, his way of qualifying the nature of *estrangement* in bourgeois society.

Divided into two parts—the first dedicated to "Money", and the second dedicated to "Capital"—the *Grundrisse* sketches have a theme running through them; they demonstrate that the specificity of bourgeois society is in its production process, a process guided by the production of a specific wealth, and that exchange relations, in the most varied forms of money, are suitable for this process (Marx, 1987a: 36). Starting with the polemic around political economy and the French socialists who followed Proudhon, Marx sought to demonstrate that social changes (or reforms) centred only on changing the form of exchange (abolition of money, wages, hourly bonuses, etc.) would not solve the social ills produced by bourgeois society. This is because, for him, an exchange process centred on money does not characterise this society. It is its important component, but it does not constitute its specificity (idem: 84).

To delineate the specific characteristic of bourgeois society, Marx suggests that its (bourgeois) social relations are characterised by personal independence and a dependence on *things*. Unlike a society based on personal interdependence, in which social position is established based on the degree of kinship, religious precepts and/or direct domination over other social groups, in bourgeois society, it is the relationships between the products of labour of each individual producer that mediates our relationships (idem: 93–96). Thus, individual producers participate in social production in proportion to their contribution to this production (or taking ownership of the production of others)—a contribution that is measured by the labour time embodied in the use values produced by them in the exchange, and expressed in how much each person carries, "[...] in his pocket" (idem: 94).

For this pattern of social relations to be established, Marx points out that a substantial change in human relations occurred. In addition to the growth of commerce, industry, transport, communications, etc.—in short, human exchange in the form of "business"—there is also the expropriation of humans, as workers, as well as the means of production and the means of subsistence, marked by the transformation of land into mobile private property—i.e. property able to be bought and sold (idem: 206–207).

Such expropriation has radically changed the nature of human exchange, because by establishing "human activity turned *thing*" as a means of accessing social production, it has relegated personal relationships to the background. Humans have been established as independent from each other ("free and equal" before the law) to exchange their *things*—even if the only *thing* they have is themselves, their own capacity for work, so turning themselves into *things* (idem: 206–207).

With the institution of wage labour, together with a degree of human exchange, there was a transformation in human relations—characteristic of a social process of production that Marx sought to understand through the category of *capital*. In criticising the notion, from political economy, that capital is the *things* (tools, machines, etc.) that mediate the labour process and provide a certain income, Marx argues that capital is the contradictory movement of the production of "exchange value" embodied in use values. In this sense, capital takes various forms throughout this movement, because it is the reproduction of exchange value which needs the form of use to continue to exist (even if its use is to represent exchange values, such as money) (idem: 202–204).

The movement of reproduction of exchange value is explained by the unity of the production process and the circulation of goods. In the latter, there is an exchange between equals: the representative of capital appropriates the labour force, which receives enough to reproduce itself in the social position of workers (idem: 213–214). In production, the exchange relationship occurs when the workforce is put to work. If during that time, labour is done beyond the time necessary for its reproduction—i.e. the exchange value for which it was contracted—then this results in surplus labour time that is appropriated by capital, as such time takes the form of exchange values embodied in use values (idem: 246–249).

Once sold, these exchange values must again assume the forms of the labour force and the means of production, so re-forming the movement. The representative of capital, who *knows* that this unity is necessary, seeks, whenever possible, to re-form the movement on an expanded scale, as its inclusion in social wealth comes from the *quantum* of labour that it produces compared to the *quantum* of labour produced by the social group. For Marx, enrichment occurs through the increasing production and realisation of exchange values embodied in use values, in which the amount of value added to the values advanced for production is increased.

Marx notes that, it is precisely in this continuously increased reproduction of exchange value that the contradiction of this production process opens up the possibility for overcoming it and moving towards human emancipation. Because, to continuously increase surplus labour time, capital generates an increase in human exchange and reduces the labour time necessary to reproduce labour capacity in relation to surplus labour time. Each new increase in human exchange decreases the already reduced labour time required, causing a small increase in surplus labour time (idem: 259–266). Consequently, the growth in the amount of labour time appropriate to the surplus tends to increasingly decrease and, in bourgeois society, it cannot be zero, since the growth in exchange value only occurs for active labour (idem: 263).

Marx's explanation for this trend lies in a historic transformation of working practices, as the rise in the "productive output of labour" took a dizzying leap upward with the change of labour processes towards large-scale manufacturing industry. Concomitant with this leap, limits on the working day were established through an intense, and sometimes bloody, struggle by workers.

In manufacturing, the pace of work and the strength of production are dictated by the workers themselves, so that decreases in the labour time required to produce goods are dependent on their capacity, the unilateral and mechanical division of labour and the organisation of the process of labour (idem: 505–508). In large-scale industry, the pace of work and the level of production are dictated by mechanical systems, so that the division of manufacturing labour and its principles of organisation are maintained, and the workforce is reduced to an appendage of the machine—i.e. another one of its cogs (Marx, 1987b: 82–86). As a result, reductions in the labour time required to reproduce labour capacity can be increased regardless of the natural limits of the workforce's own capacity, expanding surplus labour time not only through continuous and extensive working hours, but also by increasing its intensity, and thereby increasing its productivity.

As the growth of bourgeois social wealth, under large-scale industry, occurs due to the reduction of the necessary labour time in relation to the surplus labour time, Marx notes that such growth will continuously decrease because it happens within the working day—which imposes a limit. As it is a limit that has been overcome by a long process of workers' struggle, there is no a priori impediment to increasing the working day as a way of increasing the surplus, so that Marx, in pointing out this tendency of the production of exchange value to decrease, affirms only a general tendency of a society so constituted.[15]

Despite the substantial growth in material wealth and human exchange, a decline in the rate of growth of bourgeois social wealth is taking place. What marks a contradiction in the production process is that it constitutes a production potential that makes it possible to reduce the working day to the minimum working time necessary for the social group. But this power is not effective because it takes on the capital form through a mode of labour that incorporates the division of manufacturing labour into the machine system, thus constituting a labour process whose characteristic is to be a means of extracting *quantum* labour (Marx, 1987a: 108–109; 1987b: 93–94).

So, instead of freeing humans from continuous, extensive and intense working hours, intended solely for the reproduction of increasing exchange value embodied in use values, the productive potential constituted by the advance of capital reproduction keeps humans confined to this narrow horizon of production and thereby degrades their existence. Far from establishing the effective development of human individuality, there is a reduction in the time dedicated to these aspects of human life, while labour time is extended, which can be seen today with the advance of labour time over sleeping time.[16]

For Marx, the development of human individuality is made possible precisely by appropriating the productive potential engendered by the growth of human exchange. This means forming a production process whose objective is to produce available time to allow humans to develop the most varied aspects of their being.[17] In other words, a social life in which human development is wealth, and poverty is only the absence of exchange between humans, leaving labour with a declining position in the set of social relations.[18]

In critiquing the understanding of money and capital by the field of political economy and its critics, Marx developed an exchange relationship centred on money, configured as a form of social wealth capable of acquiring anything that arises from a specific social process of production. This process stems from a pattern of social relationships in which humans are independent of each other and dependent on the results of their labour, measured by the money in their pockets. This explanation is possible because Marx introduces an entirely new concept of capital into the debate, which allows bourgeois society to be classified as capitalist—a concept of capital that, despite the social transformations of the last two centuries, remains analytically relevant for understanding contemporary society.

From the point of view of understanding wealth and poverty, which is of direct interest to the theme of this chapter, we note that, in *Grundrisse*, Marx sets out a social process of production of a specific form of wealth—exchange values embodied in use values—so that wealth is effectively this set of values produced on an expanded scale. In other words, capitalist social wealth is the ever-growing *quantum* of labour, so that material abundance only means wealth insofar as it expresses and engenders the *quantum* of growing labour. Otherwise, it does not constitute wealth.

This is an affirmation of the duplicity of capitalist social wealth not found in the *Manuscripts*. Furthermore, the foundation of this wealth is, in an explicit and structural way, the impoverishment of humans, who, confined to the relationship of estrangement, are degraded because their lives are reduced to continuous, extensive and intense working hours, as well as to a horizon of social reproduction framed by the contradictory movement of the capitalist social wealth production process.[19] In the *Manuscripts*, Marx's criticism of bourgeois society points to the estranged human condition within a world he himself produces; then, in *Grundrisse*, this condition is explained by the very form of social relations—personal independence and dependence on *things*—whose reproduction points to the possibility of a new society, based on *disposable time*. In *Capital*, Marx explains how this form of social relationship is founded on an abstract social dominance.

As is well known, Marx starts *Capital*, one of his most important works, by introducing the elementary *form*[20] of capitalist wealth: the commodity form. If it is both use value and exchange value, then commodity has the capacity to satisfy both our physical needs and our dreams, and is something, tangible or intangible, destined for exchange (Marx, 1996: 45–46). This happens because the meaning of production, in a society in which its dominant social form is merchandise, has become exchange. For this reason, all concrete labour has become no more than human labour—removed from any quality other than that of being a labour cost (Marx, 1996: 46–49).

It does not matter that they are the diverse products of different human activities, because these specificities are erased by the value form. This is because, in Marx's argument, this form becomes the means for human subsistence, so that, in this mode of socialisation, social recognition of individual labours is essential. It occurs only when the exchange of the goods takes place (Marx, 1996: 83–86, 704–705).

In this sense, commodities have their value expressed in their exchange, and the basis of its exchange value is its value, with labour as its substance and time as its measure (Marx, 1996: 48–49). Although this measure is composed of abstract units, the amount of value incorporated into a given commodity is measured in social terms. This means that the time spent working on the production of a certain commodity is standardised by the social average to produce that commodity,[21] so that private labour is not directly social (Marx, 1996: 83–86). They must pass the *exchange test* to become part of capitalist social wealth—that is, the *quantum* of labour per unit of *social time* embodied in use values.

Precisely because the labour expended on producing goods is not directly social, it expresses its values in a single commodity, which lends itself and its values to become the "general equivalent form" of social wealth. This commodity thus becomes money, the capacity of which to buy any commodity is an expression of the constitution of the generalised exchange of commodities as the mode of production of social life (Marx, 1996: 69–70, 80).

This mode of production is established by a qualitative change in the division of human beings: on the one hand, there are those without the personal means to sustain their livelihood and who need to sell their labour power to survive, and on the other, the owners of the means of production, whose social reproduction consists of the continuous appreciation of their property, which requires putting themselves in contact with the labour force to obtain goods. So, regardless of whether they are in one condition or the other, people need to transform the results of their activity—or ownership of the activities of others—into commodities. The transformation lies in the *form* of the ability to work, one's own labour or the command over the labour of others, as the form of social mediation. It should be noted that, within this relationship, property is no longer just property, but a value that is only preserved through its continuous appreciation. In a word, as capital.[22]

This new form of social mediation embodies the divisions between people, in which they become, even if they do not know it, the makers of their own domination. The explanation for this lies, once again, in the social form of wealth: value. As part of total social labour, each commodity is a certain portion of the total social value.

As already stated, it is a given "value quantity", so that the result of the labour expended on the means of production is a set of commodities that express a part of total social labour, this "part" being determined by the average time in which society produces such goods (Marx, 1996: 49–50, 83–86).

For example: if the production of a given commodity is carried out, on average, at the rate of 50 units/workday at a value of £500, then industries that produce at a lower rate will receive below average (and vice versa). In this example, if you produce 10 units/workday, you will receive £100 (if you produce 60 units/workday, you will receive £600).

Thus described, individual labour that counts as social is that posted by the average production in each branch of production. The generalised production of goods is not referred to in individual production, but in the group of producers. Producing more of a certain commodity in less time than other producers of this commodity becomes everyone's production goal, because the difference between individual productivity and the abstract social norm (socially necessary labour time) can be appropriated by an individual capitalist in the form of extraordinary surplus value. Once sold, that would mean more money for their producer and, therefore, greater access to total social labour. This establishes competition as the mode of relationship between producers.

The results are, firstly, a type of social relationship in which individual production must occur at least close to the social average, the average productivity being imposed as a temporal norm formed by all the individual manufacturers producing for exchange and, secondly, a society in which the reproduction of social life is conditioned by people's participation in total social labour through the production of goods. In summary: each person will be able to satisfy their needs as long as they can do their jobs (either by selling their own labour or by appropriating it in the form of surplus value) as part of the total social production. Repeated exchange is, therefore, an imperative of this social form.

As well as being widespread, exchanges need to increase, both in terms of use values and in terms of value. For individual producers, the transformation of the fruits of their individual labour into a means of accessing larger portions of social production, expressed in money, appears as the only means by which to satisfy their growing needs. However, the growth in exchanges is not explained by individual requirements, but by the very meaning of capitalist social production: valuing *value*. In fact, the requirements themselves grow due to the appreciation process, as it generates increasing value embodied in a myriad of use values.

Before explaining how value is expanded, it should be noted that the search for increasing productivity effects the value of goods that then reinforces the social dynamics mentioned above. Starting from the previous example, if the average of social production is 50 units of merchandise per workday, then if an individual producer doubles productivity they will produce 100 units of merchandise per workday. With that, you will get double the value of other producers (according to the example, £1000). The generalisation of this labour process, however, establishes a new "social average" for producing this commodity at 100 units per workday. So, the value returns to its initial level and reduces the value per unit of merchandise. This then forces a new round of productivity increases, as producers operating under the new standard no longer obtain the doubled value, but the same value for double the goods. In other words, the individual value of the goods fell by half, but the total value of production remains identical to the value before the increase in productivity. Indeed, everyone involved in the production process is compelled to increase productivity, regardless of the type of personal relationship they have—including, so that the personal relationships of domination can compete in favour of this effect.[23]

In *Grundrisse,* Marx observes that the component of production that allows the expansion of value is the labour force, but in *Capital*, labour, under capitalism, is explicitly seen as the means by which human beings are part of society. It is the expenditure of labour on transforming the means of production into something new (value embodied in use values) that reproduces and expands its value. Since the means of production are dead labour, they are transformed into new goods, with increased value, only through contact with living labour. As Marx explains, it is the difference between the value of the labour force and the value added to dead labour in the production process that produces the portion of the value that is appropriated by the owner of the means of production. Since these owners pay workers the value of their labour while employing it beyond the time necessary to reproduce that labour, they obtain a surplus value in the production of goods. Thus, the extension, intensity and continuity of the workday have a central place in determining the surplus value generated by social production (Marx, 1996: 180–186, 204–208).

With the transition from manufacturing to large-scale industry, a concept already developed in the *Grundrisse*, "relative surplus value" became the main means of extracting surplus value.[24] For this reason, the relationship between the workforce and the means of production, in terms of value, has developed so that an ever smaller share of capital is locked up in the workforce in relation to the machines and equipment that it has in operation. Thus, the proportion of capital responsible for the increase in value is also reduced. This also forces the concentration and centralisation of capital into a few hands. There are at least two consequences of this reduction in the mobilised workforce in relation to the means of production: firstly, the decline in the growth of surplus value, forcing capital to expand its sphere of domination and to complexify its forms of growth, and secondly, from the point of view of capital, an increasing portion of the workforce becomes surplus (Marx, 1996: 607–634).

The main result of this, "general law of accumulation", is that the production of material wealth starts to generate ever less return on the expenditure of labour. As long as labour is *the* form of social mediation, the effect of the increasing uselessness of people as workers is, at the very least, to increase competition among them, to the point that they mobilise an increasing part of their lives to be able to put themselves in a position where that can be exploited by capital. On a similar line, if social wealth is the value embodied in use values, then increasing production of it results in human impoverishment, because it increases the estrangement of people from the objective world created by them and confronting them—the growing domination of capital over the most diverse spheres of life—as it establishes as an ad infinitum *praxis* of increasing production of commodities in a shorter time. What commodifies human relations is giving them the function of producing more goods in less time. Or, as Postone summarises (2020: 157):

> While agreeing that Karl Marx's category of capital refers to the structuring of society as a whole [...] it not only delineates a determinate mode of class

exploitation, but also, more basically, grasps a unique form of social mediation that structures capitalist modernity as a historically specific form of social life. This form of mediation is socially constituted and, yet, abstract and temporal.

If the concept of capital expresses the heteronomy of people by generalising their activities as the commodity form, it can be characterised as a social process of production of life that appears to be independent from our social practices and, consequently, from the thinking that they support, the essence of which is the reduction of these activities to a certain *quantum* of labour. This quantity is abstract, continuous and devoid of human meaning, but is how, in this society, we mediate our relations. Or, in Marx's synthetic formulation (idem: 84—our edit):

> [...] the relations connecting the labour of one individual with that of the rest appear, not as direct social relations between individuals at work, but as what they *really are*, material relations between persons and social relations between *things*.

According to Marx (1996: 751), overcoming this form of social domination, one based on labour as a mediator of our social relations, requires, "the expropriation of a few usurpers by the mass of the people". The question remains, however: what will be expropriated? In this case, in addition to private property, transformed into socialised production, one must also abolish what shapes the practice itself and its views regarding the production process: the value. It will be overcome, in short, through the expropriation of surplus labour time, which will allow people the *disposable time* to form a production process whose expansion of material wealth does not imply human impoverishment (Marx, 1998: 806–807). However, if these material conditions are the product of the development of capital accumulation, then their advance seems to have taken with it the subjectivity necessary to enable this, "mass of people" to free itself.

* * *

Returning to Marx's writings to understand wealth and poverty in capitalist society remains relevant to contemporary debates because, despite the significant social and economic transformations of the past two centuries, Marx treats wealth and poverty as polar opposites, which are mutually defined in the process of reproducing capitalism. This view is absent, if not directly rejected, in studies on inequality of income and wealth. These studies, as a rule, have a more or less common conclusion: that the problem of inequality cannot be solved by a new form of producing, distributing, exchanging and consuming human production, but by the equitable division of the means of acquiring value, giving the potential of each person an environment in which, with due effort, they can attain a certain standard of consumption.[25] Especially because, as some authors point out, under a capitalist system a certain level of inequality is welcome since it encourages production while maintaining social cohesion (e.g. Atkinson, 2015: 9–10). The problem, they maintain, lies in disruptive levels of income and wealth inequality, or "hyper-inequality" (e.g. Piketty, 2020: 3).

In revisiting Marx's writings, one perceives the abstract character of social domination, in societies where the commodity form predominates, as the necessary and inescapable means of expressing the results of human activity. Under this domination, a social structure is created whose reproduction dynamics engenders a material abundance, concentrated and centralised in the capital form, and the impoverishment of people—impoverished because they are confined to the social position of workers or capital managers, whose social practice is characterised by exhausting themselves for the enrichment of an objective world that ends up oppressing them.

The phenomenon of persistent income and wealth inequality, empirically observed by numerous scholars on the topic, is explained *in capitalism*, instead of being explained *from capitalism.* It is no accident, then, that the solution to the problem is not in the distribution plan. As paradoxical as this may seem, this conclusion is understandable.

If social relations, when reproduced, generate a concentration and centralisation of social wealth—value embodied in use values—which represents a form of oppression of its producers, then overcoming this situation lies in the abolition of the core of this social relationship: the commodity form of labour products and labour as a social mediator. The material conditions for this abolition are established by capitalism itself, since by expanding social wealth and, consequently, human poverty, and by increasing labour productivity it becomes possible to create production that does not require continuous, intense and long working hours to provide for a sociability that allows human enrichment. It would mean a society in which human production had, at its core, the development of human individuality, instead of the opposite, as objects of value in search of becoming surplus value.

From this perspective, overcoming (*Aufhebung*) persistent income and wealth inequality, and poverty, lies in a radical change of institutions, to use the language of literature on the subject. However, this transformation does not lie in the institution of *fair competition* within an unchanged social process of production but, for the reasons explained, in a different organising principle for social production: that of *disposable time*. In a sentence, the principle for forming the production of social life would be to provide *disposable time* for human enrichment. The route by which this principle is to be reached is still open.

Notes

1. The concept of autocracy is used here in the sense attributed to Brazilian sociologist Florestan Fernandes. In *Revolução Burguesa no Brasil* (1975), Fernandes forged the idea of "bourgeois autocracy" to analyse the persistence of radically anti-democratic principles in the shaping of the State, society and the market in contexts marked by formal democracy. Currently, levels of social, racial and regional inequality are as alarming as those presented by Fernandes in his study, and they remain signs of an organised society working against democratisation and social integration.
2. It is worth noting that the Gini Index of income distribution measures the distribution by means of the difference between the curve of perfect equality of income and the curve of the accumulated income distribution of a certain sample, the latter being calculated through the polynomial of income distribution, which starts with the income from the lowest percentile to the highest percentile. Thus, the greater the difference between the perfect equality curve and the income distribution curve of a certain sample, the greater the income inequality, so that, in the extreme inequality case, the Gini Index reaches the 100 and, for the limit case of perfect equality, zero. Thus, the closer to 100, the more unequal the distribution of income. The Brazilian case is, therefore, a case closer to extreme inequality, while the Russian situation is closer to perfect equality. For the demonstration of the calculation of the Gini Index, see Hoffmann (1998).
3. It is worth mentioning that until 2014, this data was not accessible for academic research.
4. Regarding this, it is worth remembering the efforts of The International Consortium of Investigative Journalists: Offshore Leaks Database

in mapping the tax havens in which these diverted funds are deposited (*ICIJ Offshore Leaks Database* [s.d.]).

5. It is important to note that the book caused few repercussions on its first publication in France, in 2013. The exponential growth in sales of the English version, which went down in history at the Harvard University Press, can be attributed, in great part, to the fact that the author contradicts, with a large-scale empirical study, the proposals implemented since the 1980s in the United States. Piketty's book was published in Brazil in 2014 and had widespread repercussions even though the study did not present data on Brazil. The work of Souza (2018) is in direct dialogue with the general hypothesis of and the methodology used by Piketty.
6. As the British economist Michael Roberts (2017) highlights, the level established by the World Bank is significantly low. If a level were to be established that would permit a global life expectancy of 70 years, it would need to be US$ 7.40 per day. So, instead of 0.767 billion people being below the poverty line, there would be 4.2 billion living in a precarious situation.
7. See the observation of Brazilian Marxist Mario Duayer (2020: 119), supported by the formulations of English philosopher Roy Bhaskar: "[…] from the truism that any human activity has as necessary presupposition the existence of social structures, Bhaskar concludes that society provides means, rules and resources for everything we do. He means that society with its structures is a necessary condition for any teleological activity. From this, it can be inferred that we do not create society, but it always pre-exists our actions. What we do with our practice is to reproduce and/or transform the—material and spiritual—social structures, which are the condition for our daily practice. […] And if the intentional practice acts on the pre-existing structures, reproducing or transforming them, it follows that some knowledge of the structures is a condition for the practice. Put another way, we can concluded that our understandings of reality are not a result of what we 'capture with sensorial perception, but the result of the theories [and/or representations—MD] by which our understanding of *things* is organised". For a demonstration of this methodological starting point, see Bhaskar (2005).
8. As an example, one can contrast the commodity form with gifts, one of the most widespread forms of human exchange in non-capitalist societies: "In non-capitalist societies […] people produce objects as aspects of themselves in relationship to other agents that are expressly aimed and understood to transform one type of social relation into another. Because gifts are inseparable from sociality and because that sociality is culturally and historically specific […] there is no abstract form of the gift (as there is of the commodity) to be universalised […] Gifts are, first and foremost […] social imaginaries whose meaning derives from the way that agents

apprehend the strategic intentionality of the event. Gifts are not, accordingly, *things* but functions. [...] There is thus no beginning or end to gift giving because each act of giving and receiving is performative in that it presupposes the event that it is attempting to create [...]" (LiPuma & Postone, 2020: 169–170). As the authors argue, the commodity form is specific to capitalism because, in this society, "[...] labour functions as a social mediation in such a way that the commodity emerges as the universal form of the object in capitalist societies" (idem: 169). For this specificity, there are commodities in non-capitalist societies that are not in the commodity form (idem: 170).

9. According to the Canadian historian Moishe Postone (2015: 4), this justifies the resumption of Marx's critique of capitalism, since it criticises, "the core of a social formation that is generative of a peculiar dynamic of identity and non-identity, of pointing beyond itself while reasserting itself".
10. These conditions, which Postone (2003: 37) highlights, may or may not be implemented and, above all, are not a priori in the capitalist social process itself, as if they were a nature of a certain social class.
11. As Mészáros (1972: 14–15, 313—note 3) observes, the term estrangement (or alienation) is, in Marx, fraught with complexity, because it seeks to calculate the difference between the relationships between man, nature and other people to point out how they constitute dominance—that is, a degradation of human beings and of nature itself. This complexity has led Brazilian and Argentine scholars of the *Manuscripts* to revise their translations, proposing different versions for the words *Entäusserung* and *Entfremdung* which, in the German language, are interchangeable. To see the controversies surrounding the debate, see Ranieri (2000, 2004), Infranca and Vedda (2012), Aren et al. (2015), Netto (2015), and Martorano (2017).
12. This difference is highlighted by Erich Fromm (1961).
13. Such enrichment of the objective world, which is expressed by the growing power of money, makes it the means by which human achievements can be accessed, making the possessor of money the effective owner of such exploits, even if he does not have any gift for them. It appears, therefore, that it has properties developed within itself, when in fact it does not. In this regard, see Marx (1975: 299–300, 306–307, 324). This understanding of money and its relationship with estrangement is taken up again when the author discusses the fetish of merchandise and money in *Capital*. In this regard, see Marx (1996: 81–87, 98–103).
14. This is the core of the author's criticism of Proudhon (Marx, 1975: 280).
15. Given the relationship between surplus time and the necessary time needed within an unchanged working day, one can synthesise the effect of expanding productive forces on the increase in surplus labour through

a numerical formula. Assuming that x is the portion of the workday dedicated to the necessary labour and y is how much the productive forces multiply the labour capacity, the first term of the sequence can be expressed by the x/y ratio, in which the increase in the productive force of labour reduces the number of hours needed to reproduce labour capacity. This reduction implies adding surplus labour time, as the working day is kept constant. The next term in the sequence is the new necessary labour time divided by how much the productive forces multiply the capacity for work. Each new term will, therefore, be the previous term divided by the effect of the increase of the productive force on the capacity of work. We note that, under the strict conditions developed here, the increasing expansion of productive forces tends to produce an ever-smaller increase in surplus labour time. To be more exact, an addition that tends to zero. The sum of this numerical sequence is therefore convergent. It is worth highlighting that this does not mean less surplus labour with the increase of labour productive forces, but, rather, a continuous decline in the growth of surplus labour. In "*Capital*", this trend is developed more deeply, especially when combined with accumulation, producing the famous, "General law of capitalist accumulation". On the behaviour of the numerical sequence above and for a demonstration of this convergence, see N. S. Piskunov (1969: 710–714).

16. On this subject, see the essay, *24/7: Late Capitalism and the Ends of Sleep*, by Jonathan Crary (2013).
17. Regarding this, it is worth highlighting Marx's explicit reference (1987b: 94) to *disposable time*: "The more this contradiction develops, the more obvious it becomes that the growth of the productive forces can no longer be tied to the appropriation of alien *Surplus Labour*, and that the working masses must, rather, themselves appropriate their surplus labour. Once they have done so—and *Disposable Time* has thereby ceased to possess an antithetical existence—then, on the one hand, necessary labour time will be measured by the needs of the social individual; and, on the other, society's productive power will develop so rapidly that, although production will now be calculated to provide wealth for all, the *Disposable Time* of all will increase. For real wealth is the developed productive power of all individuals. Then wealth is no longer measured by labour time but by *Disposable Time*. Labour time as the measure of wealth posits wealth itself as based upon poverty, and *Disposable Time* only as existing in and through the opposition to surplus labour time; or the whole time of an individual is posited as labour time, and he is consequently degraded to a mere labourer, subsumed under labour. Hence the most developed machinery now compels the labourer to work for a longer time than the

savage does, or than the labourer himself did when he was using the simplest, crudest implements".

18. The problem was formulated by Marx in his *Manuscripts* (1975: 304): "It will be seen how in place of the wealth and poverty of political economy come the rich human being and the rich human need. The rich human being is simultaneously the human being in need of a totality of human manifestations of life - the man in whom his own realisation exists as an inner necessity, as need. Not only wealth, but likewise the poverty of man [...] receives in equal measure a human and therefore social significance. Poverty is the passive bond which causes the human being to experience the need of the greatest wealth—the other human being. The dominion of the objective being in me, the sensuous outburst of my life activity, is passion, which thus becomes here the activity of my being".
19. It is worth highlighting that Marx's formulation is corroborated by studies in the field of the Sociology of Work, particularly those of Juliet B. Schor (1991), Ludmila C. Abílio (2015), Sadi Dal Rosso (2017) and Pietro Basso (2018).
20. Argentinian philosopher Alberto Bonnet (2020) notes that Marx uses the term *form* with various meanings, and that this precludes its definition as, "one dimension of the couple form/matter" (Bonnet 2020: 206). In Marx, he notes, "this means that the forms in question are not only subjective but, at the same time, objective; that, both in objective and subjective terms, they are products of historical development; and that, in subjective terms, therefore, they are not attributes of human being in general but of individuals socialised in specific historical conditions" (idem, 2020: 217).
21. It should be noted that the incorporation of time as a socially determined variable was not present in the *Grundrisse*. This suggests that Marx understood the abstract nature of social dominance in a new way. On this new position of time, it is worth noting the following passage from Marx: "The labour, however, that forms the substance of value, is homogeneous human labour, expenditure of one uniform labour power. The total labour power of society, which is embodied in the sum total of the values of all commodities produced by that society, counts here as one homogeneous mass of human labour power, composed though it be of innumerable individual units. Each of these units is the same as any other, so far as it has the character of the average labour power of society, and takes effect as such; that is, so far as it requires for producing a commodity, no more time than is needed on an average, no more than is socially necessary. The labour time socially necessary is that required to produce an article under the normal conditions of production, and with the average degree of skill and intensity prevalent at the time" (Marx, 1996: 49).

22. Brazilian philosopher Mauricio Vieira Martins (2020: 194) states that, by substantiating his argument in this way, Marx shows that, "the reduction of all commodities to labour-time is not only a product of thought but also takes place within society itself. Marx unveils a process of abstraction (in the core sense of reduction) at work in the real proper, even though this statement is at odds with common sense [...]".
23. This movement of the re-establishing of the social unit of time was highlighted by Postone (2003: 289–290) and called the "*treadmill effect*". At the level of social structures, and as already highlighted, it is worth noting how two processes operate on the *treadmill effect*. The first is the movement of value, which expands for the individual producer and generalised in productivity, establishes a new measure of value that returns to where it started. As a result, its magnitude per unit of commodity declines as the value produced per unit of time remains constant. The second process is the concrete transformation of working practice, from the rhythm to the tools and, therefore, to the training of the workforce. This culminates in a concrete change in the production process, in its temporality, which manifests itself in the larger number of units produced. The relationship between value and abstract time remains constant, but this value framework puts the level of productivity into a permanent and directional movement, constituting a specifically capitalist historic time mode (Postone, 2003: 292–293).
24. It is important to note that the extraction of surplus value in its absolute form also implies elevated production, technical development and other changes to the production process, contribution to the growth in value through the reduction of the value of the workforce. This said, the preponderance of relative surplus value over absolute surplus value indicates that, for large-scale industry, the changes to the process of accumulation drive the reduction in the value of the workforce that results for the expansion of the workday—and not the reverse, as in manufacturing. Even if the workday seems stable, the generalisation of a new level of production makes explicit that the new workday concentrates more expenditure of labour time. For the *treadmill effect*, this is the new expenditure norm, with no growth in value.
25. Studies conducted by Piketty (2014, 2020) are exemplars in this respect; therefore, its conclusion is that capitalism, without proper regulation, tends to generate a vicious circle of inequality. A somewhat obvious conclusion, even if one ignores, as the author does, the dynamics of capitalism exposed by Marx. Even with this conclusion, Piketty does not indicate any another possibility for social organisation. Rather, he suggests ways to tame capitalism, the very cause of the effect he finds.

References

Abílio, L. C. (2015). *Sem maquiagem: o trabalho de um milhão de revendedoras de cosméticos*. Boitempo Editorial.

Aren, F., Rotemberg, S., & Vedda, M. (2015). *Manuscritos económico-filosóficos de 1844*. Editora Colihue.

Atkinson, A. B. (2015). *Inequality: What can be done?* Harvard University Press.

Baltar, P. (2015). *Crescimento da economia e mercado de trabalho no Brasil* (No. 2036). Texto para Discussão.

Basso, P. (2018). *Tempos modernos, jornadas antigas: vidas de trabalho no início do século XXI*. Editora da UNICAMP.

Bhaskar, R. (2005). *The possibility of naturalism: A philosophical critique of contemporary human sciences*. Routledge.

Braga, H. P. (2016). *Limites e possibilidades do capitalismo: uma introdução ao estudo da riqueza e da pobreza na crítica à economia política*. http://acervus.unicamp.br/. Accessed May 19, 2020.

Braga, H. P. (2018). Notas sobre a relação entre estranhamento e capital: uma análise dos Manuscritos Econômico-Filosóficos e do Grundrisse. *Marx e o Marxismo-Revista Do NIEP-Marx, 6*(10), 29–43.

Braga, H. P., & Kawahara, I. Z. (2021). O tempo no capitalismo: uma reflexão a partir de Moishe Postone. Tematicas, 29(57), 347-369.

Bonnet, A. (2020). The concept of form in the critique of political economy. In *Marx and contemporary critical theory* (pp. 203–225). Palgrave Macmillan.

Carvalho, L. (2018). *Valsa brasileira: do boom ao caos econômico*. Editora Todavia.

Crary, J. (2013). *24/7: Late capitalism and the ends of sleep*. Verso.

Dal Rosso, S. (2017). *O ardil da flexibilidade: os trabalhadores e a teoria do valor*. Boitempo Editorial.

Duayer, M. (2020). Marx: The method of political economy as an ontological critique. In *Marx and contemporary critical theory* (pp. 113–128). Palgrave Macmillan.

Fernandes, F. (1975). *A revolução burguesa no Brasil: ensaio de interpretação sociológica*. Zahar Editora.

Fromm, E. (1961). *Marx's Concept of man*. Frederick Ungar Publishing.

Hoffmann, R. (1998). *Distribuição de renda: medidas de desigualdade e pobreza*. Editora da Universidade de São Paulo.

Hoffmann, R. (2017). *Desigualdade da distribuição da renda no Brasil: o que mudou em 2015*. Texto para Discussão n° 38 do IEPE/Casa das Garças.

Hoffmann, R. (2019). Distribuição da renda no Brasil em 2017. *Economia & Região, 7*(2), 5–27.

Hoffmann, R., Jesus, J. G., & Almeida, S. S. P. (2018). *A distribuição da renda no Brasil conforme a PNAD: 1995–2017*. Texto para Discussão n° 45 do IEPE/Casa das Garças.

ICIJ Offshore Leaks Database. ([s.d.]). https://offshoreleaks.icij.org/. Accessed August 28, 2020.

Infranca, A., & Vedda, M. (2012). Introducción: Sobre la génesis de la categoría de alienación. In *La alienación: historia y actualidad*. Herramienta.

Kurz, R. (1993). *O retorno de Potemkin: capitalismo de fachada e conflito distributivo na Alemanha*. Editora Paz e Terra.

Lakner, C., & Milanovic, B. (2013). *Global income distribution: From the fall of the Berlin Wall to the Great Recession*. The World Bank.

LiPuma, E., & Postone, M. (2020). Gifts, commodities, and the encompassment of others. *Critical Historical Studies, 7*(1), 167–200.

Lukács, G. (1969). *Conversando com Lukács*. Editora Paz e Terra.

Lukács, G. (1980). *Ontology of social being: Labour. v. 3*. Merlin Press.

Marx, K. (1975). *Marx/Engels Collected Works* (Vol. 3).

Marx, K. (1987a). *Marx/Engels Collected Works* (Vol. 28).

Marx, K. (1987b). *Marx/Engels Collected Works* (Vol. 29).

Marx, K. (1996). *Marx/Engels Collected Works* (Vol. 35).

Marx, K. (1998). *Marx/Engels Collected Works* (Vol. 37).

Martins, M. V. (2020). On real objects that are not sensuous: Marx and abstraction in actu. In *Marx and contemporary critical theory* (pp. 191–202). Palgrave Macmillan.

Martorano, L. C. (2017). *Manuscritos econômicos-filosóficos*. Editora Martin Claret.

Mészáros, I. (1972). *Marx's theory of alienation*. Harper Torchbooks.

Milanovic, B. (2012). *Global income inequality by the numbers: In history and now-an overview*. The World Bank.

Morgan, M. (2017). *Extreme and persistent inequality: New evidence for Brazil combining national accounts, surveys and fiscal data*, 2001–2015. World Inequality Lab Working Papers.

Netto, J. P. (2015). Apresentação. In *Cadernos de Paris & Manuscritos Econômico-Filosóficos de 1844*. Editora Expressão Popular.

Piketty, T. (2014). *Capital in the twenty-first century* (A. Goldhammer, trans.). Belknap.

Piketty, T. (2020). *Capital and ideology*. Harvard University Press.

Pinheiro-Machado, R., & Scalco, L. (2020). From hope to hate: The rise of conservative subjectivity in Brazil. *Journal of Ethnographic Theory, 10*(1), 21–31.

Piskunov, N. (1969). *Differential and integral calculus*. MIR Publishers.

Postone, M. (2003). *Time, labor, and social domination: A reinterpretation of Marx's critical*. Cambridge University Press.

Postone, M. (2015). The task of critical theory today: Rethinking the critique of capitalism and its futures. In *Globalization, critique and social theory: Diagnoses and challenges*. Emerald Group Publishing.

Postone, M. (2020). Capital and temporality. In *The Marx revival: Key concepts and new critical interpretations* (p. 157). Cambridge University Press.

Ranieri, J. J. (2000). *Alienação e estranhamento em Marx: dos manuscritos econômicos-filosóficos de 1844 a ideologia alemã*. http://acervus.unicamp.br/. Accessed July 7, 2020.

Ranieri, J. J. (2004). Sobre os Chamados Manuscritos Econômico-Filosóficos de Karl Marx. In *Manuscritos Econômico-Filosóficos*. Boitempo Editorial.

Roberts, M. (2017, April 5). Bill Gates and 4bn in poverty. *The Next Recession* (blog). https://thenextrecession.wordpress.com/2017/04/05/bill-gates-and-4bn-in-poverty/. Accessed July 31, 2017.

Sampaio, P. A., Jr. (2017). *Crônica de uma crise anunciada: crítica à economia política de Lula e Dilma*. SG-Amarante Editorial.

Schor, J. (1991). *The overworked American: The unexpected decline of leisure*. Basic Books.

Souza, P. H. G. F. D. (2018). *Uma história da desigualdade: a concentração de renda entre os ricos no Brasil, 1926–2013*. Hucitech editora/ANPOCS.

World Bank Group. (2016). *Poverty and shared prosperity 2016: taking on inequality*. World Bank Publications.

World Bank Group. (2020). Poverty and equity data: GINI index (World Bank estimate). https://databank.worldbank.org/source/poverty-and-equity. Accessed August 3, 2020.

CHAPTER 4

Financialisation, Work and Gender: Violence and Barbarism in Ultraliberal Brazil

Ana Paula Colombi and Lívia de Cássia Godoi Moraes

Introduction

Changes in the productive and social arrangements of contemporary capitalismover the past fifty years have resulted in lower growth rates, increased intra-country inequality, and increased unemployment and poverty in core countries. In peripheral countries, these features are consistent with structural characteristics, such as the disruption of labour markets, the permanent existence of an industrial reserve army, pockets of poverty and labour informality,[1] which have deepened barbaric traits in those societies in late capitalist development, such as Brazil. Recently, this situation has been aggravated by the ultraliberal project that has taken shape in the country. This project, intertwined with conservatism in

A. P. Colombi (✉)
Department of Economics and Post-Graduate Program in Social Policy, Federal University of Espírito Santo, Vitória, Brazil

L. de C. G. Moraes
Department of Social Science and Post-Graduate Program in Social Policy, Federal University of Espírito Santo, Vitória, Brazil

G. M. de C. Mello and H. P. Braga (eds.), *Wealth and Poverty in Contemporary Brazilian Capitalism*, Marx, Engels, and Marxisms,
https://doi.org/10.1007/978-3-030-82298-9_4

morals and customs and intensified workforce exploitation, is deepening job insecurity and validating the subordinate position of women.

The objective of this chapter is to discuss recent institutional changes in Brazil that express a universal movement towards a capitalist mode of production that accumulates value through violence, i.e. one that accumulates poverty through the accumulation of capital. In the first section, we set out the theoretical basis of capital accumulation through violence,to expose the intrinsic relationship between economy and power from which exploitation and oppression can be discussed as parts of a single totality, even though their spatial and historical particularities may be expressed in different ways. Among the various forms of oppression, those of gender and sexuality seek to place human labour at the centre of the debate. Criticising political economy, and its recent barbaric nature in Brazil, demands an analysis of production and reproduction, and we have used Social Reproduction Theory (SRT) as the theoretical basis.

In the second section, the text discusses two trends that express this process of capital accumulation through violence in contemporary Brazil. The first is the adverse effects of fiscal austerity in a country with a subordinate position in the processes of the globalisation of production and under financial dominance. It discusses how the institutionalisation of fiscal austerity has sought to reduce spending on social policies in an environment that, since 2015, has been one of low rates of growth and high unemployment. The second trend is the implementation of a reform agenda, with unpopular legislative changes, that has attacked hard-won workers' rights. The objective is to analyse, with an emphasis on women, how the approval of measures, including the ongoing labour reforms, have accentuated the vulnerability of workers in Brazil. Starting with an analysis of production and reproduction, this section ends with a discussion of the impacts of austerity policies, which have hollowed out, and reduced the rights of Brazilian workers. This exercise demonstrates the degree to which the work done by women, many times in situations of violence on both the personal and structural levels, is a praxis that constitutes the logic of capital reproduction.

This chapter shows how the institutionalisation of fiscal austerity, and the attacks on the hard-won employment rights of Brazilian workers, are manifestations of a universal movement of capitalist production at the periphery, a process that accumulates capital through violenceand that has a distinct hint of barbarismtowards women.

Capital Accumulation Through Violence: Theoretical Foundations for Considering the Brazilian Reality

Karl Marx (1975, 1996), undertook a great exercise in opposing bourgeois thinking, expressed as a *law*, in which the existence of the rich and the poor is natural. Such a *law* advocates that, in a meritocratic way, wealthy individuals are wealthy simply because they work harder. Marx aimed, in this task of denaturalisation, to focus on the political praxis of the working class.

As Kohan (2016) emphasises, Marx's concept of law differs from the positivist concept of law in bourgeois logic. It is not fixed or permanent, but functions as a trend, especially because, in its social theory, there is no separation between objectivity and subjectivity, or between economics and politics. In other words, the political struggle directly impacts objective social conditions, in a dialectical movement in which the determinant is also determined.

Laws, according to Marxist theory, must be historicised. When analysing such a theoretical movement, we see that what is presented as a law is neither indispensable nor inevitable but responds to the movement of the class struggle. In revealing the historical determinants of the conditions of social wealth and poverty, Marx (1975,1996) does so without relapsing into economic determinism or subjectivist voluntarism. The contradictions in action and the dialectical movements are fundamental to this understanding.

In criticising classical political economy in his *Economic and Philosophic Manuscripts of 1844* (1975), Marx claims that, in theoretical analyses, one starts from the "present", that is, from the concrete. Although this analysis is expressed more thoroughly in *Capital* (1996), the general foundations are already present in this work.

The key point of interest in this chapter is the fact that, "the worker becomes all the poorer the more wealth he produces [..]" (Marx 1975: 271).

> [...] all methods for raising the social productiveness of labour are brought about at the cost of the individual labourer; all means for the development of production transform themselves into means of *domination over, and exploitation* of, the producers; they mutilate the labourer into a fragment of a man, degrade him to the level of an appendage of a machine, destroy

> every remnant of charm in his work and turn it into a hated toil; they estrange from him the intellectual potentialities of the labour process in the same proportion as science is incorporated in it as an independent power; they distort the conditions under which he works, subject him during the labour process to a despotism the more hateful for its meanness; they transform his lifetime into working time, and drag his wife and child beneath the wheels of the Juggernaut. (Marx 1996: 639, author's edit)

The theory of the accumulation of povertybeing driven by capital accumulation is perfected in chapter twenty-five of *Capital* (1996), "The general law of capitalist accumulation". In it, Marx explains how, in the historical development of capitalism, simple reproduction, which continuously reproduces the relationship between capitalists and wage earners, develops towards an expanded reproduction of capital, producing more capitalists and more wage earners. It concludes that the, "accumulation of capital is, therefore, [the] increase of the proletariat" (Marx 1996: 609).

Furthermore, in chapter twenty-six of *Capital*, "The so-called primitive accumulation", Marx (1996) demonstrates that the secret of accumulation lies in the violent forms of expropriation, coercion, torture, codes of discipline, forced labour, among others, predominant in the process of colonisation. The contemporary reproduction of capital would also be unsuccessful were it not for the violent relationships imposed by the need to appreciate value on an ever-expanding scale, contrary to the aim of responding to the material and spiritual development needs of the worker himself.

A fetishistic inversion prevails, in which the product, as dead and objectified work, appears as the subject in relation to its producer, the working class. "As, in religion, man is governed by the products of his own brain, so in capitalistic production, he is governed by the products of his own hand" (Marx, 1996: 616).

It is worth noting that violence is, therefore, an economic power (Kohan, 2016), and that this violenceis not linked to a distant barbaric past which is somehow diametrically opposite to contemporary "civilized" capitalism. The law of capitalist accumulation, which produces wage earners to a degree that, when developing their productive force, it also produces a relative overpopulation, causes an accumulation of povertyas a direct result of capital accumulation. "Accumulation of wealth at one pole is, therefore, at the same time accumulation of misery, agony of toil, slavery, ignorance, brutality, mental degradation, at the opposite pole [...]" (Marx, 1996: 640).

This necessary production of a workforce has also involved the control of women's education and bodies. According to Federici (2009), in the sixteenth and seventeenth centuries the State implemented punishment for any action that obstructed population growth, with the so-called witch hunts,[2] and imposed disciplinary sanctions to regulate procreation and prevent women having control over reproduction. Federici's research (2009: 88) found that, at the height of the implementation of mercantilist political and economic measures in France and England,

> [...] the state adopted a set of pro-natalist measures that, combined with PublicRelief, formed the embryo of a capitalist reproductive policy. [...] The family was given a new importance as the key institution providing for the transmission of property and the reproduction of the work force.

In different ways, by reproducing the violent expropriation of the popular and oppressed classes in a broader form and in a new paradigm for each historical particularity, capitalism engenders the transition from the formal subsumption to the real subsumption of labour to capital. So, it is evident that capital is not only an economic relationship, but also a relationship of power,

> [...] understanding 'power' not as a crystallised thing but a relationship, not a hypostasised and all-encompassing moment, without name and without history, but a moment inscribed in the social relations of a historically determined social economic formation. (Kohan, 2016: 359)

Assuming that exploitation and oppression are part of the same historical totality, then there is structural oppression, such as of gender, sexuality, and race, in capitalist societies that should not be ignored in the analysis of the criticism of political economy. Such dominating relationships are, however, expressed in different ways depending on their historical particularities.

When looking at the specifics of the impositions on women, Orozco's (2014) analysis states that the accumulation of capital does not only (re)produce wage labour, but also abundant free labour: not free labour that responds to satisfying needs and achieving the full multidimensionality of the social being, but free labour that serves capital appreciation.

Orozco proposes an update of the, "capital *versus* work" conflict to "capital *versus* life" (Orozco, 2014: 108–109).

As explained earlier, capital accumulation sustains itself through violence and produces poverty, the opposite of a meaningful life. According to Mészáros (2002), capital produces nothing but destructive self-reproduction.

> In the worst case, sustaining life is a nuisance: it is more profitable to destroy life than to generate or sustain it, as occurs with speculation on food; or also with dimensions of life that occur at the expense of others, or that makes the process as a whole produce a final balance more destructive than regenerative. (Orozco 2014: 110)

In SRT analysis, the (re)production of the workforce is thought of as a systemic part of the totality of capitalism (Bhattacharya, 2017). In addition to feminist theories centred on reproduction in domestic and family spaces, authors on the theme of feminism consider that the everyday reproductive regeneration of work does occur in homes, but also in schools, health centres, hospitals, prisons, etc. SRT, therefore, does not analyse reproduction separately from production, but as a whole:

> SRT is primarily concerned with understanding how categories of oppression (such as gender, race, and ableism) are coproduced in simultaneity with the production of surplus value. In this aspect, it seeks to overcome reductionist or determinist representations of Marxism while at the same time creatively exposing the organic totality of capitalism as a system. It is important thus to retain the term *social reproduction theory*, as it declares its heritage to be within the Marxist tradition. (Bhattacharya, 2017: 14, author's edit)

To denaturalise social inequalities, SRT reinforces the tendential and historical-concrete procedural character and it encompasses government policies and the State's performance into the analysis, whatever the current conjunctural and structural aspects. By doing so, it allows a more in-depth interpretation of the condition of working-class women in contemporary Brazil, in the context of the counter-reforms that occur in the process of capital accumulation through violence.

Ultraliberal Counter-Reforms in Contemporary Brazil

Capital crises, as a necessary mechanism for the recovery of the conditions for accumulation, have continuously reinforced the need for economic and labour reforms in national plans. In the Brazilian case, its subordinate position in the process of financialisation over the last 40 years has produced successive waves of counter-reforms[3] the objective of which has been to guarantee the conditions for capital accumulationat the capitalist periphery, which has had profound consequences for the social issue. As Prado (2018) states:

> The capitalist reforms proposed and implemented by neoliberalism have their logic: they aim, in the final analysis, to recover the rate of profit and, thus, accumulation, enabling capitalism to continue. Therefore, they may slightly increase the rate of economic growth, but in doing so, they also increase the rate of exploitation in the Brazilian capitalist economy. They also produce a worsening in the distribution of family income, as well as a reduction in social spending by the State. In seeking to regulate the economic system through the generalised imposition of a competitive rationale, not only among companies but also among individuals in general, considered as companies, society will trend in such a way that, ultimately, there will not be more civilization but more barbarism. (Prado 2018: 135)

Two processes are essential in understanding how the dynamics of capital accumulation guarantees the production of wealth and the intensification of social barbarism in Brazil. One is the fiscal austerity paradigm, as a fundamental component of a prescription aimed at the production of financial wealth at the expense of social spending, as discussed below. The other refers to repeated efforts to reduce the workforce, opening a process that Antunes (2018) called a “new era of structurally insecure work” in which a limited set of stable and regulated work is replaced by diverse forms of insecurity: outsourced work, cooperativism, entrepreneurship, voluntary and intermittent work. This is a process related to the restructuring of companies that want a full-time workforce, along the lines of what Abílio (2020: 117) has called *just in time workers*, i.e. “to be available to be used immediately, but only be paid for what you produce”.

This counter-reform agenda, in the economic and labour spheres, has been gaining momentum nationally since 2012,[4] but it only truly materialised in 2015 and has deepened following the impeachment of Dilma Rousseff in 2016. This is not, however, a new agenda.

Paulani (2017) explains that it was in the 1990s that Brazil actively entered the era of financialisation through the building of an institutional framework aimed at making the country an "international platform for financial appreciation". This framework included the opening-up of the Brazilian market for private and public securities, the gradual withdrawal of controls guaranteeing the free international flow of capital, the granting of tax exemptions on the financial gains of non-residents, the adoption of a regime for targeting inflation, and a monetary policy of highly elevated real interest rates and strict fiscal control aimed at producing primary surpluses (Paulani, 2012, 2017).

In the 1990s the results were low economic growth and increased poverty and unemployment. The average growth of Gross Domestic Product (GDP) under the two Fernando Henrique Cardoso governments was 2.4% between 1995 and 1998 and 2.1% between 1999 and 2002. The decline in employment opportunities occurred mainly in manufacturing industry, with displacement of jobs from large industrial companies to smaller establishments through subcontracting. The process of employment informalisation[5] was expressed in the increase in the number of; jobs with unsigned work-cards; employers; self-employed workers; unpaid workers; and workers in paid domestic service. Finally, with more than half of the active population not absorbed, and the consequent increase in unemployment, the structural changes to the Brazilian economy, stimulated by commercial and financial opening-up and the reduction in the role of the State in the dynamics of the economy, have led to a narrowing of the waged labour market" (Baltar, 2003: 146).

Social welfare and labour reforms also occurred in the 1990s. The first, approved in 1998, consisted of yet another measure to promote economic stability and state reform, under the paradigm that the structure of social protection should be evaluated from the point of view of the economic viability of the expenditure, and not the guarantee of rights. Among the main points, this reform replaced "length of service" with "period of contribution" in pension calculations (30 years for women and 35 for men), established the minimum retirement age (48 years for women and 53 for men), and established a nominal ceiling for benefits, unrelated to the minimum wage (Andrietta, 2015).

A clear path to the reduction and flexibilisation of labour rights was adopted, as shown by Krein (2013).These include, the introduction of new forms of contracting (fixed term contracts), banked hours, the move from a wage policy to variable remuneration practices and the implementation of new, private, forms of conflict resolution such as the Comissão de Conciliação Prévia (Preliminary Conciliation Commission). These changes were approved despite resistance from a part of the union movement that, in confronting the dismantling of labour right and assimilating the participation and negotiation dynamics of the neoliberal State, found itself involved in a series of contradictions and difficulties (Galvão, 2007). Two other aspects were not approved but remained on the agenda and were revisited in the following Bills: Bill 134/01 which provided for the power of negotiation over legislation[6] and Bill 4,302/98 which broadened the use of outsourcing,[7] a process that has spread in Brazil despite a lack of regulation.

In the 2000s, the Partido dos Trabalhadores (PT)[8] governments continued to follow the fundamental guidelines for inserting the Brazilian economy into the global cycles of financial accumulation and to that end they approved new pension reforms but were unable to stop the process of the relaxing of labour relations already underway. Maintaining the macroeconomic tripod (based on the upward revision of inflation rates, increasing the base interest rate within the primary surplus target, and the maintenance of the floating exchange rate policy) set the tone of the Lula governments, leading to the deceleration of economic growth in 2005, despite the good performance of the external sector. Under the second Lula government, and especially after 2006, the adoption of government policies to increase income and boost credit and consumption had positive effects on the economy, delivering an average growth rate of 4.5% between 2006 and 2010, with a consequent impact on employment growth.[9] The result of this growth model, based on increasing domestic consumption and the maintenance of the macroeconomic tripod, was the absence of structural changes, which meant that the country remained in the financialisation trap with continuing deindustrialisation and the re-primarisation of exports (Medeiros 2015; Paulani, 2017).

Pension reform of civil servants' retirement arrangements was a fundamental aspect of this process. This reform approved the adoption of the General Social Security Regime (RGPS) pension ceiling for the retirement of civil servants and the creation of complementary social security (through closed pension funds managed on an equal basis by Federal entities and workers' representatives, which, in practice, turned the worker into a rentier) through voluntary contributions by civil servants. In December 2003, this proposal was approved and in 2012 a complementary law put into practice the supplementary pension plan, establishing the Supplementary Pension Foundation for Federal Government Employees (Fundação da Previdência Complementar do Servidor Público da União [Funpresp]), which started operating in 2013.

The PT governments were marked by the promotion of a model of labour market inclusion and by forms of consumption characteristic of contemporary capitalism.The expressions of this process, from the point of view of labour, were the generation of low-quality jobs and the continuing tendency to make labour relations more flexible (Colombi, 2018).

The poor quality of formal jobs generated is evident in the prevalence of occupations in poorly structured sectors, with lower pay (between a half and two minimum wages) and a higher level of job insecurity, particularly those in civil construction. At the same time, although legislative changes were timely and did not dismantle labour codes, the play of forces in the capital-labour relationship resulted in the deepening of the insecurity and vulnerability of workers through the promotion of disguised employment modes with an emphasis on outsourcing and encouraging entrepreneurship as a policy for combating informality (Colombi & Krein, 2019).

So, throughout PT's period of government, although to a lesser extent when compared to the 1990s, the contradictions surrounding fiscal, labour, and social security policies have continued to exist. They led to a series of contradictions for the political forces that supported these governments. This included the union movement, which, in return for its political support, was able to condition the possibilities for advancing the labour agenda (Colombi, 2018). It was from 2015, under the Dilma Rousseff government, that a new cycle of neoliberal measures gained strength. These represented the end of the class mediation process of the PT governments and were expressed in the processes of labour market inclusivity and stimuli to consumption intended to maintain accumulation in the sphere of financial accumulation.

The Institutionalisation of Fiscal Austerity

The neoliberal agenda, that has gained strength since 2015,is characterised by the introduction of fiscal adjustment policies in response to the economic crisis, such as an increase of 1.75% in the primary surplus, contingency in budgetary authorisation, and the suspension of contracts for new public positions (Dweck et al., 2018); the approval of Provisional Measures (PM)[10] that restrict access to sickness insurance, to the receipt of a pension by a dependent in the event of the death of the insured (PM 664/2015), and to unemployment insurance and salary bonuses (PM 665/2015); and the launch of the employment protection programme (PPE), which allowed the reduction of the working day with reduced wages. After the impeachment of Dilma Rousseff, this agenda took more solid form, driving an intense and rapid institutionalisation of the deconstruction of the already fragile pillars of social protection.

Constitutional Amendment 95[11] (CA 95) approved in 2016, under Michel Temer, defined the New Tax Regime. Under this new regime, a constitutional limit was established for the annual growth of primary Federal expenditure. The maximum increase is being set at the inflation rate of the previous year, with a term of 20 years, and with revision of these rules only possible after the tenth year. Rossi and Dweck (2016) explain that, in practice, this New Tax Regime implies a real-term freeze on total Federal government expenditure and that public spending will not, therefore, keep pace with population growth. This is, Rossi and Dweck clarify, the institutionalisation of fiscal austerity for the next 20 years.

The Brazilian economy has witnessed declining growth since 2015, when the government of Dilma Rousseff bet on fiscal adjustment to balance public accounts and regain support from the private sector. The Temer government deepened this strategy with CA 95, creating a negative growth trajectory in the country between 2015 and 2016 (Fig. 4.1). The strategy underlying this proposal is called an "expansionary fiscal adjustment", according to which a fiscal adjustment does not cause aggregate demand to contract, but improves the confidence of the private sector, resulting in an expansionary effect on income and employment (Giavazzi & Pagano, 1990).This is an economic policy intended to counter the view that austerity policies weaken demand and employment and compromise social spending (Krein & Colombi, 2019).

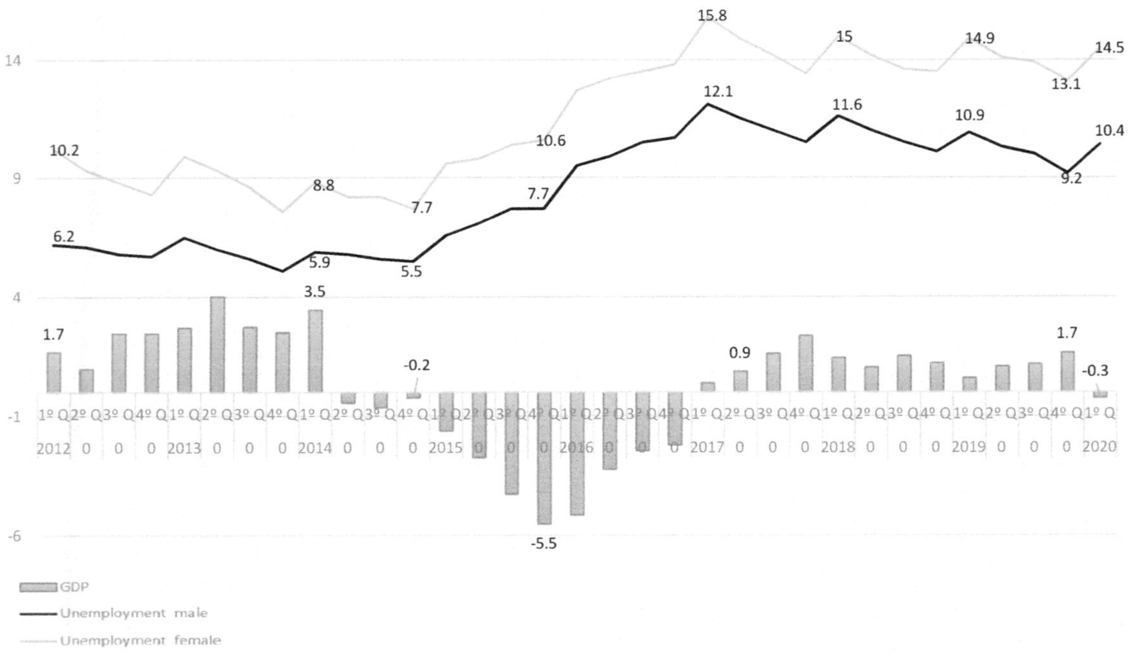

Fig. 4.1 GDP growth rate and unemployment rate (male and female)—quarterly % (*Source* Authors' production, based on the Sistema de Contas Nacionais [SCN–PIB: Change in volume in relation to the same quarter of the previous year] and Pesquisa Nacional por Amostra Domiciliar Contínua [PNADC/IBGE])

The policy of fiscal austerity must, therefore, be understood within the context of class struggle, that is, as a demand from the market and economic elite. This can be seen in the effect of the fall in economic growth on unemployment and its consequent impacts on the reduction of labour costs: between the years 2015 and 2016 there was a reduction from 50.3% to 18.5% in the percentage of workers who achieved wage readjustments above inflation (DIEESE, 2018). In 2019, the policy for increasing minimum wage[12] was abandoned by President Jair Bolsonaro.

As shown in Fig. 4.1, from 2015 the unemployment rate took on an upward trajectory and particularly affected women. This is a historical phenomenon that shows how the accumulation of capital is also the production of the working class, partly resulting from relative overpopulation and from working time absorbed by and purged from the labour market, with women forming a proportionally larger part of that cohort. In the first quarter of 2017, after two consecutive years of negative GDP growth, unemployment reached 14.1 million, the highest level in the historical series beginning in 2012, with women representing 7.1 million (50.6%) and, among them, black women 4.5 million (63.2%).

The commodification of social rights is another objective of the permanent fiscal adjustment policy. Cardoso Jr. (2016), analysing Exposição de Motivos Interministerial 83/2016 (EMI)[13] (Inter-ministerial Motives Exposition 83/2016), which followed the processing of the Constitutional Amendment Proposal (known at the time as PEC 241/2016[14]), shows that the down-scaling of the social protection system as set out in the 1988 Constitution appeared to be one of the desired results. The data collected in the analysis indicates that to comply with the limits imposed by the Constitutional Amendment, a reduction in social spending, which makes up 65% of primary Federal expenditure, would necessarily have to occur.

Before the effects of the coronavirus crisis and allowing for an average annual GDP growth rate of 2.5%, Dweck et al. (2018) projected a reduction in primary spending, from 17% of GDP in 2017 to 12% in 2037. This represents a reduction in social spending, and, in practice, this is what is happening. Since 2015, social spending cuts have occurred, principally in non-mandatory areas of expenditures. According to the systematisation of budgetary data carried out in the INESC report (2020), between 2014 and 2019areas including education, employment and culture have lost around 50% of their discretionary resources.[15] In education, the loss of resources was close to R$ 20billion, with higher education being the most affected. Considering all areas of social expenditure, discretionary social expenditures decreased by 29% between those years.

In the context of the pandemic, government expenditure has been made beyond the spending cap rule, as permitted by legislation in cases of "public calamity". Even in a recession, the government has, however, reiterated the importance of maintaining the rule, reinforcing the need to approve a reform agenda for both taxation, administration, and unemployment management policies, as discussed below. Furthermore, to maintain the ceiling rule, the government has proposed redirecting funds that fall outside the rule, such as the Basic Education Maintenance and Development Fund (Fundeb),[16] the main source of basic education resources, which accounts for more than 60% of the financing of all basic education in the country. The Leader of the House rejected the proposal, not because it represented a reduction in funds for education, but because it would make a "mockery" of the spending ceiling.[17] The tax reforms are based on the creation of a new tax and the reduction of payroll obligations, as a "sweetener" for the business sector, including a reduction from 8 to 6%of the proportion of salaries deposited by companies in the Severance Pay Fund (FGTS).[18]

The reduction in social spending has unequal effects on men and women as the dynamics of relations between the State, the market and the family are guided by the socio-gender-racial division of labour. As raised in Sect. 1 of this chapter, a fundamental theoretical exercise, from a critical perspective, is to demystify natural laws. It is therefore necessary to historicise the determinations that place women in a subordinate condition without disengaging from economics and politics. That is, to consider the relationships of domination and oppression that plague working-class women in the productive and reproductive environment.

The INESC report (2020) shows a reduction in spending on the implementation of public policies aimed at women, among them the "Policies for Women: Promotion of Autonomy and Confronting Violence" programme".[19] In 2014, expenditure amounted to R$ 185 million. In 2019, that amount dropped to just R$ 46 million, a reduction of 75% in real terms. The survey also shows that, in 2019, no resources were set aside for the Women's Service Centres, one of the country's main initiatives to combat gender-based violence.In 2018, R$ 7.4 million was spent on this service, in 2017 it had been R$ 33.6 million.

In addition to increasing violence, the reduction in social spending requires that working-class women, whose family members, or cohabitants are unable to access public services, are directly affected by having to take on care tasks and unpaid work. Many are forced to leave their salaried jobs (formal or informal) to care for children, the elderly and even men of working age. This "returning home" for women, as it has been named, is echoed positively in conservative discourse on morals and customs, validated by a religious reinforcement and implemented in public policies by elected representatives on a "religious bench" (Catholic and Evangelical) which has become institutionalised within the structure of Brazilian governments for, at least, the last two decades (Moraes, 2020). So, from the perspective of production and reproduction, austerity policies not only compromise the budgets for policies aimed at guaranteeing greater autonomy for women, but also subject them to less secure relations in the labour market and increase their responsibilities for caring for their families (Teixeira, 2018).

One area where the effects on women of the reduction in social spending can be seen is in analysing the effects of the consequent crisis on the structure of the labour market, where unemployment is always higher among women, and especially among black women. Another aspect of this inequality is in the reduction of expenditure under the pension reforms approved in 2019, under the administration of Jair Bolsonaro. Constitutional Amendment Proposal 06/2019 changed the constitutional text, modifying both the Regime Geral de Previdência Social (RGPS[20]) (General Social Security Regime)and the Regimes Próprios de Previdência Social (RPPSs[21]) (Specific Social Security Regimes).Among other measures, the reforms increased the minimum retirement age for women from 60 to 62 years, increased the minimum working time required to receive a pension from the Instituto Nacional de Seguridade Social(INSS) (National Social Security Institute) from 15 to 20 years, and removed pensions calculated on "timeserved".

The potential for exclusion under these reforms lies in the obstacles they pose to receiving a pension, especially for women (DIEESE 2019). Given the difficulties of remaining in formal employment in the Brazilian labour market, most Brazilians are unlikely to achieve the 40 years of contributions necessary to receive the full benefit, especially women who have a more intermittent working life. For this reason, most women's pensions are based on age.

To achieve a partial pension, individuals will have to contribute for 20 years, and 40% of the population were unable to reach this level even before the approval of the labour reforms (Fagnani, 2019). Women, as a reflection of the traditional structural sexual division of labour in the country, work less time in activities considered "productive" and with lower remuneration, which implies less capacity to contribute to social security. Women are, therefore, more affected by this reform, by both the increased minimum contribution time and significant reductions in the amounts of benefits due to changes in the calculation rules. This is yet another dimension of social protection in which gender inequalities and family relationships tend to be aggravated. Another dimension is changes in labour legislation.

Labour Reforms[22]

The dismantling of labour rights is a process dating back to the 1990s and it has not yet ended. The approval of laws 13,467 and 13,429, in 2017, sparked a new cycle, intensifying this process. The first introduced new types of contracting, changes in the working day, forms of remuneration and working conditions and the second deals with temporary work and how employees provide their services. Beyond this significant change in the legal framework, there are also other measures that indirectly affect labour legislation: Provisional Measure (PM) 881, approved in 2019, and called the "PM for economic freedom"; PM 905, on the Green and Yellow Work-card Contract, which was revoked in 2020 due to difficulties in gaining Senate approval, but which remains a government objective; and PMs 927 and 936, approved in the context of the Covid-19 pandemic. Table 4.1 summarises the impact of each of them on labour:

In all these measures, the prevailing logic is that increased flexibility is the way to combat unemployment and informality, showing that the process is indeed a broad labour counter-reform that has not yet ended. The current effort is to reintroduce the PM on Yellow and Green Work-cards. These work-cards would replace the "Blue" work-card for young people entering the job market, by reducing the costs for employers who hire young people in their first job and people over 55 who had been outside the formal job market. In these cases, workers would individually negotiate all terms of employment with the employer. On May 29, 2020, the Minister of Economy, Paulo Guedes, affirmed that informal workers

Table 4.1 Provisions of labour reforms from 2017

Legislation	*Alterations*
Law N°. 13,467/2017 and N°. 13,429/2017	• Flexibility in modes of contracting, the working day and renumeration (Liberalisation of Third Party contracting, increased temporary contracts, extension to all sectors of a 12 × 36 workday, non-payment of overtime at home and others) • Weakening of public institutions and of union organisations (The preference for the negotiated over the legislated, ending obligatory union contributions and the results of collective bargaining, union assisted homologation to cease)
PM for Economic Freedom (Law 13,874/2019)	• Restricted the clock-in and clock-out rules to companies with more than 20 employees and allows the registration of a "point by exception", that is, simply by signing an individual agreement with the employee clocking-in and clocking-out is only required when the worker has a different schedule than usual for any given type of company. These measures aim to hinder the payment of overtime • Altered the rules under which a legal status can be disregarded, deepening the separation between the company's assets and those of its owners. This complicates the process of indemnification and recovery of unpaid funds to workers in case of company bankruptcy
PM 927/2020	• Allowed remote working, bringing forward of holidays, individual and collective vacations, use of banked hours, and the suspension of administrative requirements for Health and Safety at Work to be carried out by individual agreement with the worker, without the endorsement of the unions

(continued)

Table 4.1 (continued)

Legislation	*Alterations*
Conversion Bill No. 18/2020 which expired in July 2020 due to the government's disagreement with the extension of the suspension of the payment of FGTS and INSS by companies until the end of 2020	• Allowed the postponement of deposits into the Guarantee Fund for Time of Service (FGTS) between March and May 2020
	• Suspended obligatory occupational medical examinations, including those related to dismissal, for short-term employment contracts • Allowed a negative hours bank, that is, if the employee does not work, for reasons beyond his control, he receives wages and becomes indebted for the later fulfilment of these hours • Allowed the employer to bring forward holidays, without ensuring the bringing forward of holiday payments
PM 936/2020	• Introduced the ability to reduce the workday with a proportional reduction in wages for up to 90 days, in percentages ranging from 25%, 50% to 70%, with payment by the government of a benefit calculated with reference to the value of unemployment insurance (the average of the last three payments)
Converted into Law 14,020/2020 Emergency Employment and Income Maintenance Programme, valid until 31 December 2020	• Authorised the temporary suspension of employment contracts for up to two months

Legislation	*Alterations*
	• When the cut is 25%, the changes can be made by individual agreement between the employer and the employee, regardless of the salary range. In the case of reductions of 50% and 70% or suspension of contracts, individual agreements can only be signed with employees who earn less than R$ 3,135 or more than R$ 12,202.12 per month. Workers who receive between R$ 3,136 and R$ 12,202.11 will only be able to have their contracts modified by collective agreement or convention, with the participation of the union

Source Authors' production

in Brazil are the target group for the green and yellow work-card[23] that, in its new guise within the *Renda Brasil* programme (Brazilian Income Programme), is seen as a mechanism that permits hourly payments, and to be "employed" by several companies at the same time, with a definitively lowered level of rights.[24]

The same logic remains embedded in laws approved in 2017: in the face of permanent fiscal austerity and low economic growth, the management of the surplus labour force must be achieved through mechanisms that allow insecure access to employment without the rights associated with employment. In these measures, the idea persists that excess labour legislation creates obstacles to the free market, economic activity, and investment.

In the name of this flexibility, Law No. 13,467 ensures that negotiation between the parties prevails over what is provided for in legislation and ensures that negotiation takes place on an individual basis for cases in which the employee has higher education and a monthly salary equal to or greater than two times the ceiling on social security benefits. PM 936, approved during the pandemic, also reinforces the sense of attack on the legitimacy of unions, as less protected employees (those who receive less than R$ 3,135 about USD 580 per month) can have their workdays reduced, with reduced wages, or their employment contracts suspended without union involvement. The aim is to decentralise the spaces for the standardisation of labour relations within the scope of the company and to transfer the defining of the rules to the negotiation between the parties, so reducing the bargaining power of the unions. This is taking place at a time when male and female workers—the latter still subject to harassment and broad sexism—have no strength to negotiate against less unfavourable working conditions in the face of the real threat of unemployment.

There are other aspects of legislative changes whose effects are worse for women. One of them was the permitting of intermittent work in 2017. This form of hiring allows the worker to establish a contract with more than one company, being paid only for the hours worked.[25] As Oliveira (2020) states, this is not a new form of employment relationship, but the legalisation of a form of work that already occurs in the informal sector. Although male and female workers have access to rights in proportion to the hours worked, given the instability of this form of employment this does not guarantee either work or income.[26] Part-time work already existed but has been extended from 25 to up to 32 hours per week, and with the ability to work overtime. Law 13,467 also changed the provisions on remote working, allowing it to be carried out without controls over the working day. PM 927, issued in the context of the pandemic, approved the alteration of the presential work regime for remote working, which had previously taken place by mutual agreement, allowing it to be freely implemented by the employer. Finally, Law 13,467 allowed even pregnant and breast-feeding women to work in unhealthy places, but this measure was overturned by the Supreme Court in 2019.

All these measures profoundly alter labour relations and increase the pace and intensity of work, with women being the ones most exposed to these changes and new forms of hiring. Historically, part-time work is already more prevalent among women. PNAD Continuous data for Q1-2020 indicates that among employed men, only 29% worked less than 40 hours a week while among women this percentage was 45%. This is an indication of the high number of part-time workdays among women, especially in the areas of education, health, and social services. It confirms the importance of analysis based on SRT, which theorises reproductive work beyond the domestic space and considers the totality of social reproduction.

Intermittent work, which deepens employment insecurity and hinders the conditions for the reproduction of the workforce, and which corroborates the increase in relative overpopulation, still does not, however, represent an expressive reality in the new forms of contracting: among total hirings between November 2017 and December 2019, 40% were women (Oliveira, 2020).

Both part-time work and remote working are justified as being beneficial to women, as they can work "less", or at home, which allows them to respond to domestic demands and the care of their children. However, these forms of work, especially remote working, which intensified during the period of social distancing, results in different degrees of productivity for men and women,[27] and was consistently lower for women. With no other option, many women remain in informal work, which has increased since the 2017 labour counter-reforms. It is in this way that labour counter-reforms tend to perpetuate the conditions for inequality, recreating and expanding the forms of exclusion and segregation.

All these changes show that, as an object of permanent dispute, the legislation which had reduced the violent entrepreneurial forms of exploitation of the working class is experiencing another attack (Fontes, 2017) intended to maintain the conditions of wealth accumulation of the business-financial ruling class. The significance of so many changes remains the same: flexibilisation as an alternative approach to the problems of unemployment, informality, and overcoming the economic crisis.

However, the results of the more than two years since the beginning of this dismantling process, point in another direction. What we see is a failure to deliver on these promises, and this has reaffirmed the subordinate position of women both within and outside the labour market. It is worth noting that this affirmation was already in motion before the Covid-19 pandemic which only worsened an already dramatic situation.

In Q4-2019, the working population was 106.2 million people, of which women represented 47%. From 2012 to 2019, their participation in the labour market increased, an increase that continued after the economic crisis of 2015 and the labour reforms initiated in 2017. This demonstrates the continued demand from women for employment against a background of high unemployment. Only in Q1-2020 was a drop in the participation of women in the workforce observed. This movement is linked to the effects of the pandemic which caused a reduction in the number of people in the workforce, both among men (−0.7%) and women (−1.4%).

The growth in female employment does not, however, represent their true incorporation into the labour market, as unemployment was increasing until Q1-2017 (Fig. 4.2), especially for them. This demonstrates how unemployment among women is a phenomenon related

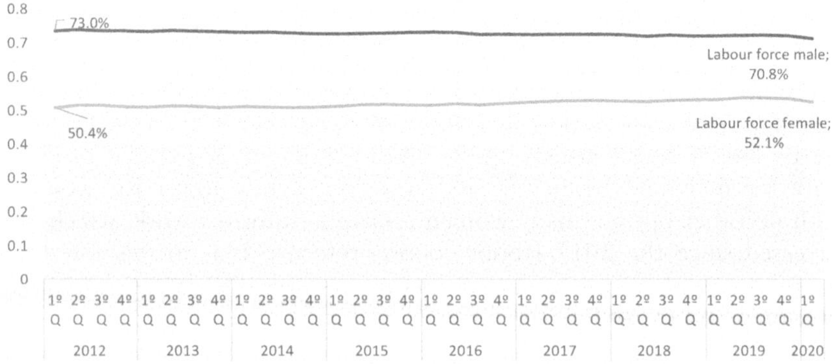

Fig. 4.2 Persons of 14 years or older in the workforce (%), by gender (Q1-2012 to Q1-2020) (*Source* Authors' production. PNADC/IBGE)

to gaining entry to the workforce and, from there, to the search for continued employment. For men, increasing unemployment originates mainly in the loss of occupied posts.

The solution to the exposed condition of working women in ultraliberal Brazil does not lie in the liberal agenda of equal opportunity access to the labour market. The conditions for women's participation in the labour market are fundamental to their inclusion. These range from the more immediate perspective of social rights, to the perspective of social transformation in the emancipation of women around substantive equality and freedom (Moraes, 2018).

Far removed from the liberal, or revolutionary, agenda, the weak fall in unemployment from 2017 cannot be attributed either to the easing of legislation or to the achievements of feminist militancy, as this process occurred with a concomitant increase in informality, underutilisation, and a sluggish recovery in formal employment. From 2017, informality[28] has increased for everyone (Fig. 4.3). In Q4-2017, there were 43.3 million workers in informal employment. Two years later, in Q4-2019, there were 45.5 million, and in the same period the number of unemployed fell by only 635 thousand. Informality is greater among men. Of the total of 45.5 million in this condition in Q4-2019, 57% were men and 43% women. However, in the same period, the increase in informal workers was 11% among men and 14% among women.

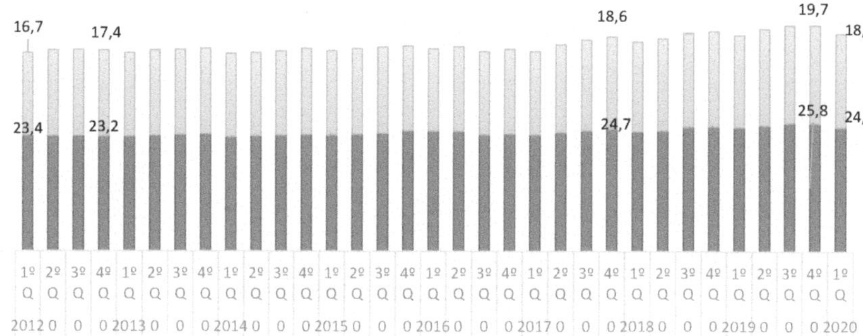

Fig. 4.3 Persons of 14 years or older in informal employment, by gender (Millions) (*Source* Authors' production. PNADC/IBGE)

Among informal occupations, the growth in self-employment stands out, with a more significant increase among women (an increase of 29% for women and 15% for men between Q4-2012 and Q4-2019), a process that labour reforms have not reversed as between Q4-2017 and Q4-2019, self-employment grew more (6.3%) than occupations in the formal private sector (1.3%). It is also noteworthy that women are more involved in these informal activities (see Fig. 4.4).

Self-employed women are mainly involved as shopkeepers, home-based retailers, beauty treatment specialists, hairdressers, and seamstresses. Self-employed men are mainly involved in civil construction (as bricklayers), as farmers and skilled agricultural workers, shopkeepers, and professional drivers. The profiles of informal occupations for women and men reveal the predominance of the genders according to a "traditional" gender division of labour, because even in insecure employment men and women participate differently.

Informality only fell in Q1-2020 because of the negative impacts of the Covid-19 pandemicon the labour market. The reduction in informality occurred because these workers left the labour force, particularly workers without a work-card and the self-employed. That is, these workers stopped working and did not go looking for a job because of the pandemic. Noteworthy, is the greater intensity of the reduction in vacancies in domestic work (385 thousand positions, formal and informal, disappeared between Q4-2019 and Q1-2020), which is carried out principally by women.

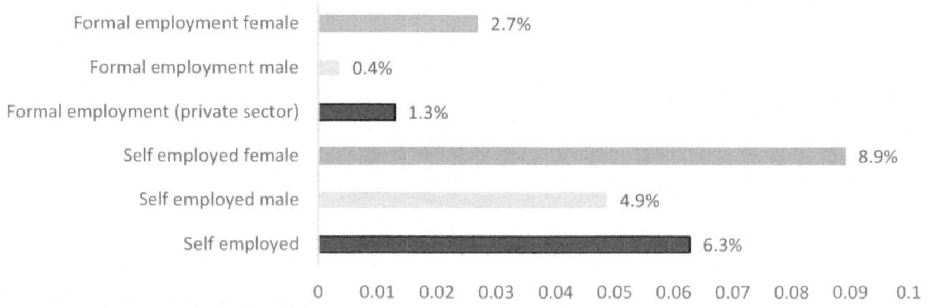

Fig. 4.4 Persons of 14 years or more by employment type, by gender (Rate of variation between Q4-2017 and Q4-2019) (*Source* Authors' production. PNADC/IBGE)

In the context of the pandemic, the greater fall in informal vacancies in relation to formal ones means that the remedial measures taken by the government to maintain positions (even with reduced wages) did not reach workers at the margins of mainstream employment. The government's intention is to provide for this cohort through the *Renda Brasil* programme, that is, to permit and encourage intermittent employment with reduced rights as an alternative to unemployment. It is an institutional measure that, when approved, will legitimise a "turning point", to a reliance on sporadic employment opportunities (Abílio, 2017), with more workers joining the ranks of a new proletariat of workers with no fixed working hours or fixed remuneration, with no defined work-space, and with no union representation (Antunes, 2018).

The low economic dynamism of the commercial and services sectors have maintained the employment profile generated after the approval of these labour reforms. In Q4 of 2019, 65.5% of employed people received up to 2 minimum wages. In the same period, 61% of men and 71% of women received up to 2 minimum wages and the average income of women was 78% of that for men. Even at the height of the crisis, in 2015 and 2016, this difference remained unchanged. In comparison with 2012, the variance was slightly reduced by the effects of the crisis, which containing the income of the poorest without representing a change in the wage structure or the gap between women and men.

Another change in the Brazilian labour market is increased underutilisation of the workforce. The vulnerability of Brazilian workers is not being reversed by Labour reforms. In Q1-2020, the under-employed, unemployed, and potential workforce,[29] gave a total for underutilised workers of more than 27 million, most of whom are women. Throughout the course of the data series, the underutilisation rate among men has been close to 20%, while among women the rate approached 30% (see Fig. 4.5). In absolute terms, in Q4-2012 there were 16.9 million underutilised workers. This valuehas continued to increase, even after the start of the reform process, and in Q2-2019 it peaked at 28.4 million people (15.7 million women and 12.7 million men, see Fig. 4.5).

With the outbreak of the Covid-19 pandemic, the underutilisation rate increased again between Q4-2019 and Q1-2020. This movement is a regular occurrence at the turn of the year. However, the effects of the economic and health crisis seem to indicate a permanent tendency for this indicator to increase, as it reflects the situation of those who remain in

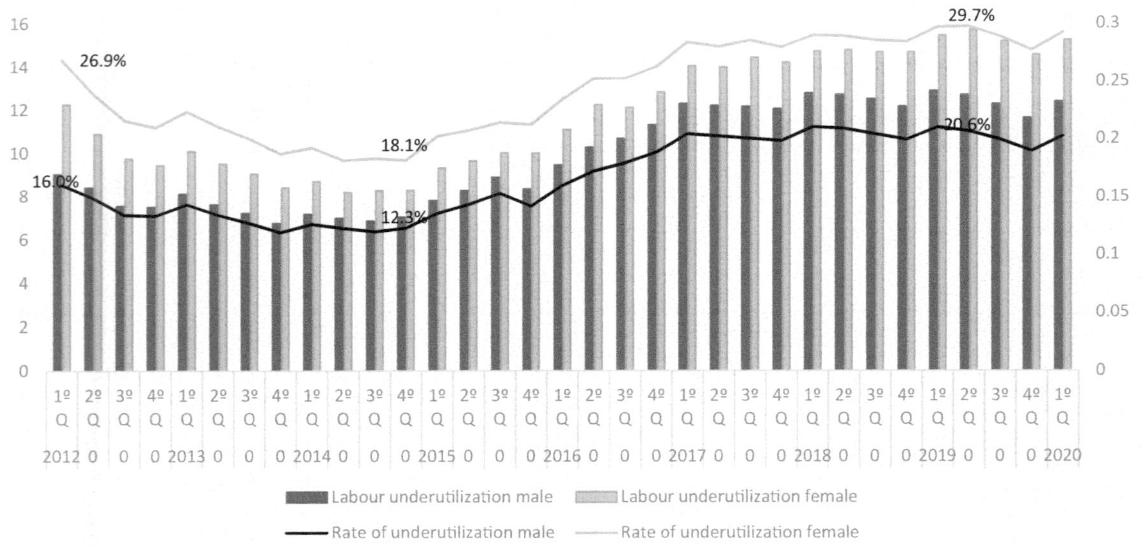

Fig. 4.5 Underutilised persons of 14 years or more (Millions) and the rate of underutilisation (%), by gender (Q1-2012 to Q1-2020) (*Source* Authors' production. PNADC/IBGE)

the labour market seeking employment (unemployed) and those who are unable to seek employment due to the pandemic (potential workforce).

Analysis of the evolution of the labour market between 2012 and 2019 shows that the effects of the economic crisis, worsened by the health crisis, have had negative consequences for a labour market that is already historically unstructured. These consequences are not being reversed by the legislative measures to increase flexibility. On the contrary, what the indicators show is that the weak fall in unemployment between 2017 and 2019 occurred at the expense of increased informality and underutilisation. At the same time, the participation of women in the labour market was already increasing and this trajectory has been maintained since 2017. However, a significant portion was not able to enter the labour market, reflected by a higher unemployment rate in this group. Finally, the increase in informality, especially for self-employed workers, has happened at a higher rate than in previous formal employment, indicating a drop in the quality of labour relationships in Brazil. Unemployment, informality, and underutilisation are indicators of a heterogeneous and low-level labour market that, in a context in which the difficulties around the health crisis and fiscal austerity are combined, aggravate the challenges for the livelihoods of both male and female workers.

Conclusion

Chico de Oliveira (2000: 20) states, "the class conflict has the use of public funds as its main divider". The institutionalisation of fiscal austerity proves this assertion, since, anchored in counter-reforms that reduce social rights, it promotes a real programme for concentrating income and wealth. One of its fundamental pillars is the ongoing labour counter-reforms that makes labour law more flexible and reduces social protection with the purported objective of creating jobs, an outcome that our investigation shows did not occur.

Part of the government's ultraliberal project is the removal of the rights of the employed, a process that continued under the provisional measures introduced during the pandemic. Another part, already in place pre-Covid-19, was the so-called Green and Yellow Work-card Project, but with the arrival of the pandemic the true objectives of this project were comprehensively revealed by the identification of 40 million Brazilians working in the informal sector. This project consists of the managing the increasing surplus mass through the logic of "cycling", that is, providing a continuous, intermittent ability to earn income, but without rights. On both fronts, what prevails is a strategy for intensifying labour exploitation, legitimising, legalising, and trivialising the transfer of costs and risks to workers.

In this process, women are hit hardest. In the socio-gender-racial division of labour, they have historically occupied subordinate and more insecure positions, whether in the labour market or in the free use of their workforce in care and domestic work within their families. In the context of ultraliberal counter-reforms, it is mostly women who have joined the ranks of part-time work, underutilisation and unemployment and find themselves, in times of austerity and pandemic, challenged to precariously integrate into a labour market that is already reduced for them by the demands of the responsibilities for caring for the family. Historically and contemporaneously, the precariousness of the condition of women in the labour market and their responsibility for reproductive work are two faces of the same process that, by perpetuating inequality and barbarism, simultaneously produces the accumulation of both wealth and poverty.

Faced with this barbaric situation, what should one do? SRT theorists have called for the holding of social reproduction strikes, intended to be creative spaces in which the "impossible" must be demanded (Ferguson, 2020). Unlike feminists movements in the 1970s and 1980s, that called for strikes in domestic space and demanded wages for work traditionally performed free of charge, the strikes proposed by SRT feminists foresee solidarity between different sectors of social reproduction, such as state schools, public health, public transport, and environmental conservation. The key being the solidarity of militants from these diverse agendas. "They are examples of people who collectively insist on putting need over profit by demanding the resources for social reproduction be expanded—who attempt, that is, to take life back from capital" (Ferguson, 2020: 133).

We then return to Orozco's (2014) proposal in which the SRT theorists place "life above profit" and propose to bring life back from the bonds of capital. Only a policy of "life" can oppose the policy of violence, barbarism, destruction, and death imposed by increased capital accumulation. Perhaps feminist epistemology, which promotes the denaturalisation and historicisation of inequalities imposed by the integrated relationship between exploitation and oppression, and enhanced by the concrete life relationships of women, can make an important contribution to an emancipatory political praxis for the Brazilian working class.

Notes

1. The term informality refers, here, to the phenomenon of illegal earning, that is, when workers are hired outside the current labour rules. In the case of Brazil, these rules are united in the Consolidação das Leis do Trabalho (CLT) (Consolidation of Labour Laws). Workers who enjoy these rights are called "carded workers" because they have the document that allows contracted employment. They are also known as having a "blue card", a reference to the colour of the document. "Uncarded workers" are those not registered for a work-card and who have no rights to a guaranteed employment relationship.
2. In the middle of the sixteenth century, a redefinition of what would be considered a "reproductive crime" occurred and women began to be prosecuted on a large scale, some were executed for infanticide or "witchcraft", related to "child murders" and other violations of reproductive norms. According to Federici (2009: 89), this policy remained in place for more than two hundred years and, "[…] their wombs became public territory, controlled by men and the state, and procreation was directly placed at the service of capitalist accumulation".
3. The concept of counter-reform is understood here as a set of regressive changes, actively instituted by a neoliberal State, that sets out to politically mould economic relations and social rules to guarantee competition, thus guaranteeing the conditions for capital accumulation at the periphery of capitalismand removing the meagre social protection previously achieved in national regulatory frameworks.
4. In 2012 the document "The 101 proposals for the modernisation of labour relations" of the National Confederation of Industry was published, which served as a reference for the labour reforms approved in 2017. "A bridge to the future" was the other document presented by the Party of the Brazilian Democratic Movement (PMDB) in 2016, catalysing the interests of the elite around the austerity agenda and the concretisation of the coup against President Dilma.
5. See Note 3.
6. This is a normative proposal aimed at increasing the prevalence of negotiations between workers and owners (collective norms) regarding what is established by law. In the Brazilian case, collective bargaining has historically only played a complementary role in the regulation of rights, as a model of legislated labour relations has prevailed. Collective bargaining should not lower the level of protection provided for in legislation. This proposal is aimed at opening the possibility of negotiations so as to reduce regulations registered in the legal framework. It was not approved in 2001 but remained on the agenda of businessmen and even some unions

that believe that this measure could strengthen their bargaining power. In 2017 it was approved, as discussed below.

7. This is a bill aimed at allowing the use of outsourcing for any type of activity within a given company, without limitations.Although there was no specific legislation that vetoed outsourcing, the Superior Labour Court's understanding prevailed that the practice could only occur in middle activities and not in end activities. This project also remained on the businessmen's agenda and was approved in 2017 under the terms of Law 13.429/2017, allowing the outsourcing of any type of activity by companies.
8. Luiz Inácio Lula da Silva (2003–2011), Dilma Vana Rousseff (2011–2016).
9. In 2003 Brazil had a rate of unemployment of 9.7%. In 2014, this rate had fallen to 6.9% (PNAD, IBGE).
10. A Provisional Measure (Medida Provisória, MP) is enacted by the President of the Republic and has legal force.It is enacted without the participation of the Legislature, which is only called upon to discuss and approve it at a later date.
11. A Constitutional Amendment is a modification of the constitution, resulting in specific changes to the constitutional text. In the phase prior to approval, a Constitutional Amendment must appear as a proposal, called a Constitutional Amendment Proposal (PEC).
12. In 2004, the appreciation of the national base began to correspond to the annual inflation adjustment measured by the INPC-IBGE (National Consumer Price Index, of the Brazilian Institute of Geography and Statistics) and to the real increase in the GDP variation.
13. An Inter-ministerial Motives Exposition is a set of arguments addressed to the President of the Republic by a Minister or by several ministries in defence of a given project.
14. PEC 241/2016 is the New Brazilian Fiscal Regime. Henrique Meirelles. Available at: https://www2.camara.leg.br/atividade-legislativa/comissoes/comissoes-temporarias/especiais/55a-legislatura/pec-241-2016-novo-regime-fiscal/documentos/audiencias-publicas/ApresentaoPEC241Ministro_v4.pdf. Accessed on 10 April 2020.
15. Mandatory government expenditure is that which the government is required by law to pay, such as payroll, social security benefits, welfare benefits and subsidies. Discretionary expenses are those that can be cut, "adjusted" without the need to change the law. Among the areas that make up social spending are: Health; Education; Social assistance; Housing and Sanitation; Culture; Job; Agrarian Organisation; Social Security.

16. The Primary Education Maintenance and Development Fund is a set of funds formed from resources from the three levels of public administration in Brazil to promote the financing of public primary education.
17. "Government gives in and proposes an even bigger increase". Available at: https://valor.globo.com/politica/noticia/2020/07/21/governo-cede-e-propoe-aumento-ainda-maior.ghtml. Accessed on 21 July 2020.
18. FGTS is a monthly deposit, a percentage of the employee's salary, which the employer is required to deposit in a bank account in the employee's name.The objective being that these amounts help the worker if he is dismissed or in any case of termination of the employment relationship.
19. This programme was launched in 2012 and set out to broaden the country's women's protection policy. To achieve this, actions to consolidate the assistance network and awareness campaigns were undertaken.
20. RGPS is affiliated with urban and rural wage earners, optional insured self-employed workers, family farm workers, individual microentrepreneurs and housewives, and public servants from more than 3,400 municipalities that have not implemented their own social security systems.
21. RPPS refers to social security for public servants in entities that have their own social security system.
22. The data on the labour market in this section refers to research on the impacts of the labour reforms carried out jointly by CESIT/UNICAMP.
23. Guedes promises employment plan within 40 days. Available at: https://valor.globo.com/brasil/noticia/2020/05/29/guedes-promete-plano-de-emprego-em-ate-40-dias.ghtml. Accessed on 25 June 2020. 13th salary, paid vacation and Guarantee Fund for Time of Service would be maintained, but only in proportion to the hours worked.All other guarantees, such as: unemployment insurance, working hours control, union representation, night pay premium and others would be disregarded in this modality.
24. Proposal to permit the registration of hourly paid work. Available at: https://valor.globo.com/brasil/noticia/2020/06/30/proposta-permite-registro-por-hora-de-trabalho.ghtml. Accessed on 30 June 2020.
25. The primary difference between intermittent work and the Programa Renda Brasil (Brazilian Income Programme), intended to hire informal workers and pay them by the hour, is that it is not possible for a contract to be continuous.
26. Dieese (2020) identified that of the 62 thousand temporary contracts in December 2018, only 36 thousand registered some activity in the last month of the year. Of those working, 43% received income below the minimum wage (R$ 954, USD 180) and only 17% of temporary contracts generated wages equivalent to two minimum wages or more, in that month.

27. For example, the articles by Kitchener (2020) in The Lilly and by Flaherty (2020) in Inside Higher Education stand out internationally. And nationally, Girard's report (2020), in *Estadão*.
28. Corresponds to a person employed in the private sector without a work-card, public sector without a work-card, domestic work without a work-card, on their own account, or in auxiliary family work.
29. This means: the total number of people who worked less than 40 h a week and would like to work more; together with unemployed people who sought employment in the past 30 days and were able to start employment immediately, and those outside the workforce who would like to work and who did not seek employment in the last 30 days or were not available to work at the time of the survey.

References

Abilio, L. C. (2017). *Uberização do trabalho: subsunção real da viração*. Available at: https://blogdaboitempo.com.br/2017/02/22/uberizacao-do-trabalho-subsuncao-real-da-viracao/. Accessed on 1 July 2020.

Abilio, L. C. (2020). Uberização: A era do trabalhador just-in-time? *Estudos Avançados, 34*(98), 111–126.

Andrietta, L. (2015). *A mercantilização do sistema previdenciário brasileiro 1988–2014*. 2015. UNICAMP.

Antunes, R. (2018). *O privilégio da servidão: o novo proletariado na era digital*. São Paulo: Boitempo.

Baltar, P. E. (2003). Estrutura econômica e emprego urbano na década de 1990. In M. W. Proni & W. Henrique (Eds.), *Trabalho, mercado e sociedade: Brasil nos anos 90*. Unesp.

Bhattacharya, T. (Org.) . (2017). *Social reproduction theory*. Pluto Press.

CARDOSO, Jr. J. C. (2016). Uma Análise Técnica das Justificações da PEC no 241/2016. Available at: https://plataformapoliticasocial.com.br/wp-content/uploads/2016/10/As-justifica%C3%A7%C3%B5es-da-PEC-241-2016-10-12.pdf. Accessed on 12 January 2009.

Colombi, A. P. F. (2018). *A institucionalização do consenso: atuação da CUT e da FS durante os governos do PT (2003–2014)*. Tese de Doutorado, UNICAMP.

Colombi, A. P. F., & Krein, J. D. (2019). Labor market and labor relations under the PT governments. *Latin American Perspectives, 47*.

DIEESE. (2019a). *Balanço das negociações dos reajustes salariais de 2018*. N° 90, agosto.

DIEESE. (2019b). *PEC 06/2019: a desconstrução da Seguridade Social*. Nota técnica 203, março.

DIEESE. (2020). Contratos intermitentes na gaveta. *Boletim emprego em pauta*. N.14, janeiro.

Dweck, E., Silveira, F., & Rossi, P. (2018). Austeridade e desigualdade social no Brasil. In P. Rossi, E. Dweck, A. Oliveira (Eds.), *Economia Para Poucos: impactos sociais da austeridade e alternativas para o Brasil*. Autonomia Literária.

Fagnani, E. (2019). Da seguridade social ao seguro social. Reforma previdenciária pretende sepultar o pacto de 1988. Available at: http://www.ihu.unisinos.br/159-noticias/entrevistas/586966-da-seguridade-social-ao-seguro-social-reforma-previdenciaria-pretende-sepultar-o-pacto-de-1988-entrevista-especial-com-eduardo-fagnani. Accessed on 1 April 2019.

Federici, S. (2009) *Caliban and the witch*. Autonomedia.

Ferguson, S. (2020). *Women and work: Feminism labour and social reproduction*. Pluto Press.

Flaherty, C. (2020, April 21). No room of one's own. *Inside Higher Education*. Available at: https://www.insidehighered.com/news/2020/04/21/early-journal-submission-data-suggest-covid-19-tanking-womens-research-productivity. Accessed on 13 July 2020.

Fontes, V. (2017, January/June). Capitalismo em tempos de uberização: do emprego ao trabalho. *Marx e o Marxismo*, *5*(8).

Galvão, A. (2007). *Neoliberalismo e reforma trabalhista no Brasil*. Revan/FAPESP.

Giavazzi, F., & Pagano, M. (1990). *Can severe fiscal contractions be expansionary? Tales of two small European countries* (NBER Working Paper). Cambridge, EUA, n. 3372.

Girard, G. (2020). Produção científica de mulheres e mães despenca em meio à pandemia de coronavirus. *Estadão* 18 de maio. Available at https://ciencia.estadao.com.br/noticias/geral,producao-cientifica-de-mulheres-despenca-em-meio-a-pandemia-de-coronavirus,70003306675. Accessed on 13 July 2020.

INESC. (2020). O Brasil com baixa imunidade. Balanço do Orçamento Geral da União 2019. Available at https://www.inesc.org.br/wp-content/uploads/2020/04/Balanco-OGU-Inesc.pdf. Accessed on 3 September 2020.

Kitchener, C. (2020, April 24). Women academics seem to be submitting fewer papers during coronavirus. 'Never seen anything like it,' says one editor. *The Lilly*. Available at https://www.thelily.com/women-academics-seem-to-be-submitting-fewer-papers-during-coronavirus-never-seen-anything-like-it-says-one-editor/. Accessed on 13 July 2020.

Kohan, N. (2016). La violencia como potencia económica. In *Seminario El Capital*. Nuestra América.

Krein, J. D. (2013). *As relações de trabalho na era do neoliberalismo no Brasil*. Editora LTr.

Krein, J. D., & Colomi, A. P. F. (2019). A Reforma Trabalhista em Foco: desconstrução da proteção social em tempos de neoliberalismo autoritário. *Educ. Soc.*, Campinas , v. 40.
Marx, K. (1975). *Marx/Engels Collected Works* (vol. 3).
Marx, K. (1996). *Marx/Engels Collected Works* (vol. 35).
Medeiros, C. A. (2015). *Inserção externa, crescimento e padrões de consumo na economia brasileira*. IPEA.
Meszaros, I. (2002). A taxa de utilização decrescente e o Estado capitalista: administração da crise e auto-reprodução destrutiva do capital. In *Para além do capital*. Boitempo.
Moraes, L. C. G. (2018). Mészáros, sobre a emancipação das mulheres. *RTPS - Revista trabalho, política e sociedade, 3*(5), 121–140 1 out.
Moraes, L. C. G. (2020). O discurso da "cortina de fumaça" e o desvelamento das relações entre capitalismo e patriarcado no brasil conservador e ultraliberal. In M. L. Garcia, & F. Bernardes (Orgs.), *Contrarreformas ou revolução*: respostas ao capitalismo em crise. São Paulo: Editora Cortez.
Oliveira, F. (2000). Passagem na neblina. In: Stédile, J., Genoíno, J. (orgs.) *Classes sociais em mudança e luta pelo socialismo*. São Paulo: Perseu Abramo.
Oliveira, R. V. (2020). Trabalho Intermitente: a que veio? Para onde vai? *Blog Remir*. 06 de maio. Available at: https://www.eco.unicamp.br/remir/index.php/condicoes-de-trabalho/148-trabalho-intermitente-a-que-veio-para-onde-vai. Accessed on 13 jul. 2020.
Orozco, A. P. (2014). *Subversión feminista de la economía: Aportes para um debate sobre el conflito capital-vida*. Traficantes de Sueños.
Paulani, L. (2012). A inserção da economia brasileira no cenário mundial: uma reflexão sobre a situação atual à luz da história. *Boletim de Economia e Política Internacional* (IPEA), n.10, abril.
Paulani, L. (2017, January/April). Não há saída sem a reversão da financeirização. *Estudos Avançados, 31*(89). São Paulo, IEA/USP.
Prado, E. (2018). *Ciência da Economia: demarcações*. CRV.
Rossi, P., & Dweck, E. (2016). Impactos do novo regime fiscal na saúde e na educação. *Cadernos de Saúde Pública, 32*(12).
Teixeria, M. (2018). A crise econômica e as políticas de austeridade: efeitos sobre as mulheres. In P. Rossi, E. Dweck, & A. Oliveira (Eds.), *Economia Para Poucos: impactos sociais da austeridade e alternativas para o Brasil*. Autonomia Literária.

CHAPTER 5

Marx and the Category of Fictitious Profits: Some Notes on the Brazilian Economy

Adriano Lopes Almeida Teixeira and Mauricio de Souza Sabadini

Introduction

Although the debacle surrounding real socialism in the late 1980s caused a setback in Marxist research, in which it was unceremoniously dumped as anachronistic and was overshadowed by the supremacy of neoliberal thinking, the beginning of the twenty-first century has reaffirmed those who have continued to state the importance of Marx's work in understanding the transformations that have taken place within contemporary capitalism. Among other themes, the issue of financialisation has occupied a prominent place. Indeed, transformations in the economic world

A. L. A. Teixeira
Department of Economics and Post-Graduate Program in Social Policy, University of Espírito Santo, Vitória, Brazil

M. de Souza Sabadini (✉)
Department of Economics and Post-Graduate Program in Social Policy, Federal University of Espírito Santo, Vitória, Brazil

G. M. de C. Mello and H. P. Braga (eds.), *Wealth and Poverty in Contemporary Brazilian Capitalism*, Marx, Engels, and Marxisms, https://doi.org/10.1007/978-3-030-82298-9_5

over the last few decades, the spread of financial practices driven by technological developments and the global economic crisis of 2008, have all been great stimuli for Marxists like David Harvey, Michael Heinrich, Fred Moseley, Michael Roberts, François Chesnais, Anwar Shaikh, and others.

This chapter takes advantage of the enthusiasm of the Marxist field for debate and for its continuing interest in revisiting Marxist works to turn the spotlight on a specific item, albeit one that it is immersed within the larger context of studies on financialisation. We are referring to the category of fictitious profits. Studies on this category were received by some allies, who had occasionally been critical of financialisation theories, with manifest indifference or, at times, with a high degree of distrust regarding the need for a new economic category to interpret contemporary capitalism, given that in Marx, the category of fictitious capital already exists.

This chapter will subject the category of fictitious profits to the filter of Marx's method of presentation in *Capital,* to verify the relevance of its development from the category of fictitious capital and its legitimacy within the theoretical-conceptual universe developed by Marx. This legitimacy will be investigated by analysing the kinship of fictitious profits using Marx's dialectical method. In the first section, the development of categories originally established by Marx will be analysed up to the point that it results in the category of fictitious capital. In the second section, we will unveil the determinations of fictitious capital that signal its subsequent development towards the category of fictitious profits. The dichotomy of totality versus individuality is an indispensable part of the analysis required for understanding this theme. It is absent in the research of other representative Marxist authors who, from various angles, recognise the importance of the fictitious character (or, as some say, financial character) of contemporary profits. In the following section, some elements of the long-standing debate around the relationship between the historical and the logical in Marx's theory will be revisited, combining that debate with another extremely importance theme, which was not often dealt with by Marx and his followers, namely, the distinction between the research method and the presentation method. The final section is an overview of the Brazilian economy. It is a closer look at the concrete, with a survey and analysis of data that highlights the financialisation process since the final decades of the last century, with a particular emphasis on the categories of fictitious capital and fictitious profits within the research. This is followed by the final considerations.

From Commodity to Fictitious Capital

The substantiation of value and the gradual unravelling of the forms of capital to its most mystified state, fictitious capital, reveals a central path and a reminder for us: the need for a total reading of Marx's great work, *Capital.*[1] Book I explains wealth in capitalist society from the perspective of totality, and surplus value plays a central role in this discovery. Book II deals with aspects of circulation and in Book III, in Marx's own words, "Our concern is rather to discover and present the concrete forms which grow out of the process of capital's movement considered as a whole" (Marx, 1991: 117). On the one hand, these concrete forms are more visible, which makes them easier to understand, but on the other, their degree of fetishism intensifies and discovering their true nature becomes more difficult, requiring prior knowledge of the categories developed by Marx.

Following this path is, or should be, an indispensable trajectory for critics, who always seek to find gaps and non-existent themes in Marx's work. This is true for his followers too, who often read only the first book of *Capital*. We will examine some of Marx's development of categories, to highlight elements of a striking feature of contemporary capitalism, financialisation, which will then make it possible to understand the intensification of the capitalist process of appreciation founded on capital with fictitious dynamics and an illusory origin-fictitious capital (M-M').

Fictitious capital, which has no productive or real base and therefore does not produce value, disguises its connection with the capitalist process of appreciation. We observe it through variations in prices and the speculative game of buying and selling shares in its financial assets, in which, "... these securities actually represent nothing but accumulated claims, legal titles, to future production. Their money or capital value either does not represent capital at all, as in the case of national debts, or is determined independently of the real capital value they represent" (Marx, 1991: 599). According to Marx, its formation is called capitalisation.

The appreciation of fictitious capital, loaded with its internal contradictions, manifests itself in the commercialisation of a variety of roles within the financial system, or, for Marx, the international credit system, a system which has been at the centre of capitalist crises, manifested as financial crises, over the last decades of the 20th and early twenty-first century.

The journey to this more mystified form of capital in Book III of *Capital*, starts in Book I, where Marx follows the path from commodity to money to capital (commodity → money → capital) with labour value as the central component of the appreciation process. In Book III, Marx goes on to explain that this process is cyclical and is involved in a more extensive mystification process that includes not only capital but also commodity (commodity → money → capital → commodity)—the latter being the commodity of capital form.

The path followed by Marx begins with commodity, following on from the discovery of money and capital, as outlined in Book I, but the commodity presented at the beginning of the first paragraph of Chapter 1 has a different starting point to that of classical economists on the theme of value and will be metamorphosed in the other books of *Capital*. Although its determinations are discussed in Chapter III and its transformation into capital is clarified in Chapter IV, in Chapter I, money appears as a representative of value, consolidating, in a predominant way, the movement of value in substance and content. Commodity and money both appear as forms of capital.

The whole capitalist dynamic is then linked to continuously expanding accumulation, whose central axis is a long process of generating surplus value, a form of surplus that takes on a primary role in the capitalist mode of production. This process of appreciation culminates in capital value and in the historical and theoretical specifics of the mechanisms of wealth generation typical of a new form of social organisation that emerged from the crisis of and transition from the feudal system of production.

After his initial indication of commodity being the form in which wealth appears in society and the discovery of its true origin centred on the labour force as a special commodity, producing surplus labour in the form of surplus value, Marx started to follow the path that capital took with the development of this mode of production within, the then, modern societies. Having presented the general formula of capital in Book I, Book II presents the functional forms in which this capital, as a value that appreciates, is manifested as money-capital, productive-capital, and commodity-capital.

It is noteworthy that Marx exposes the functional forms in three moments, but they express both phases of the capital appreciation process—the circulation phase. This is the moment in which each configuration of capital results in new developments and new functional forms, but in a process that is now autonomous and in which each function further develops from a division of labour among capitalists, in which their roles are expanded and diversified. The historical process of forming this mode of production demands autonomy, in which capitalists assume different functions in the circulation and production phases.

This movement is a central element in this constant transformation and specialisation of capital. Marx makes this clear in a passage from Book II,

> Capital, as self-appreciating value, does not just comprise class relations, a definite social character that depends on the existence of labour as wage-labour. It is a movement, a circulatory process through different stages, which itself in turn includes three different forms of the circulatory process. Hence it can only be grasped as a movement, and not as a static thing. Those who consider the autonomisation [Verselbststiindigung] of value as a mere abstraction forget that the movement of industrial capital is this abstraction in action. Here value passes through different forms, different movements in which it is both preserved and increases, is appreciated. (Marx, 1992: 185)

In Book III, Marx was confronted, from a methodological point of view, with this incessant movement of capital in the search of appreciation, with the movement of categories and their concrete expressions. It is here that the surplus value manifests itself in the form of profit, where the value in the form of the buying and selling price no longer corresponds to the value of the goods—the hypothesis initially adopted throughout the work—and the process of the autonomisation of the forms of capital undergoes significant developments.

Book II and Book III were not finished by Marx, it was Engels who organised and published them, which may have produced mistakes. Marx does, however, leave us a fundamental legacy for discussion of the whole capital cycle and the particularities of capitalist circulation. Capital had appeared in its functional forms and these forms had become autonomous, in a complex tangle of functions of different capitalists through the phases of production and circulation. There was no longer a single capitalist, but a group, competing to appropriate the largest possible fraction of the surplus in the form of surplus value. Competition, until then only assumed was now a permanent more explicit feature.

In this way, money-capital became autonomous as interest-bearing capital (M-M-C-M'-M')—interest appears here as a fraction of surplus value. Commodity-capital becomes autonomous as commodity-dealing capital, with commodity traders, and as money-dealing capital, with money traders (banks). This is all enveloped within a credit system, although Marx did not present this in an organic way, which increasingly permeates and conceals the existing connections between real, productive, and financial movements, much of which is speculative.

Regarding interest bearing capital, the figure of the lender appeared, who grants loans and cedes the use-value of his capital to be used in production, generating surplus in the form of surplus value. In return, the lender receives remuneration in the form of interest, a fraction of the surplus value, while the borrower keeps the profit or gain of the entrepreneur. One of the elements that characterises this autonomous form of interest-bearing capital is that,

> The lending capitalist parts with his capital, transfers it to the industrial capitalist, without receiving an equivalent. But this is in no way an act of the actual cyclical process of capital; it simply introduces this circuit, which is to be effected by the industrial capitalist. This first change of place on the part of the money does not express any act of metamorphosis, neither purchase nor sale. Ownership is not surrendered, since no exchange takes place, and no equivalent is received. (Marx 1991: 468–469)

In this situation, we note that there is a direct relationship between interest-bearing capital, as an autonomous form, and productive-capital, its own formula indicates this. Fictitious capital, on the other hand, is based on interest-bearing capital, at an even higher level of fetishism, but its value is disconnected from the production of value. Hence its fictional character, and its cycle shortened to M-M'. It is important to highlight the relationship between interest-bearing capital and fictitious capital, the former as a mere assumption of the latter, because consolidating its fetishised character in a legal relationship that legitimises the appropriation of income in the form of interest, without a direct link with production, engenders the perception that all capital is a source of interest. Going forward, the right to any future income stream materialises in the form of securities that legally guarantee the appropriation of those flows, as if they resulted from real capital, but that, in fact, does not have and does not itself generate any value: i.e. fictitious capital. So, if this capital does not generate value, it therefore has to appropriate wealth generated in production, in an relationship with work, the genesis of value. In this sense, fictitious capital can originate from three sources: negotiable securities, the apparent doubling of the value of interest-bearing capital, and the speculative valuation of different types of financial assets (Carcanholo & Sabadini, 2015).

As a result, in the contradictory dynamics of fictitious capital, "all connection with the current process of capital's valuation is lost, right down to the last trace, confirming the notion that capital is automatically valued by its own powers" (Marx 1991: 597). The classic forms of this type of capital, according to Marx, are stocks and bonds. It is not overreaching to reaffirm the temporal character of wealth that will be produced in future, but that is already commercialised in the present.

It is also important to highlight another form of fictitious capital known as derivatives. For Mello and Sabadini,

> It is worth mentioning another mode of fictitious capital that develops from those analysed by Marx, derivatives. Derivatives have gained enormous importance, linked to so-called securitisation, the transformation of debts into negotiable securities through capitalisation. These are financial assets, referenced to exchange rates, interest rates, mortgages, stock indexes, student loans, futures securities and commodities prices, climate events, other derivatives (such as *collateralised obligations*, referenced in *bonds, loans, mortgages, debits*, etc), and the estimated risk of investments in these assets (with emphasis on *credit default swaps* [CDS]), which have reached a monumental volume in recent decades. (Mello & Sabadini, 2019: 150)

In Book III, Marx did not fully develop all elements of the process of autonomisation of the functional forms of capital, but he added the credit system and its complex potential for functioning within, and disrupting, the capital cycle, and its published records help us to understand the speculative financial movements, in a contemporary capitalism characterised by a strong speculative dynamic.

The most fetishised stage of the autonomised form of capital, fictitious capital (M-M'), had already been identified by Marx by the end of the nineteenth century.[2] Its development followed a path of countless transformations both in the form of the organisation of, mostly fictitious, bank capital, and in the development of the institutions responsible for the custody of money, loans, accounting, etc. This, coupled with the recent developments in information and data transmission using new technologies, further exacerbates the degree of crises in the global economy.

In effect, the principal route by which capital assumes its reified form is as fictitious capital. Fictitious capital is real and fictitious at the same time, real because it can represent a gain for the individual, and fictitious because it does not produce value or surplus value (Carcanholo & Sabadini, 2015). So, we suggest that this mystified form of capital could appropriate the transfer of wealth from production, for example, through the mechanisms for transferring public debt and/or dividend payments to shareholders, maintaining a close link with productive-capital, and/or it could come from profits arising from the speculative appreciation of asset prices, the so-called fictitious profits discussed in the next section.

The Advent of the Category of Fictitious Capital

It is no accident that the first citation of the category of fictitious profits, as far as we can ascertain, was made by Carcanholo (2003) in a text analysing various aspects of the concealment of the origin of surplus value. Carcanholo argues that, during a process of progressive and increasing mystification, the source of profit is increasingly obscured. Starting from an analysis of categories including cost price, salary, fixed capital, and circulation and advancing to the theme of transforming values into production prices, Carcanholo, following Marx, demonstrates how surplus value becomes invisible, from a purely empiricist perspective.

The last dimension, or category, presented in his text is fictitious profit[3] a category that the author acknowledges was not suggested or intuited by Marx, but which, according to him, would serve to a largely explain the survival of contemporary capitalism[4] The final phase of which is marked by the unprecedented growth of fictitious wealth and is being extended by finding a way to feed the appreciation of that wealth with fictitious profits, which the surplus value, as the output of real wealth, would no longer be able to meet because, "the growth of fictitious capital occurs without corresponding to the true production of surplus value … comes from a profit that does not originate from surplus value" (Carcanholo, 2003: 94). In this sense, Carcanholo points out, that current capitalism, marked by the excessive growth of fictitious capital, or what he calls parasitic speculative capital, has forged an even more powerful instrument for hiding the exploitation of the labour force, namely, fictitious profits.

At this moment, Carcanholo makes a methodological consideration that seems intended to strengthen the basis of his argument. He states that he is averse to employing a procedure that he views as recurrent in the world of science, namely, "the empiricism of one who only sees the apparent" as the only explanation of the real. Although he emphasises that he does not consider his method to be false, because it maintains close links with the empirical essence. For him, the thinking or methodology used to evidence the category of fictitious profits is the distinction between the individual and the totality,

> Fictitious capital and, in particular, parasitic speculative capital, from the point of view of the individual and isolated act, is real capital; in the hands of any entrepreneur, it can be converted into any other form of capital or real wealth. On the other hand, from the point of view of totality it is real and fictitious at the same time; real, for demanding remuneration like any other; fictional, for having no material substance and in no way contributing to the production of surplus, surplus value. (Carcanholo, 2003: 94)

Carcanholo resorts to a methodological expedient common to Marx, namely *totality*, and seeks to lift the category of fictitious profits beyond a simple deduction resulting from the observation of numbers, indices, and data from international financial markets. This procedure underlies his refusal to consider the *apparent* world as decisive for understanding the *real*, which is one of his numerous merits, but which does not seem to account for the inescapable task of explaining the historical-logical process underlying the advent of the category of fictitious profits[5] Except for a minor digression in the final part of the text on content and form in Marx, there are no other methodological movements that demonstrate the category's place in the theoretical presentation of capital, not least because this was not the specific objective of the work. In short, it can be said that the theoretical contribution made by Carcanholo and continued in subsequent texts by Nakatani (2007) and Sabadini (2015), values Marx's dialectic and reclaims it as an essential analytical instrument, despite the absence in it of methodological developments that explain the theoretical transition from the category of fictitious capital to culminate in the category of fictitious profits.

By revitalising this dialectical method for analysing the category, it contributes to demystifying the apparent autonomy of current financial markets, whilst reinforcing the links with Marx's theory of value. This procedure seems to be totally unfeasible regarding interpretations that attempt to extract both fictitious capital and fictitious profits directly from reality or in those that "fix" (in the sense of immobilising) the category of fictitious capital, as defined by Foley (1991: 116), because these interpretations understand that the fictitious character of this form of capital lies in the detachment of the value of the securities that represent it and the value of the real capital that served as a reference:

> In this situation the ownership shares of the firm represent a claim on a certain flow of income arising from the residual profit of enterprise. Holders of money can either lend their money and receive a flow of interest on it or buy shares and receive a flow of dividends. The price of shares will be established to make them attractive as investments, in competition with loans, given the higher risk attached to the flow of residual profit relative to the flow of interest. But this price of shares may exceed the value of the capital actually invested in the firm's operations. Marx calls this excess fictitious capital, since it is part of the price of shares which does not correspond to the capital value actually participating in the firm's production. (Foley, 1991: 116)

The low importance given to *totality* by some Marxists, therefore, seems to be the key for explaining some approaches to the category of fictitious profits. Firstly, authors who deny its existence,[6] such as Lapavitsas and Mendieta-Muñoz (2016: 05), for whom, "financial profits are thus a highly complex economic category; one notion that could be immediately dispensed with, however, is that they are somehow 'fictitious'", and Durand, according to whom,

> The counterpart to the growth of fictitious capital relative to wealth produced is financial profits' increasing share of overall profits. But these financial profits are not themselves fictitious. Paid in hard cash, they have all the attributes of monetary power, first of all in terms of what is usually called purchasing power – the immediate drawing rights on wealth produced. (Durand, 2017: 155)

They are satisfied to use, with various nuances, the term "financial profits" to express the growth of profits derived from financial activities. For Lapavitsas and Mendieta-Muñoz, "there is a close relationship between industrial profit and financial profit, although the latter could also arise from sources different from the former" (Lapavitsas & Mendieta-Muñoz, 2016: 05). While, for Durand, "Financial profits incarnate value but do not result from value production. We should thus conceive of them the transfers of income away from those activities that do produce value..." (Durand, 2017: 156). Durand further deepens the argument when he credits the gains of some to the losses of others, that is, a zero-sum game[7]: "Whatever the type of assets under consideration, capital gains result from a zero-sum game among the various participants on the market: the fictitious capital accumulated through price rises becomes a reality for a given vendor when a buyer on the market himself takes over this fiction" (Ibidem: 173). These are hasty interpretations of a recurring phenomenon in contemporary capitalism, and they do not account for the fact that fictitious profits have no connection with the generation of surplus value.

Secondly, there are authors who welcome the category of fictitious profits, but whom, without a properly Marxist methodological perspective, are quick to submerge it into their empirical investigations, as with Smith et al. (2014) and Duman (2014), who disregard the need to account for different levels of abstraction. Lapavitsas and Mendieta-Muñoz (2016: 03) also carried out direct empirical analyses of the category of financial profits, and they seem to foresee the need for further theoretical development when they state that, "a moment's thought would suffice to show that this general approach must be further elaborated if theory is to account for financial profit. For one thing, the content and form of financial profit are not immediately apparent". Regarding this, Carcanholo and Sabadini (2015: 135) warn that, "thinking about an empirical demonstration of its existence is something completely outside the scientific logic; within the dialectic perspective it is meaningless".

Finally, in a third strand, there are those authors who, more concerned with the fall in the average rate of profit over the last decades and the possibilities and methodologies for its measurement, recognise the existence of fictitious profits and try to analyse them by mobilising a somewhat dialectic method. For Peter Jones, contrary to Durand,

> Worse still, fictitious capital can itself create forms of profit. Rising share prices, for example, create profits for owners of share certificates. Because an expansion of the total market value of corporations' outstanding shares is (correctly) not usually treated as an expansion in anyone's liabilities, rising share prices can, by themselves, create profit without creating corresponding losses. In principle, share traders could produce this wealth without limit. (Jones, 2013: 10)

Although developing another theme and not intending to offer a specific methodological for dealing with the category of fictitious profits, Carchedi points out that,

> If loan capital is fictitious, its profits are fictitious too. They are fictitious not because they do not exist (as in some fraudulent accounting practices). They are the appropriation of a representation of value (money), and in this sense they are real. But they are fictitious because this appropriation springs from a relation of debt/credit rather than production. Financial capital sells titles of debt with no intrinsic value for a representation of value, money. It appropriates value. (Carchedi, 2011: 5)

As already mentioned, this section further develops analysis around a methodology that brings together, into the same dialectical whole, the individual and isolated point of view with the perspective of *totality* in Marx. To this end, Chapters XXI and XXII of Book I of *Capital* are important, as they explicitly open-up space for the discussion of the *totality*, which was already present and presumed in the analysis of commodity at the beginning of the work.

Marx's quote regarding the theoretical explanation made in *Capital* is well known. He took the trouble to return to the topic in what is considered by many to be Marx's last economic text, his *Marginal Notes on Adolph Wagner's 'Lehrbuch der Politischen Ökonomie'* of 1879. "De prime abord, I do not proceed from 'concepts', hence neither from the 'concept of value', [...] What I proceed from is the simplest social form in which the product of labour presents itself in contemporary society, and this is the 'commodity'" (Marx & Engels 1989: 545).

For Marx, selecting commodity as his starting point was not an arbitrary choice. He placed it there precisely because he, as a researcher, did not accept a priori the logic of previous work on the object, but by investigating the subject found a logic in it that led him to this decision. In selecting it, Marx was applying what he had learned from Hegel in calling upon to the idea of *totality*. As an elementary "cell" of capitalism, it constitutes a simple *totality*, an ontological category, which contains, albeit at a highly abstract level, the entire web of relationships and contradictions existing in capitalist society. Marx did not arbitrate a way to start the science, nor did he formulate a methodological introduction, even though he partially gave in to the temptation in *The Introduction of 1857*.

It was not pure empiricism that placed commodity as the starting point of the theoretical pathway, so the directly observable empirical data of reality cannot be the starting point for defining the concept of fictitious profits. It is the perspective of *totality* that will allow the demystification of what is apparent and of what is seen from the perspective is the individual and isolated act. So, let us return to Marx.

According to Marx, "The matter takes quite another aspect if we contemplate not the single capitalist and the single worker, but the capitalist class and the working class, not an isolated process of production, but capitalist production in full swing, and on its actual social scale" (Marx 1990: 717). Later, in a similar quote, Marx better qualifies his argument by exposing the category of *totality*, which, in the capitalist universe, is remote from the agents' individual perception. He says:

> To be sure, the matter looks quite different if we consider capitalist production in the uninterrupted flow of its renewal, and if, in place of the individual capitalist and the individual worker, we view them in their totality, as the capitalist class and the working class confronting each other. But in so doing we should be applying standards entirely foreign to commodity production. (Marx 1990: 732)

It was evident to Marx that both analytical perspectives, the individual and the global, needed to be considered, in an overlapping movement in which one determines and is determined by the other. What the economic agents noticed, with the naked eye, were the exchanges that took place between individuals in a certain period and within an anarchic society without central control. This is the measurement standard. Exchanges do not take place between classes globally, that is, the entire capitalist class buys in a coordinated manner from the entire proletarian class or vice versa.

The explanation that Marx makes in *Capital*, vital for understanding the production and distribution of surplus value, seems to be a development of the analysis he made in the *Introduction of 1857* in which he argues that production and distribution are not isolated spheres, but are part of an organic whole. Bourgeois economists were right to perceive production and distribution as spheres of material life but were unable to include them in the same totality. Marx continued his argument, contesting the procedure followed by John Stuart Mill, who had separated these spheres indistinctly: "The conclusion we reach is not that production, distribution, exchange and consumption are identical, but that they all form the members of a totality, distinctions within a unity" (Marx 1993: 99). For Marx, it was imperative that these spheres showed themselves as organically linked, by a dialectical procedure, expressed in the form of, "[...] a regular syllogism; production is the generality, distribution and exchange the particularity, and consumption the singularity in which the whole is joined together" (Marx 1993: 89). Economic structure can only be understood through a process that not only recognises this logical chain, but also, and principally, the real determinations that express the impossibility that each sphere is autonomous and independent from the others. This is to say, "that production is also consumption; that production is distribution; exchange is circulation, and exchange is production" (De Paula, 2010: 99).[8]

It is possible, therefore, that many of the challenges to the concept of fictitious profits, or indifference to it, lies in a misunderstanding of the different levels of abstraction between categories. Fictitious profits are situated at a level of abstraction different from that of surplus value and it may be useful to revisit the syllogism developed by Marx in the *Introduction*, between *universality*, *particularity*, and *singularity*, and outlined by him in the *Grundrisse*.

If production is *universality*, then the added-value located within it is a synthesis of the generation of value that occurs in the sphere of production and a space for affirming the law of value. This occurs *particularly* in the sphere of distribution and exchange, in the moment of circulation, and in the movement of the autonomised functional forms of capital that, in the process of theoretical revelation, steer the categories of fictitious capital and fictitious profits. And finally, the *singularity*, "in which the whole is unified", this is the moment of interaction between the various competing capitals, of the forms in which capital exists, in which fictitious profits, like the ghosts that they are, are expressed through the monolithic body of the same elements that embody the existence of fictitious capital, namely, stocks, government bonds, derivatives, and the many other vehicles being continuously created by new capitalisation processes carried along by an unprecedented wave of financial innovation.

As elements belonging to a lower level of abstraction, these concrete types of fictitious capital unify the whole as an expression of the singularity that they are, but in themselves, they do not reveal the line from which they were constituted by fictitious profits, a category that is situated at a higher level of abstraction. It is, therefore, not possible to subject fictitious profits to the economists' own instruments of empirical verification. It is in this same sense that Rieser, discussing the capitalist appearance and its forms of manifestation, summarises his argument.

> We have thus outlined three levels of propositions: 1) the general law of value; 2) the general laws of buying and selling the labour force and the capitalist decision-making system; 3) the particular proposals on the march of wages and on the organisation of the factory. Of these three levels, only the third consists of proposals directly subject to empirical verification. (Rieser, 1977: 127)

Our interpretation is somewhat akin to that of Moseley (2014), the difference being that Moseley divided Marx's theory into two levels of abstraction only, *universality* (capital in general, the *locus* of the generation of surplus value) and *particularity* (competition, the *locus* of distribution of surplus value), since, according to him, Marx would have paid little attention to *singularity*.

To better understand fictitious profits, we consider three levels of abstraction, and even though Marx placed competition as an element of *particularity* (which is incorporated by Moseley)—and, in fact, this is presupposed in the action of the autonomised forms of capital—it is better placed at the level of *singularity*, due to the free action of the diverse forms of capital. De Paula's interpretation is similar to Moseley's, which is reproduced in the previous footnote. De Paula seeks to rehabilitate the *singularity* by understanding that it is only possible to build a theory of competition based on it, "by explaining its singular aspects" (De Paula, 2003: 122), aspects which were not developed by Marx either in *Grundrisse*, or in *Capital*. On the contrary, Harvey (2013: 178) surprises us by offering a rather poor interpretation of *singularity*; "Marx was not at all comfortable with exploring such 'singularities' as the inner workings of the spirit of entrepreneurship, the psychology of expectations, and the role of trust in financial affairs [...]".

From the above, the misunderstanding of Foley's definition of fictitious capital is more evident, as it only considers fictitious capital as the part of capital that exceeds the value of the capital invested in the company's activities. This means to say that, to the extent that a speculative valuation of the shares occurs, both the portion of the value of the shares that corresponds to the true estate and the portion that exceeds it, compose a monolithic whole, in such a way that the totality of that title will move through the financial system without being viewed as distinct. The same understanding applies to attempts to place fictitious profits in the empirical data set provided by governments and research bodies.

An analysis that seeks to organically link *totality* and *individuality* is what will allow us to understand the nature of fictitious profits. At the level of *singularity*, of the interaction between the various actions of the individual agents, what the proportion of fictitious capital, composed of fictitious profits or not, transformed into real wealth might be, does not matter (and may even be impossible to differentiate). So, at this level of abstraction, fictitious profits are real, while from the perspective of *totality* they are fictitious. It is a matter, therefore, of trying to illuminate how, in the process of exposure, the logical-genetic and historical process generates profit from fictitious capital. The task of the next section is to historicise fictitious profits, demonstrating how logical development abstractly reflects the real historical process which, in turn, can only be understood if the internal connections of the logical process are clarified.

The Relationship Between the Logical Method and the Historical Method

The relationship between the logical and the historical in Marx has turned out to be a costly, complex, and controversial issue within the Marxist tradition. Authors who have dealt with this phenomenon—for some as fictitious profits, for others as financial profits—have apparently ignored this theme and cite the category as if it can be understood idealistically, through the free functioning and exercise of the thinking mind. In other words, simple analysis of the empirical data generated by contemporary capitalism would supposedly give the researcher direct and immediate access to the real, as if it could present itself without the appropriate mediations. This type of empirical-immediate analysis, typical of classical economists, is foreign[9] to Marx's conceptual universe, although Marx took advantage of it.[10]

Just as wrong, albeit in the opposite direction, are those who reject history, attempting to retrieve from Hegel, the elements of a logic that make it possible to reconstruct the development of categories in Marx's work,[11] and which could also be applied in the case of fictitious profits. As we will see later, our proposed path will be neither.

In addition to the discussion of the logical-historical, and as an important precursor, we need to discuss a theme that has been little studied in this tradition, the relationship between the research method and the presentation method. It is possible that the differentiation made briefly by Marx in the postscript to the second German edition of *Capital*, and the scant attention paid to it by Marxists in general, is the key to understanding why many authors do not account for the distinction and present their investigations as if they were the very process of expounding the theory.

Commonly, studies of the relationship between the historical and logical in Marx's work starts with comments made by Engels (2008) on Marx's *Contribution to the Critique of Political Economy*, where he says that the logical method, "is, in reality, but the historical method stripped only of its historical form and disturbing casualties. There, where the story begins, the process of reflection must also begin" (Engels, 2008: 283). Engels immediately disputes Marx when Marx says in the *Introduction* that,

> It would therefore be unfeasible and wrong to let the economic categories follow one another in the same sequence as that in which they were historically decisive. Their sequence is determined, rather, by their relation to one another in modem bourgeois society, which is precisely the opposite of that which seems to be their natural order, or which corresponds to historical development. The point is not the historic position of the economic relations in the succession of different forms of society. Even less is it their sequence' in the idea' (Proudhon) (a muddy notion of historic movement). Rather, their order within modern Bourgeois society. (Marx, 1993: 107–108)

All this controversy seems to flow into the discussion around the method of presentation in *Capital*. The heart of the matter does not lie in whether the explanation of the categories directly expresses the order in which historical development proceeds, it lies in analysing how the evolving logic appropriates history, at the same time as the history to be captured, in its internal nexuses, requires the instruments of logic. Let us look again at Marx in the *Grundrisse*:

> On the other side, much more important for us is that our method indicates the points where historical investigation must enter in, or where bourgeois economy as a merely historical form of the production process

points beyond itself to earlier historical modes of production. In order to develop the laws of bourgeois economy, therefore, it is not necessary to write the real history of the relations of production. But the correct observation and deduction of these laws, as having themselves become in history, always leads to primary equations - like the empirical numbers e.g., in natural science - which point towards a past lying behind this system. These indications [Andeutung], together with a correct grasp of the present, then also offer the key to the understanding of the past - a work in its own right which, it is to be hoped, we shall be able to undertake as well. (Marx 1993: 460–461)

Commenting on the above quote, Reichelt (2013: 140–141) says that the distinction between effective history and presentation requires that the way in which effective history penetrates the categorical framework be brought into the light, together with the "internal logic of the value movement" from which one can conceptually understand the "history of production relationships". In a similar vein, Machado points out that,

The historical character of the categories does not lie in the fact that they succeed one another in *Capital* in the order in which they were historically determinants, but that they succeed one another in the order that specifies and determines more and more a particular historical form, with the determinations that are its own. The much-vaunted logical need in the chain of categories thus follows the logic of their particularisation or historical determination. (Machado, 2018: 267)

For Müller (1982), the result of not understanding Marx's method is the theoretical dilution of the concept of dialectics, and especially that of "presentation". According to him, when the dialectical character of the method of *Capital* was rejected, claiming that it represented a Hegelian compromise, then the presentation lost its philosophical specificity, taking up Marx's counterpointing of the method of exposure and the method of research, with an emphasis on the latter. It is essential, therefore, to understand how the elements of the investigation (empirical data, indexes, statistical information, etc.) are appropriated by the presentation. This incorporation which, according to Ilienkov, consists of the elevation of the abstract to the concrete, is characterised as, "the elevated form, which organically unites the analysis of the facts with the analysis of the concepts, [and] it is precisely the form that passes from the abstract to the concrete of which Marx speaks" (Ilienkov, 1978: 49).

Marx's process of theoretical presentation advances through successive incorporations of historical elements arising from research, which are not directly integrated with the development of categories. It is not possible, then, to capture reality, the essence, directly from observation, and simply add it to the next step of the presentation without first having those results subjected to a critical operation within the framework of dialectics. The investigation feeds the presentation, in the same way that the presentation clarifies the elements of logic for a better understanding of the effective historical reality. Corazza clarifies the issue considerably,

> Although Marx affirms that the correct scientific method is what starts from the abstract to arrive at the concrete, this does not mean that the real starting point is not the sensible reality, as he is referring to the moment of the exhibition, which was preceded by a whole research work, when abstractions are made. (Corazza, 2003: 51)

The process of creating categories in Marx demands real abstractions of a historical nature. It is not a matter of observing a certain phenomenon and naming it, or as Marx (1992: 303) says, "What is at issue here is not a set of definitions under which things are to be subsumed. It is rather definite functions that are expressed in specific categories". The genesis of the category of fictitious profits in the theoretical presentation follows the appearance of fictitious capital, as already indicated above. Furthermore, the gaps pointed out in the previous section give the impression that the character of fictitious profits results solely from empirical observations, because, in Marxist terms, a category cannot appear, or be named, before it is properly (historically and logically) deduced.

Hence, the need to historicise the category, to understand how history is appropriated within the development of categories that takes us from fictitious capital to fictitious profits, indicating, in accordance with Marx's method, "[...] the points where historical investigation must enter in" (Marx 1993: 460).[12] Primitive accumulation was only analysed by Marx after he had studied the nature of capitalist accumulation in the three preceding chapters. Had he begun with primitive accumulation, the result would have been the compiling, in a single chapter, of a variety of historical information and disconnected empirical data, removed from the logical links necessary to elucidate its genesis and its internal mechanisms of operation.

Let us return to the distinction that Marx makes between research method and presentation method in which there is no indication of "how to do it, how to research". He says that,

> Of course, the method of presentation must differ in form from that of inquiry. The latter has to appropriate the material in detail, to analyse its different forms of development and to track down their inner connection. Only after this work has been done can the real movement be appropriately presented. If this is done successfully, if the life of the subject-matter is now reflected back in the ideas, then it may appear as if we have before us an a priori construction. (Marx 1990: 102)

In addition to the fact that the investigation is dealing with a chaotic reality, Marx does not risk violating the fundamental methodological principle of his dialectical analysis, according to which the method cannot be defined a priori, and the object must be accompanied in all its various shades and in its evolution.[13]

Although it is common to find references to presentation as being Marx's preferred method, it is clear that presentation, as a moment of critical reconstruction, on the ideal plane, of reality, is only one of its moments. To a certain extent, this is what Marx argues when he says,

> Thus, if I were to begin with the population, this would be a chaotic conception [*Vorstellung*] of the whole, and I would then, by means of further determination, move analytically towards ever more simple concepts [*Begriff*], from the imagined concrete towards ever thinner abstractions until I had arrived at the simplest determinations. From there the journey would have to be retraced until I had finally arrived at the population again, but this time not as the chaotic conception of a whole, but as a rich totality of many determinations and relations. (Marx 1993: 100)

Since reality presents itself as the multiple of many determinations, empirical observation alone is not able to decipher the means of the capitalist mode of production by externalising its laws and general tendencies. For this reason, real abstractions seek to isolate specific aspects of the real, remove elements that cloud the essence of the phenomena and reveal determinations that will lead to new abstractions that are increasingly less concrete.

The starting point, therefore, is the concrete. From it, it is possible to construct a chaotic mental representation that cannot be confused with the real, as it is always external. Through a process of abstraction, abstract determinations are reached, in which the part is separated from the whole and is also considered as a whole. This leads to concepts that, as moments of thought, reproduce the real. The investigation methodology is, therefore, "the study or investigation of determinations, both simple and complex, through analysis, [...] the first moment of the theoretical method" (Dussel, 2004: 51).

As, in Marx, the abstractions are neither ideal nor arbitrary, then investigation of the concrete is a mandatory step and precedes the act of abstraction. But, with the abstraction accomplished, the following steps can only be taken through new abstractions, which, in turn, will also be preceded by investigations or as already mentioned, by penetrations of history at specific moments of the presentation. If fictitious profits are a distinctive phenomenon of contemporary capitalism, their development, as a new abstraction, must be justified and demonstrated logically and historically. The logical demonstration will not be accomplished by merely recognising the degree of proximity and similarity to the category of fictitious capital, nor the historic demonstration through the simple observation of empirical data and historical specificities of contemporary times.

What is proposed here is that, despite the speculative appreciation of the bonds that represent fictitious capital being an integral element of its own definition, fictitious profits constitute an abstraction capable of explaining structural features of current capitalism. Before the 1970s and throughout the process of debt securitisation that occurred from the 1980s onwards, we might have considered fictitious profits as an occasional phenomenon, present periodically in all the historic stages of capitalism, and which could be contained by good regulatory practices, but today they have become a distinctive brand. Fictitious profits potentially arise at the birth of capital, regardless of whether they are verifiable at any given time. It could be argued, for example, that trading companies in the seventeenth century were already companies capitalised under commercial logic (and not industrial) as they were already issuing shares. It is not, however, this historical evidence that confirms the existence of fictitious profits at a concrete level within capitalist society.

The question, therefore, is no longer whether fictitious profits came into existence recently, or have done so forever. We consider them integral to the concept of fictitious capital, as discussed in the previous section. Like a virus incubated by the capitalist organism—and sometimes controlled by "healthy" feeding practices i.e. through the regular extracting of surplus value—fictitious profits started to subordinate the functioning of the organism, and the antibiotics prescribed by neoliberalism have only contributed to opening new ways for it to proliferate. The corollary of this is that the logic of the securitisation process needs to be understood, and this process, as a historical phenomenon, needs to be investigated for a better foundation of the logical genesis of the category of fictitious profits. This is a suggestion for future work.

From this, we can see that the debate around the logical and the historical in Marx needs to be analysed within the scope of the classical distinction that he made between the method of investigation and the method of presentation. Investigation and presentation are distinct moments of theoretical development that interpenetrate, intertwined as a theory, as an ideal description of reality in thought. Investigation is, therefore, a decisive moment in the presentation of the subject, as it means the moment in which elements of the appearance are appropriated, that at some subsequent moment in the theoretical development will be linked. This is the same sense in which Marx indicates points where historical analysis must be introduced.

It is not our intention to indicate a mechanical process, and therefore, nothing dialectical or explicit on the subject, which can only be understood throughout its process by investigating its determinations. The attraction to the empirical represents an approximation, not of the essence, but of the form of the manifestation of categories that cannot appear in the real world because they belong to lower levels of abstraction. The next section reflects this. It is not an attempt to extract data from the real world that delivers the exact percentages that correspond to the total for fictitious profits. It is a search for elements of the empirical that reflect the prominence of fictitious capital and, therefore, of fictitious profits in contemporary capitalism. As in Marx's method, subsequent categories redefine previous ones. The elements of *singularity* have, at some point, to be articulated for a better definition of what was proposed as belonging to *particularity* and *universality*. Fictitious profits cannot be proven by a direct and immediate incursion into the concrete, but, as a theoretical component of the definition of fictitious capital itself, it can be evidenced by the exponential growth of so-called financial wealth in the contemporary capitalist system. The following section describes some aspects of the Brazilian economy, immersed in so called financialisation, to seek evidence of fictitious profits. In the same way that flattening wage indices and the intensification of exploitation reflect an increasing extraction of surplus value, the elements that form fictitious capital, stocks, government bonds, and derivatives, among others, only evidence the increase in fictitious profits as a decisive aspect of the financial logic guiding the process of contemporary capitalist accumulation.

The Case of the Brazilian Economy

We start from the assumption that the integration of peripheral markets into the process of the financialisation of the capitalist world economy has become more integrated over the final decades of the 20th and early twenty-first century. It is no coincidence that this moment is associated with a period of commercial, productive, and financial liberalisation that marks both central and peripheral capitalist countries. Hannan (2018), analysing what he calls Emerging Markets and Developing Economies (EMDEs), directs us to some of the peculiarities of this process, highlighting, for example, the growth and composition of capital flows, where,

> ...the composition of net capital flows to EMEDEs changed over the decades. The dramatic rise of foreign direct investment flows, especially in the 1980s and 1990s, stood out. While other investment flows constituted the highest share amongst all capital flows. Compared to foreign direct investment, other investment flows and portfolio flows exhibited more volatility and swings, with gross inflows in portfolio and other investments around two and four times more volatile than foreign direct investment (...). On the other hand, net portfolio investment flows continued to rise until the mid-1990s and then faced a downward trend until early 2000. (Hannan, 2018: 5)

Bearing in mind the particularities of each country in the exact form of this integration into the financialised world economy, we suggest that Brazil has, especially since the 1990s, inserted itself more strongly into external capital flows, where the liberalisation of the balance of payments capital account has contributed to the gradual entry of, mostly speculative, capital.

Although our interest in the Brazilian economy lies in this most recent historical period, it is important to note that the form of Brazil's economy suggests a model of dependence on and subsumption to the world capitalist and imperialist order which explains the inequalities that characterise the country and suggests that the current moment is just one more when the production of wealth is appropriated in large part by the holders of fictitious assets. For illustrative purposes only, 39% of the executed federal budget (paid) in 2020 was spent on interest and debt repayments, while areas such as health, education, and public safety were received just 4.2, 2.4, and 0.3% of the total, respectively, as shown in Graphic 1 below (Fattorelli et al.—Citizen Debt Audit 2021), a clear demonstration of the appropriation of wealth by the holders of fictitious capital in the form of bonds (Fig. 5.1).

This information is not just part of recent history, it is historic. The current national economy is treated by some, like Paulani (2013), as the fifth stage of the Brazilian economy, being marked as an, "international platform for financial accumulation and producer of primary goods", and

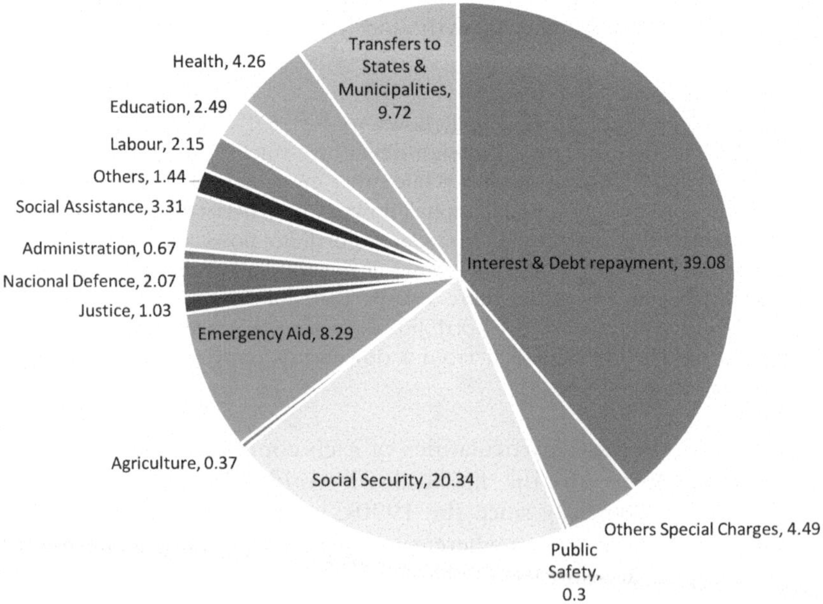

Fig. 5.1 Executed federal budget (paid) 2020 (% of GDP) (*Source* Fattorelli et al. [2021])

featuring, "active insertion into the financialisation" of the world (p. 245). It presents, according to Paulani, points in common with the period of Dos Santos (1970), who called the first phase, "colonial dependency", the second phase, "industrial-financial dependence", consolidated at the end of the nineteenth century, and a third phase, post WWII, of, "consolidated dependence based on multinational corporations", built upon industrial-technological dependence. Paulani goes on to indicate, as a first step, and in the same sense, the, "primitive accumulation", representative of a process of plundering by central capitalist countries, followed by a phase of the, "consolidation of the capitalist mode of production", with signs, "of [the] crisis of over-accumulation" at the centre of world capitalism, and of the, "affirmation and maturation of financialisation".

It is worth noting that the current economic stage does not reveal itself naturally, through its content, as an isolated moment in the establishment of the peripheral and dependent history of capitalism in the country, and it is unoriginal from the point of view of its economic and geopolitical formation. As pointed out above, the current subordinate insertion of the Brazilian economy demonstrates the dynamics of primitive accumulation of capital represented by, among others, the processes of colonial exploitation, slavery, and indigenous extermination, in the context of capitalist nation States and their mercantile policies of overseas exploitation.

Considering this, the intensification of the recent internationalisation of the financial cycle of the Brazilian economy began in the 1990s, alongside neoliberal policies, and marked its entry into global financialisation. These policies of productive, commercial, and financial deregulation have set the tone for changes since the middle of that decade.

As previously indicated by EMDEs, a sign of this process can be observed in the evolution of indicators such as Foreign Direct Investments (FDI) and Balance of Payments Portfolio Investments, in addition to other possible variables that signal the growth of fictitious capital and earnings as fictitious profits. A important point made by Marques and Nakatani (2013) was the creation, in 1991, of Annex IV of Resolution 1289/87 which, "allowed foreign capital to be invested in the Stock Exchange and in Investment Funds or Portfolios in Brazil" (p. 74), this was a milestone in the increased flexibility of the entry and exit of fictitious capital to the Brazilian economy.

Additionally, Bruno and Caffé (2015) identify some indicators of the financialisation of the Brazilian economy, among which are the participation of *income from interest* in the gross product and the macroeconomic rate of financialisation. In their conclusions, they state that, "in the specific case of Brazil, the inclusion of interest in GDP has reached very high proportions (...) the greater weight of interest income, resulting from the high domestic real interest rates, has contributed to raising the political and economic power of the financial sector and the rentier classes" (p. 41). Analysing data on the total flow of interest received and paid as a percentage of GDP, they conclude that this, "highlight is due to the high participation of the flow received 29% of GDP for the 1993–2003 period and 30% between 2004 and 2010. Almost one third of the total Brazilian product is being absorbed by interest income" (p. 43).

This, and other indicators, suggest that the rate of the financialisation of the Brazilian economy, calculated by the ratio of the total of non-monetary financial assets and the total stock of productive fixed capital, has increased significantly since 1994. According to Bruno and Caffé (2015), "in the period 1994–2010, the ratio of financial assets to productive fixed assets is being rapidly detaching from the rate of capital accumulation. This is a characteristic expression of financialisation processes" (p. 51).

Figure 5.2 shows this process of the intensifying flow of financial movements over the last decades of the 20th and early twenty-first century, represented by net FDI and Portfolio Investments.

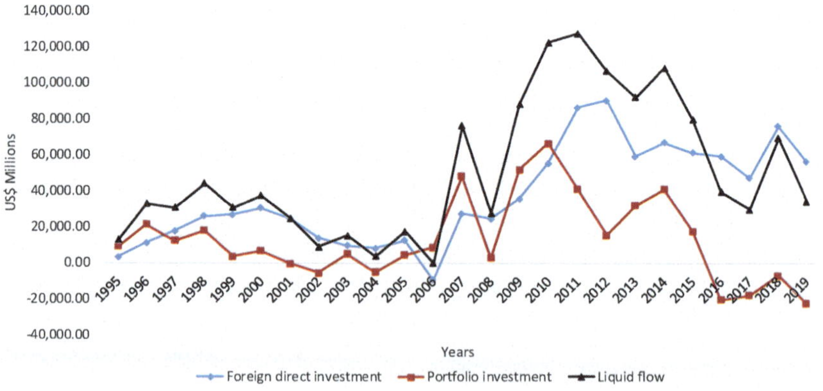

Fig. 5.2 Foreign direct investment and portfolio investment (*Source* Banco Central do Brasil [BCB-DSTAT]. Author's production)

Starting from a volume of FDI close to zero in the early 1990s, there has been effective growth until the 2000s and an even greater increase between 2006 and 2012. These initial positive variations were mainly due to the sale of state-owned companies in a process of privatisation that has expanded since the mid-1990s. As Rodrigues and Jurgenfeld (2019) inform us, under the Collor government (1990–1992) 18 companies were privatised, raising a total of USD 3.6 billion; during the administration of Itamar Franco (1992–1994), "15 companies were privatised, generating USD 3.2 billion in sales" (p. 403), and from the mid-1990s, in the first Cardoso government (1995–1998), the privatisation process intensified, "31 companies, including from sectors such as energy, telecommunications, transport and mining, were privatised, raising USD 31.9 billion" (p. 410).

It should be noted, as Nakatani (2000: 221) warns us, that, "unlike what happened historically, these investments no longer expand productive capacity. They are directed, for the most part, to acquisitions, mergers and incorporations of existing capital". It is common to see the literature stating that the beginning of FDI relates positively to improvements in production arising from the attraction of foreign capital. However, as Moreira and Almeida (2013: 14) reinforce, "the investments made in this deflationary and low growth context do not generate expansion of production capacity, focusing more on productive restructuring operations, which mean, notably, specialisation in more competitive activities and outsourcing of secondary activities. This implies focusing on the main activity, closing production units, and reducing workforce"; for this reason, "from the financing point of view, the stable and long-term nature of FDI cannot be confirmed", and it is not significant regarding the increase of what is commonly called real investment in the economy.

So, this process saw a significant increase in the amounts of fictitious foreign capital in the form of stock purchases throughout the 1990s, it caused the denationalisation of the Brazilian economy, and a commitment to send wealth abroad in the form of the remittance of profits and dividends. This intensified the entry of the national economy into the speculative movements of the world market and contradicted the official line that the sale of the state-owned companies would raise funds destined to reducing the debt. As we will see below. Paulani (2012: 92) highlights that this decade was marked by, "the opening of the Brazilian market for private and public securities and the financial opening of the Brazilian economy, with the gradual removal of controls that hindered the free flow of international capital".

This period was marked by these characteristics, and the consequences portray the subordinate position of the Brazilian economy. As Nakatani (2000) shows, Brazilian exports as a percentage of the world total decreased from 0.99% in 1980, to 0.91% in 1990 and rose to 0.94% in 1998. The capital remittance indicator is also enlightening regarding the behaviour of the Brazilian economy in the world, since "the net remittance of interest reached a total of USD 173.7 billion in the period from January 1980 to December 1998, with an annual average of USD 9.1 billion between 1980 and 1993 and USD 9.2 billion between 1994 and 1998" (Nakatani, 2000: 217).

The portfolio account, which, "moves most of the international parasitic speculative capital flows, in Brazil" (Nakatani, 2000: 222), shows an upward trend in the previous graph until the 1998–1999 crisis, followed by a retraction until 2002, the year of the election of Luiz Inácio Lula da Silva (2003–2010), and then a recovery of growth, mainly from 2006, but with a huge reduction in 2008 due to the international capitalist crisis. Usually classified as a very short-term investment (investments in bonds, shares, and fixed income), it presents speculative variations and evident volatilities throughout the historical series, showing a sharp drop after the 2014 crisis, and with a high degree of creation of fictitious profits.

Despite not having the same methodological approach adopted here, and assuming that Foreign Investment in Portfolio (FIP) is more volatile compared to FDI, Silva Filho (2015: 15) indicates that, regarding the stock of FIP, "a large part of this wealth consists of shareholdings in national companies, (…) there is also an increasingly significant volume of fixed income assets owned by foreign investors (…), in addition to other private securities such as debentures and derivative contracts". For Van Noije and De Conti (2016: 209) the, "2000s were marked by a significant inflow of capital with a speculative profile into the country, resulting in a large increase in net external liabilities, which suggests a worsening of the external vulnerability of the Brazilian economy".

We should remind ourselves that fixed income stocks and assets form the classic composition of fictitious capital, as Marx indicates in Book III, and they characterise the formation and transformation of the Brazilian economy over recent decades, in a country subordinate to financial dynamics and with distinct traces of the fictitious expansion of capital within it. Even though it was a latecomer at the international level, it was necessary to first create a more solid base, both from a macroeconomic point of view, with the control of inflation in the mid-1990s, for example, and from an institutional point of view, from the various changes in Central Bank rules for the inflow and outflow of capital flows, bringing more direct effects on the evolution of fictitious capital in more recent decades.

In view of this, we have identified, in the Brazilian economy, an expansion in the scope of the commercialisation of commodity of capital and a high degree of creation of fictitious wealth in the form of fictitious profits, represented by speculative variations in the prices of financial assets. If the 1990s mark the beginning of the economic opening-up process, then the 2000s will characterise, according to Paulani (2012: 93), "the consolidation of the Brazilian position in financialised capitalism", because several measures have been approved that deepen this insertion, such as the, "extension of pension reforms to the civil service, reform of the bankruptcy law to prioritise the interests of financial creditors, and the adoption of measures to increase the degree of financial openness".

In the case of the fictitious capital represented by government bonds, we can follow its evolution in the last two decades of the century 20th and in the first two decades of the twenty-first century in Fig. 5.3.

As in Fig. 5.2, there is an exponential growth in national indebtedness over a short period of just four decades, mainly from the mid-1990s, committing about 40% of the executed federal budget in 2020 to the servicing of debt. Over recent decades, the growth of public debt, added to the previous data, demonstrates a significant increase in transactions of financial assets that represent fictitious capital. This has had social and economic consequences for the functioning of the Brazilian economy, especially for the vast majority of Brazilians, who survive in precarious living conditions and with high levels of poverty.

The evolution of these indicators and the reflexive growth of fictitious capital indicate the way in which the insertion of the national economy within contemporary capitalism took place, and how our economy is historically dependent on the dynamics of accumulation, driven by a strong financialisation dynamic. These milestones indicate, "Brazil's subordinate insertion in the international market, with a *re-primarisation* and financialisation of exports, a pattern of capital flow from the financial account subordinated to international capital and with high capital volatility" (Sampaio, 2020: 3).

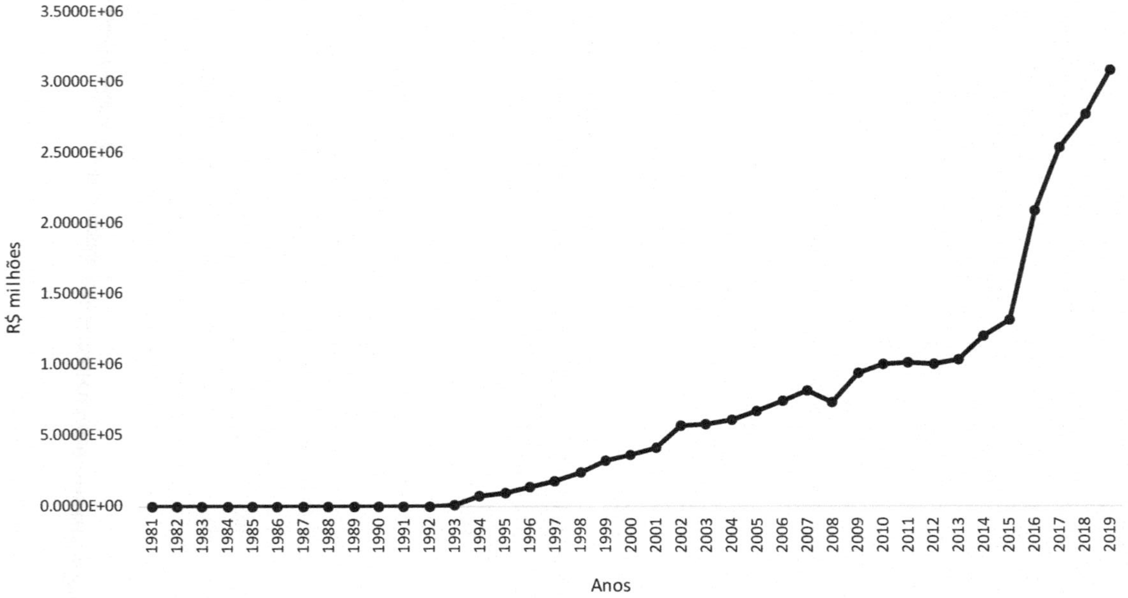

Fig. 5.3 Public sector net debt (Federal Government and Central Bank) (*Source* IPEADATA. Author's production)

Furthermore, the dependence on external capital flows has made the Brazilian economy hostage to external speculative movements which, together with the free movement of fictitious capital inflows and outflows and high domestic interest rates, have mortgaged the country's future wealth on a massive scale. National governments have also been pushing through a variety of reforms, including in labour and social security, and they have increasingly intensified their regressive, neoliberal, policies, and cut social spending to pay for these financial commitments, all at the expense of social and labour protections.

The signs of financial fragility and the vulnerability of the economy were already clear in the 1990s (Carcanholo, 2002), laying the foundation for the following decades, "the external insertion of the Brazilian economy, financially speaking, during the first decade of the twenty-first century led to a situation of excess inflow of foreign capital (in relation to the needs of current transactions), allowing a simultaneous large expansion of international reserves—which tend to improve external solvency—and the appreciation of the real—which tends to worsen current transaction deficits. This contradictory effect on external accounts seems to have led to a make-up of the PII[14] that reduced the *vulnerability-stock* of the Brazilian economy, at least in the short term; but that, in the long run, accentuated the *vulnerability-flow* and crystallised the dependence on external financing, mainly to pay the income from this huge net external liability" (Van Noije & De Conti, 2016: 237).

This intense speculative movement, marked by the expansion of fictitious capital and fictitious profits, has become a central aspect of the Brazilian economy, contributing to the understanding of phenomena such as the wide social inequality across all regions of the country, fed by the continuous transferring of wealth generated by labour to the most favoured classes, who hold the fictitious financial assets.

Final Considerations

It is possible to say, according to Marx, that although, over the past three centuries, capitalism has presented different nuances according to time and place, the nature of capital has remained the same. Within this scope, the fictitious character of capital, as a determination internal to this category, presents itself as a potentiality capable of accommodating the contradictions of capitalism, which in contemporary times, perhaps more than at any other time, claims that the category of fictitious capital is a central element to its functioning. This means that the process of capitalist accumulation occurs in a raging sea, instigated by waves of contradictions that are amplified with each attempt to increase the value of the growing masses of capital that more from one extreme to another, submitting everything and everyone to their logic of domination. One of its corollaries has been the desperate initiatives to increase workforce exploitation in all forms, ranging from the reintroduction of old-fashioned and violent practices, typical of the beginnings of capitalism, to the most sophisticated means of extracting surplus value disguised within the technological development of so-called, platform capitalism.

It is not uncommon to find analysts, connected with various theoretical matrices, publishing empirical research that expresses the unprecedented growth of so-called financial wealth in relation to material wealth. From what has already been stated above, the category of fictitious capital, as it expresses aspects of the contradictory character of capital, is essential in elucidating the internal movements of the current stage of capitalism. The category of fictitious profits gives greater density to the category of fictitious capital, as it can explain specific determinations of the latter.

While blocks of fictitious capital are waiting for a valuation that cannot be delivered by the traditional source of their support, fictitious profits contribute to understanding the resistance and survival of a social production system that has succeeded against the most pessimistic projections regarding its longevity. They do so because, by definition, they do not correspond to any fraction of the added-value generated in the production process.

However, while it illuminates the internal tensions of fictitious capital as a category, fictitious profits, themselves, cannot be discovered through conventional channels of empirical observation, as, like fictitious capital, they are located at a higher level of abstraction and can only be expressed by the concrete forms of its manifestation, negotiable securities. From the point of view of the individual transactions of these bonds, they appear as real wealth for their owners, as they can convert it at any time into material wealth. However, from the point of view of totality, it remains fictional.

The way in which the Brazilian economy has been dealt with here, even if somewhat briefly, expresses this perspective. The exorbitance of the financial channels for increasing the value of wealth in Brazil reflects the imposition of fictitious capital, and its various forms of manifestation, on any interpretation on the specific way in which the process of capitalist accumulation has taken place over recent decades in Brazil and the world.

Notes

1. "In this way, from a simple adjective of commodities, value becomes a noun in the cycle of capital. When value is no longer simple value but capital value, we witness the substantiation of value. Marx devotes only a single passage to the subject in chapter IV of Book I of *Capital* and some others in the first chapter of Book II" (Carcanholo & Nakatani, 2019: 121).
2. In the historic process of constituting fictitious capital in the form of shares, and in the implementation of mercantile policies by an absolutist state, the East India Company (1602) was, for example, a commercial company formed by an association of shareholders (merchants, bankers)—for buying and selling shares—amid the capitalist formation and expansion in financing the trafficking of slaves to the colonies in the context of the primitive accumulation of capital. Finally, in the nineteenth century, in Marx's time, "In 1884, when the Dow Jones was created, it was comprised of nine railway companies, a steamboat company and the Western Union fund transfer company" (Lohoff & Trenkle, 2014: 197).
3. This question makes a difference to the text by Vittorio Rieser (1977) since he does not discuss fictitious profits.
4. This argument appears explicitly in the article from 2007, and even more strikingly in that of 2015: "The difficulty is not in finding a justification for a possible thesis in the sense that this speculative stage has limits and will come, in a relatively short time, to an end. The most difficult thing is to explain why it has not yet sunk. How do we get out of this theoretical difficulty? Either our explanation for the current capitalist stage is totally wrong, or there is something new on the theoretical plane" (Carcanholo & Nakatani, 2007).
5. This issue is more fully considered in the third section of this article.
6. Mello and Sabadini (2019) develop a critical analysis of these authors, part of which is reproduced here.
7. This argument by Durand on the zero sum is similar to that of Hilferding (Sabadini, 2015) and is the basis of his denial of fictitious profits, since the latter indicate that some can win without others losing (Carcanholo & Sabadini, 2015).
8. In another text, analysing the syllogism proposed by Marx, De Paula (2003: 116–118) offers us a beautiful metaphor, "But if the sea is everything, it is totality, it is also its particular manifestations - the coldest of the north and south ends, the changing colours, the distinct salinities.

But this is still not all that the sea is - and so the sea presents itself in its singularities, those that from the beach, observing it from the top of the mountain, sailing it, immersed in it, we are able to experience: several seas, the same sea in various situations, the changes that time, elements and society produce in its rigorously changeable body … As far as this article is concerned, the sea, the metaphor is the capitalist mode of production, the kingdom of capital. Its first manifestation, as a simple totality, an adequate synthesis for its apprehension by reason is the law of value, … the capital considered in its ideal average, the abstraction of the particular conditions of its existence. The second manifestation of the real is the franchising of the particularity, the concrete organisation of work and capital … Finally, the third presentation of the same process, the imposition of capital, is what brings the singularity - the validity of the interaction of the various capitals, of competition, which being the possible form of manifestation of the capitalist reality, presents itself, as in the metaphor of the sea, as the space of the myriad of events and processes, of disputes and strategies, of the class struggle and of the power of the State".

9. As Muller (1982) points out, "not knowing how to use the genetic method, bourgeois political economy takes its categories directly from empiricism and uses them as descriptive concepts of economic forms in their immediate appearance, without being able to penetrate their essential relations".
10. On the empiricism bequeathed by the classics as a constituent part of Marx's thought, see Vaz (1983).
11. The authors of the new dialectic, especially Christopher Arthur, have investigated the ordering of the theoretical categories indicated by Marx from purely systematic considerations (Arthur, 2004: 64).
12. For Rosenthal (1978: 163), "The reflection of history in the logical course of thought is nothing other than the study of concrete facts, of concrete social practice". As Luporini points out (1974: 25), "In *Capital*, the genetic-formal - that is, the systematic development of 'forms', or figures, is only possible through the insertion of the genetic-historical in certain points". As an example, Luporini, in a later passage, transcribes Marx's well-known passage on the transformation of money into capital, and concludes: "The presence of that variable, that is, the presence of the historic-genetic component, is what makes the systematic building of the model possible" (ibid.: 33).
13. An additional difficulty is the number of times at which Marx uses the term investigation, not in the sense of the research procedures that precede the explanation, but as the explanation itself, as follows, "The wealth of societies in which the capitalist mode of production prevails appears as an 'immense collection of commodities'; the individual

commodity appears as its elementary form. Our investigation therefore begins with the analysis of the commodity" (Marx, 1990: 125).

14. International Investments Position—Posição Internacional de Investimentos (PII).

References

Arthur, C. J. (2004). *The new dialectics and Marx's Capital*. Brill.

Bruno, M., & Caffé, R. (2015). Indicadores macroeconômicos de financeirização: metodologia de construção e aplicação ao caso do Brasil. *População, espaço e sustentabilidade*: *contribuições para o desenvolvimento* (pp. 35–61). IBGE.

Carcanholo, M. A. (2002). *Abertura externa e liberalização financeira*: impactos sobre crescimento e distribuição no Brasil dos anos 90. Rio de Janeiro, tese de doutoramento, IE/UFRJ.

Carcanholo, R. A. (2003). Sobre a ilusória origem da mais-valia. *Crítica Marxista* (Vol. 16, pp. 76–95). Boitempo.

Carcanholo, R. A., & Nakatani, P. (2007) Capitalismo especulativo y alternativas para América Latina. *Herramienta*. Disponível em: https://herramienta.com.ar/articulo.php?id=479.

Carcanholo, R. A., & Nakatani, P. (2019). Parasitic speculative capital: A theoretical precision on financial capital, characteristic of globalization. In G. M. de C. Mello & M. de S. Sabadini (Eds.), *Financial speculation and fictitious profits*: A Marxist analysis (pp. 117–137). Palgrave Macmillan.

Carcanholo, R. A., & Sabadini, M. de S. (2015). Capital fictício e lucros fictícios. In H. Gomes (Ed.), *Especulação e lucros fictícios: formas parasitárias da acumulação contemporânea* (pp. 125–159). Outras Expressões.

Carchedi, G. (2011). Behind and beyond the crisis. *International Socialism*, n. 132. Disponível em: http://isj.org.uk/behind-and-beyond-the-crisis/#132carchedi_18

Corazza, G. (2003). O caminho de volta do abstrato ao concreto: uma introdução ao método da economia política em Marx. In G. Corazza (Org.), *Métodos da Ciência Econômica* (pp. 43–60). UFRGS Editora.

De Paula, J. A. (2003, January–March). Aparência e Realidade Capitalista: o lugar da concorrência na dinâmica do capital. *Revista Estudos Econômicos*. São Paulo, *22*(1), 115–142.

De Paula, J. A. (2010). A "Introdução" dos Grundrisse. In De J. A. Paula (Org.), *O Ensaio Geral*: Marx e a crítica da economia política (1857–1858) (pp. 89–108). Autêntica.

Dos Santos, T. (1970). The structure of dependence. *The American Economic Review*, *60*(2), 231–236.

Duman, Ö. S. (2014). A theoretical framework for the analysis of the current global economic crisis: The financial market and the real economy. *Economic and Labour Relations Review, 25*(2), 240–252.

Durand, C. (2017). *Fictitious capital: How finance is appropriating our future.* Verso.

DUSSEL, Enrique. (2004). La Producción Teórica de Marx. *Un comentario a los GRUNDRISSE.* Siglo Veintiuno Editores.

Engels, F. (2008). Comentários sobre a Contribuição à Crítica da Economia Política. In K. Marx (Ed.), *Contribuição à Crítica da Economia Política* (2nd ed., pp. 273–285). Expressão Popular.

Fattorelli, M. L., Ávila, R., & Muller, R. (Auditoria Cidadã Da Dívida). (2021). *Gastos com a Dívida Pública cresceram 33% em 2020.* Disponível em https://auditoriacidada.org.br/conteudo/gastos-com-a-divida-publica-cresceram-33-em-2020-2/. Acesso em 26 January 2021.

Foley, D. (1991). Credit and fictitious capital. In T. Bottomore (Ed.), *A dictionary of Marxist thought* (pp. 115–116). Blackwell.

Hannan, S. A. (2018). *Revisiting the determinants of capital flows to emerging markets – A survey of the evolving literature* (IMF Working Paper, WP/18/214).

Harvey, D. (2013). *A companion to Marx's 'Capital'* (Vol. 2). Verso.

Ilienkov, E. V. (1978). Elevar-se de lo Abstrato a lo Concreto. In L. Dias (Org.), *El Capital, Teoria, Estructura y Método* (Vol. 1, pp. 27–83). Ediciones de Cultura Popular.

Jones, Peter. (2013). *The falling rate of profit explains falling US growth.* Disponível em http://gesd.free.fr/jonesp13.pdf

Lapavitsas, C., & Mendieta-Muñoz, I. (2016). The profits of financialization, *Monthly Review, 68*(3).

Lohoff, E., & Trenkle, N. (2014). *La grande dévalorisation: pourquoi la spéculation et la dette de l'État ne sont pas les causes de la crise.* Post-Éditions.

Luporini. C. (1974). *Dialética marxista e historicismo.* In C. Luporini, & E. Sereni (Eds.), *El concepto de formación económico-social.* Siglo XXI (Cuadernos Pasado y Presente, 39).

Machado, G. (2018). O papel da história no modo de exposição de O capital de Marx. Verinotio - *Revista on-line de Filosofia e Ciências Humanas,* 24(1), 238–268. ISSN 1981-061X. Ano XIII.

Marques, R. M., & Nakatani, P. (2013). Crise, capital fictício e afluxo de capitaisestrangeiros no Brasil. *Caderno CRH*, Salvador, *26*(67), 65–78.

Marx, K., & Engels, F. (1989). *Collected works* (Vol. 24). Lawrence and Wishart.

Marx, K. (1990). *Capital: Critique of political economy* (Vol. I). Penguin Books.

Marx, K. (1991). *Capital: Critique of political economy* (Vol. III). Penguin Books.

Marx, K. (1992). *Capital: Critique of political economy* (Vol. II). Penguin Books.

Marx, K. (1993). *Grundrisse*. Penguin Books.

Mello, G. M. de C., & Sabadini, M. de S. (2019). Profit, interest, rent, and fictitious profit. In G. M. de C. Mello & M. de S. Sabadini (Eds.), *Financial speculation and fictitious profits: A Marxist analysis* (pp. 139–181). Palgrave Macmillan.

Moreira, C. A. L., & Almeida, A. T. de. (2013). A dinâmica recente do Investimento Direto Estrangeiro (IDE) no Brasil e impactos sobre a conta de transações correntes. *Indicadores Econômicos FEE*, Porto Alegre, *41*(1), 9–22.

Moseley, F. (2014). The universal and the particulars in Hegel's logic and Marx's capital. In F. Moseley & T. Smith (Eds.), *Marx's capital and Hegel's logic: A reexamination*. Historical materialism book series. Brill.

Müller, M. L. (1982). Exposição e método dialético em O Capital. In *Boletim SEAF* (n. 2). SEAF. Disponível em http://orientacaomarxista.blogspot.com.br/2010/10/exposicao-e-metodo-dialetico-em-o.html

Nakatani, P. (2000). Capital especulativo parasitário, capital fictício e crise no Brasil. *Revista Venezolana de Análisis de Coyuntura, VI*(2), 209–235.

Paulani, L. M. (2012). A inserção da economia brasileira no cenário mundial: uma reflexão sobre a situação atual à luz da história. *Boletim de Economia e Política Internacional* - DINTE/IPEA, nº 10.

Paulani, L. M. (2013). Acumulação sistêmica, poupança externa e rentismo: observações sobre o caso brasileiro. *Estudos Avançados, 27*(77), 237–264.

Reichelt, H. (2013). *Sobre a estrutura lógica do conceito de capital em Karl Marx*. Editora da Unicamp.

Rieser, V. (1977). La "apariencia" del capitalismo em el análisis de Marx. In M. Dobb, et al. (Eds.), *Estudios sobre El Capital* (2nd ed.). Siglo XXI.

Rodrigues, C. H. L., & Jurgenfeld, V. F. (2019). Desnacionalização e financeirização: um estudo sobre as privatizações brasileiras (de Collor ao primeiro governo FHC). *Economia e Sociedade*, Campinas, *28*(2) (66), 393–420.

Rosenthal, M. (1978). Correlación entre lo histórico y lo lógico. In P. L. Díaz (Org.), *El capital, teoría, estructura y método* (Vol. 1, pp. 160–172). Ediciones de Cultura Popular.

Sabadini, M. de S. (2015). O capital fictício e suas formas: lucros de fundador, diferencial e fictício. In H. Gomes (Ed.), *Especulação e lucros fictícios: formas parasitárias da acumulação contemporânea* (pp. 161–204). Outras Expressões.

Sampaio, D. P. (2020). Elementos de la inserción externa de Brasil en el siglo XXI. *Cuadernos del pensamiento crítico latinoamericano*, Consejo Latinoamericano de Ciencias Sociales, número 77.

Silva Filho, E. B. da. (2015). Trajetória recente do investimento estrangeiro direto e em carteira no Brasil. *Boletim de Economia e Política Internacional* - DINTE/IPEA, nº 19.

Smith, M. E. G., Butovsky, J., & Dumont, J. D. (2014). *Marxist phoenix: Studies in historical materialism and Marxist socialism*. Canadian Scholars' Press Inc.

Van Noije, P., & De Conti, B.(2016). A vulnerabilidadeexterna decorrente da Posição Internacional de Investimentos e do fluxo de rendas da economia brasileira no período 2001-2010. *Nova Economia, 26*(1), 207–239.

Vaz, H. L. (1983). Sobre as fontes filosóficas do pensamento de Karl Marx. *Revista Nova Escrita/Ensaio especial* – Marx Hoje. São Paulo, ano *11/12*, 147–160.

Zeleny, J. (1974). *La estructura lógica de El Capital de Marx*. Grijalbo.

CHAPTER 6

Dollar Hegemony Under Challenge and the Rise of Central Bank Digital Currencies (CBDC): A New Form of World Money?

Gustavo Moura de Cavalcanti Mello, Paulo Nakatani, and Erebus Wong

Introduction

Amid the so-called "New Cold War" between the United States and China, there are more and more frequent expositions on the decline of American hegemony and the rise of China. The variables employed in such analyses are diverse and relate to the ways in which each country is positioned within the international division of labour and, therefore,

G. M. de C. Mello (✉) · P. Nakatani
Department of Economics and Post-Graduate Program in Social Policy, Federal University of Espírito Santo, Vitória, Brazil
e-mail: gustavo.m.mello@ufes.br

E. Wong
Lingnan University, Hong Kong, China

G. M. de C. Mello and H. P. Braga (eds.), *Wealth and Poverty in Contemporary Brazilian Capitalism*, Marx, Engels, and Marxisms,
https://doi.org/10.1007/978-3-030-82298-9_6

to their participation in global production and trade; their military and "soft power"; their level of indebtedness; their technological capacity; the general orientation of domestic economic policies, and so on. An element of many of these investigations is whether to proclaim the resilience of American power or to foresee its imminent collapse and the prospects for maintaining the dollar as the world money.

This debate is not new and, following key moments, such as Richard Nixon's ending of the convertibility US dollars to gold and the collapse of the Bretton Woods system, and the "Volcker shock", which pushed the American and world economy into a severe recession in the 1980s, many announced the dollar's obsolescence and speculated about what might replace it in the role as the world money. In recent years, this debate has been revived by the great world crisis unleashed in 2007–2008 and the subsequent euro-zone sovereign debt crisis, in the wake of which the US national debt has risen substantially, particularly resulting from "quantitative easing" policies and other generous bail-outs for insolvent corporations. The quarrels surrounding the dollar's future have been fuelled by the continued strengthening of the Chinese economy, and by measures taken to expand its global influence and mitigate its dependence on the US economy. They have been exacerbated by geopolitical turbulence and the current arms race, in which Russia, China and India appear as the principal players, alongside the United States, as well as the recent crisis triggered by the Covid-19 pandemic. Finally, the emergence of private cryptocurrencies in the first half of the 2010s, and more recently of state cryptocurrencies, and in particular the pioneering role of China in this field, have also played an important part in this debate.[1]

This text is dedicated to this study and seeks to understand the differences between digital currencies, such as bitcoin, and sovereigns, such as the e-renminbi, in the light of the role played by money in the global dynamics of capital accumulation, and particularly its function as world money. It sets out to understand the impacts of the emergence of digital currencies on the international monetary system, and the place occupied in it by Brazil.

The Saga of the Dollar as the World Money and the Rise of China

In the middle of the nineteenthcentury, Marx (1993: 104) had already characterised the United States as "the most modern form of existence of bourgeois society". At the height of the so-called "Belle Époque", with the rumble of war drums and the escalation of colonial terror, American industrial primacy was undisputed.[2] It was the First World War that enshrined the United States as a hegemonic power, a major world creditor, the centre of European reconstruction—under the leadership of American private corporations—and the means of containing the revolutionary wave that began with the consolidation of the Bolshevik regime. Without dethroning the City of London, which still plays a crucial role in the global financial system today, American banks became the main financiers of international transactions, and the Federal Reserve (Fed), the US Central Bank, accumulated enormous monetary gold reserves, holding 50% of global reserves by 1923. In addition to the rise of the dollar as the basis of international reserves, the United States emerged as a force for exchange rate stability amid the turbulence inherent in the establishment of the gold-exchange standard.[3]

The short period of exchange rate stability in the second half of the 1920s would soon be wiped out by the 1929 Wall Street Crash and the Great Depression of the 1930s, with all its damaging social consequences, and by the geopolitical conflicts that culminated in World War II. As in World War I, the delay in the entry of the United States into the conflict, the preservation of its territory, its position as a supplier of credit, supplies and armaments to the allied nations, the immense material and human destruction in Europe and elsewhere, and its ability to rival the Soviet bloc, were all factors that catapulted American hegemony.[4] Even before the end of WWII, the main global capitalist powers were already engaged in the reconstruction of the international monetary system, based on the experience post WWI. Despite British efforts and the ingenious plan presented by the team led by Keynes at the Bretton Woods conferences, the American proposal prevailed. Among many outcomes, it established the dollar as the mainstay of the international monetary system, convertible into gold, from which a system of fixed exchange rates was structured. At that time, the United States fully embedded the dollar as the world money, having accumulated around 75% of the world's gold reserves by the end of WWII. By the second half of the 1950s it boasted a surplus balance of payments in virtually all its elements, all of which meant productive, commercial, and financial primacy. Another relevant factor was the decision, following economic and geopolitical calculations,[5] to undertake the reconstruction of the devastated powers as a strategic objective. Hence the importance that, until the present day, the dollar gained as the denomination of most international loans; the basis of

Central Bank reserves worldwide; a "safe haven" in financial crises; and the currency for the pricing of commodities, with an emphasis on oil, copper, gold, and wheat, as well as weapons, aeronautical and chemical products, and other dimensions that will be considered in due course.

We are not here to explain the mechanisms and operation of the Bretton Woods System, but it bears remembering that a decisive element of its architecture, according to the plan put forward by Dexter White, was the creation of a multilateral institution that would monitor national economies and safeguard the international monetary system. In practice, the International Monetary Fund (IMF), which was intended to fulfil this role, soon turned out to be a "toothless lion" (Eichengreen, 2007: 132), and was subordinate to the Fed, which became the central institution in this arrangement. During a process of the internationalisation of the American banking system, *pari passu* to the forming of large North American multinational conglomerates, the international monetary system became a credit system, mainly of bank credit, regulated by the Fed (Belluzzo, 1995: 168–169).

It should be remembered that one component of this process, which would eventually become a barrier to maintaining it, was the emergence of the so-called "euro-dollar markets" or "euro-markets".[6] In the 1960s, these markets had already consolidated themselves as spaces *par excellence* for the short-term investment of dollar reserves, both by American companies (industrial, as well as banking) that operated overseas, and by European Central Banks, sometimes through the Bank of International Settlements (BIS). With this, the international availability of dollar-denominated credit greatly increased, which fuelled "developmentalist" projects in peripheral countries. In any case, the euro markets have become an important interbank capital market, and the "offshore" dollars that circulate there have become a negotiable financial instrument that, to a large extent, escape the exchange control mechanisms and regulations of domestic financial markets, particularly in the United States.

Throughout the 1960s the US balance of payments deteriorated due to increasing military expenditure and unproductive spending on social security policies, as well as the relative loss of markets and competitiveness by American companies due to the recovery of economies devastated by the war, particularly Germany and Japan, although this was generally offset by large-scale issuing of new money (Mandel, 1982: 300). The "capital flight" mentioned above also played an important role because it occurred during a period of the transnationalisation of American industrial and financial conglomerates, by which they avoided the regulations and taxation in force in the USA. When added to the significant reduction in its gold reserves, this swelled the "exorbitant privilege" that the USA enjoys in this context, with its ability to attract international loans at low interest rates, through issuing state bonds, and to service its rampant debt and its growing imports with the currency that it issued itself.

It is not the scope of this essay to analyse the deterioration of American hegemony in its multiple dimensions—military, political, cultural, and economic—in a context of a global crisis of capital over-accumulation that we saw expressed in stagflation in several key capitalist countries the 1970s. Suffice it to note that this crisis of over-accumulation reinforced the trend towards financial innovations and the growth of financial markets which we see being launched from the 1980s onwards, amid a process of the securitisation of debts and the advent of huge secondary markets. So, and this point will be expanded later, there is a large overlap between the trends and processes of the transnationalisation of industrial capital and the profusion of fictitious forms of capital, linked to the complexification, proliferation and expansion of institutions, assets and financial markets, and there is a tendency towards the autonomy of these forms of capital and the prominence of the financial dimension of accumulation. For this reason, hegemonic disputes within the inter-state system, which are still relevant in a context of capital transnationalisation, have at their centre the impact on the global production and circulation of fictitious capital. This was largely due to the abandonment of the convertibility of the dollar into gold, which affirmed *de jure* something that had de facto long been in force and which, along with Volcker's interest shock and despite its strong recessive and destructive effect on traditional American industries, channelled a large part of the over-accumulated capital worldwide into the United States in the form of money capital and fictitious capital. As Maria da Conceição Tavares (1997) pointed out in the heat of events, Wall Street was reaffirmed as the gravitational centre of the international monetary and credit system and US state bonds reinforced its position as the mainstay of the system. Furthermore, part of that capital was used to finance "research & development" activities and branches of production that utilised cutting-edge technology. This gave rise to a series of algorithms and technological innovations that, protected by patents and other intellectual property rights, allowed their holders to appropriate surplus value from the four corners of the planet in the form of fees paid by companies and governments for their use. This influx of wealth was added to that from foreign direct investments, in the form of remittance of profits and dividends, and from US loans, in the form of payment of interest and amortisations.

The appreciation of the dollar that followed only deepened the deficit in US transactions and this was accompanied by an increased supply of US government bonds. During the 1980s and part of the 1990s it was mainly Japan that absorbed such bonds, and even today Japan holds the largest reserves of them, approximately USD 1.3 trillion in July 2020.[7] With its explosive economic growth dating back to the late 1970s, but which has acquired greater stability since 1990, China has come to play a decisive role. On 31 July 2020, China held a total of USD 3,298.2 billion in international reserves, with USD 3,147.3 billion or 95.4% of this holding in securities.[8] According to US Treasury Department data,[9] China held USD 1.07 trillion of its bonds on that date, which represents 34.1% of total bonds. Between 2005 and 2019, the US current account deficit exceeded USD 6.8 trillion, while the Chinese surplus totalled more than USD 3 trillion.[10] In 2019 the United States had a trade deficit of USD 854.4 billion with the rest of the world, of which approximately 40% (USD 345.2 billion) came from relations with China.[11]

It may be surprising, at first glance, that between mid-2014 and May 2020 the dollar showed a significant tendency to appreciate against other currencies in real and nominal terms, according to the US Fed's broad index.[12] The benefits of issuing the world money cannot be underestimated here. Other factors will be considered below, but an indicator of the dollar's centrality in the international financial system concerns the total volume of "market capitalisation" of the stock markets. In terms of capitalisation, the London stock exchange was just below USD 5 trillion by the end of 2019, ranked the fourth largest in the world, in third place the Tokyo stock exchange had approximately USD 5.7 trillion. The top two places in this ranking were American, with much higher volumes: Nasdaq had almost USD 11 trillion, and the New York stock exchange, about USD 23 trillion (Norfield, 2020, s/p).[13]

A touted advantage for the USA arising from the maintenance of the dollar as world money is the appropriation of the seigniorage gains of hundreds of the billions of dollars in treasuries around the world, as the cost of issuing paper money is insignificant given the values it represents. More importantly, the dollar's position as world money puts it under relatively low pressure in the face of trade deficits, as companies in surplus tend to retain, to a greater or lesser extent, the dollars they receive, and North American treasury bills are in strong demand on the world market.

The USA does not need to accumulate large foreign exchange reserves and expose itself to the volatility of foreign currencies, as they are the creators of world money. Even more decisive, as it turns out, they obtain abundant financing at low costs, in such a way that more than 50% of their obligations consist of treasury debt securities and other instruments remunerated at low interest rates, while their assets are concentrated in more profitable investments, of which more than 60% consist of foreign direct investment and equity assets. In 2019, the United States received USD 1.13 trillion from assets totalling approximately USD 29.15 trillion, and paid USD 899.3 billion from liabilities totalling USD 40.2 trillion, generating a surplus of USD 236.3 billion in primary income. By way of comparison, in the same year China received USD 235.8 billion for assets totalling USD 7.71 trillion, and paid USD 268.9 billion for liabilities totalling USD 5.59 trillion, resulting in a deficit of USD 33.1 billion.[14]

China Emerging Against the Background of Thucydides' Trap?

Now it is time to return to the relationship between the United States and China. It remains evident that to a greater or lesser extent all domestic economies establish interdependent relationships in the world market, and this is particularly important when it comes to the largest in the world. Nevertheless, the link between the economies of the USA and China is noteworthy, as the finances of the latter depend, in part, on a debt spiral on the part of the former. Despite the reciprocal benefits, and all the advantages and power enjoyed by the United States within the contemporary monetary and financial system, it is a contradictory arrangement, and its evolution over time has intensified the antagonisms between these countries.

So, with the quantitative easing policies put into place in early 2011, in the wake of the 2007–2008 global crisis, the Fed became the main holder of US treasury bills, which reduced China's importance as the lender to its current account deficit. At the same time, the United States lifted the pressure for the Chinese currency to appreciate, which, to avoid this, has continued to buy US bonds. Tensions have intensified, amid growing competition in the field of R&D, ranging from supercomputers to Tik Tok, and including "5G" technology. Such disputes imply important and possibly sinister consequences in another decisive area of the struggle for power within the interstate system, that of the weapons industry, and there are many authors who have identified an ongoing arms race involving, principally, the United States, Russia, China, and India (Barreiros, 2019; Fiori, 2018; Fiori & Nozaki, 2020). These have manifested in disputes, such as conflicts over the dominance of the South China Sea, where commercial tensions have tended to lead to military confrontation.

Even as an ascendant power in the industrial, technological, military, and commercial production fields, China remains strongly dependent on the markets and on US treasury bills. Over recent years there have been innumerable government initiatives aimed at expanding the use of renminbi in funding direct investments abroad and in international commercial transactions, including initiatives such as the launch, in 2018, of future oil contracts on the Shanghai Stock Exchange denominated in renminbi, taking advantage of its status as the world's largest buyer of crude oil. In the same vein, there has been an increasing use of foreign exchange swaps, with the establishment of bilateral agreements with dozens of countries, starting with South Korea in 2008; the establishment of compensation agreements for international renminbi operations with several financial centres in other countries; the creation of offshore renminbi centres around the world; the expansion of the volume of domestic securities that can be acquired by foreign institutional investors; and the acquisition of gold, with reserves in 2020 approaching 2 thousand tonnes (which, however, equate to less than 4% of its total reserves). Furthermore, in 2015 the *China International Payment System* (CIPS) was launched by the Chinese government, and in that same year the renminbi was introduced into the currency basket that forms the *Special Drawing Rights* of the International Monetary Fund (Cintra & Pinto, 2017). To these measures can be added other efforts directed at the internationalisation of the banking system, such as the opening of branches of its large state-owned banks abroad and the purchase of foreign banks in several countries.[15]

Among these various initiatives, it is worth mentioning the creation of the *BRICS Development Bank* (now the *New Development Bank*) and the perhaps lesser-known *Asian Infrastructure Investment Bank* (AIIB)—which has more than 100 member countries, including some aligned with the USA, such as the United Kingdom and Australia—and which has already financed projects in several countries, including Egypt, Turkey, Indonesia, India, Bangladesh, and Pakistan. Even more important is the

Belt and Road Initiative (BRI), a monumental set of infrastructure and communication works to be implemented over the next three decades, involving more than 130 countries and dozens of multilateral institutions.

Incidentally, one aspect that hinders the process of internationalising the renminbi is the relative inaccessibility of the Chinese financial sector compared to that of other economic powers, although this has become more flexible in recent years. For example, the regulation that prevented foreigners from taking majority control of investment funds in China was recently lifted, the announcement of which was immediately followed by investments by Goldman Sachs and Morgan Stanley, who acquired control of Chinese joint ventures.[16]

The recent launch of the Chinese state-owned cryptocurrency, the e-renmimbi, is just one component among a wide spectrum of actions, and we will now move onto focus on. We will start by succinctly comparing state cryptocurrencies to the private cryptocurrencies that preceded them.

Currency Race: Decentralised Digital Currencies vs Central Bank Digital Currencies (CBDC)

According to their supporters, private digital currencies would end the state monopoly on issuing money, undermining various monetary policy mechanisms and the influence of the State in the regulation, supervision, and taxation of monetary transactions. These so-called digital currencies would end the secondary issuing of currency resulting from the perverse fractional reserve system and would grant the banking system the exorbitant privilege of issuing credit in a volume that surpasses its supposed social demand. This uncontrolled production of money would tend to corrupt the system of relative prices, mitigating the virtuous self-regulatory mechanisms of the market, generating inflation and inefficiency, and turning the natural cyclical movement of the economy into a disruptive process. The idea of decentralised digital currency is apparently an inspiration of the Austrian School which implies an anti-government ideology claiming that any authority involved in economic affair would lead to adverse effect. Some advocates of the technologies related with cryptocurrency and smart contract believe that they would facilitate an ideal state of market creditability without any authoritative intermediary. Behind the enthusiasm of technological faddism is in fact a century-long ideological movement aspiring to create a utopia of pure and unadulterated market state in which an atomised or stateless society could function perfectly in which nobody trusts anybody whereas no authority is granted with the power to mediate between individuals. The advocates believe that technology could replace social interaction or communality as the foundation of trust. Or one may even envision a new form of sociality without any need of trust at all. The ideological implication of cryptocurrency apparently goes beyond economy.

There are four core technologies in present mode of blockchain: (1) Distributed ledger; (2) *Asymmetric Encryption*; (3) *Consensus mechanism*; (4) *Smart contract.* Digital currency is just one of their applications. In the case of bitcoin, the first and by far most popular cryptocurrency, its production mimics gold extraction, through a sophisticated technological process, so accurately that the creation of new coins is called "mining". The validation of each transaction made with this cryptocurrency is carried out in a decentralised manner through the solving of cryptographic problems that become progressively more complex, and whose resolution therefore requires increasing computational capacity and extremely high electricity consumption.[17] These operations receive bitcoins as a reward, at decreasing rates, and according to the architecture of this cryptocurrency, the total mass of bitcoins will reach a limit of 21 million bitcoin around the year 2140. These transactions are registered as a block, which, after verification, is inserted in a blockchain, a kind of digital ledger that records, in chronological order, all transactions made with bitcoins,[18] these are then accumulated by their holders in digital wallets. The issuing, validation, and supervision of the system are carried out in a decentralised manner, dispensing with the intermediation and interchange of a monetary authority, and are based on strict rules that are built into the bitcoin's algorithmic architecture. This requires increasing storage capacity and processing time for the validation of each operation, for each blockchain node, and must be confirmed by at least 50% plus one of the nodes.[19]

The Limits of Decentralised Cryptocurrencies That May Prevent Them from Really Functioning as Currency

There is great heterogeneity among the thousands of private cryptocurrencies that exist today; some are linked directly to gold and other commodities or to domestic currencies—the *stablecoins*—others are issued by companies in predetermined fixed quantities, but in general they have limitations that may prevent them from fully functioning as currency envisioned by advocates. By convention, a medium must fulfil four basic functions to work as money: (1) as means of exchange or payment; (2) as measurement of value or unit of account; (3) as store of value; and in addition (4) as standard of deferred payment. We may then ask whether private and decentralised cryptocurrencies could function well as money in these aspects?

As Means of Exchange

The primary and core design of cryptocurrencies is to devise a means of exchange. Admittedly its technological development is by far quite effective in this aspect.[20] However, one of the limitations of cryptocurrencies as means of exchange is precisely the plethora of digital currencies and the limitations to their use as a means of circulation or means of payment, which remain quite restricted. Furthermore, decentralised cryptocurrencies are in fact extremely costly if all the costs are taken into consideration. Some advocates claim that one of the advantages of cryptocurrencies is the relatively low cost in case of long distance or cross-border transaction without the need of clearing or wiring agents. However, the blind spot of this argument is quite consistent with the mainstream economics which often deliberately neglects the externalities when it comes to cost-efficiency evaluation. The energy and environmental cost of cryptocurrency mining is in fact staggering.[21] The decentralised cryptocurrencies at their present design are simply self-defeating. Considering how much energy has been consumed nowadays to support the relatively small total asset value of cryptocurrencies compared with global GDP, it would be an environmental disaster if one day a significant portion of global economic transactions are conducted through decentralised cryptocurrencies at their present mode. Put concisely, the world simply does not have enough energy to support the circulation of decentralised cryptocurrencies for them to really play a significant part in real economy.

Another problem that renders the logic of decentralised cryptocurrencies self-defeating is the creation and programming of a blockchain is quite expensive and complex, which limits the decentralised creation of cryptocurrencies. Strictly speaking, a cryptocurrency can only be created with its own blockchain,[22] so hundreds or thousands of cryptocurrencies are created in some blockchains as tokens, or signs. Furthermore, under current technological standards, the production and circulation of cryptocurrencies is extremely expensive and energy intensive, with serious environmental consequences. Due to these rising costs and technological requirements, mining activities have undergone a rapid process of centralisation. Furthermore, contrary to the ideals of their proponents, both the circulation and the production of cryptocurrencies have been oligopolised by large investors.[23] The utopia of a decentralised and horizontally spontaneous economic order as imagined by some advocates is simply an illusion.

As a Measure of Value

Cryptocurrencies by far do not perform the functions of measuring value and price standards. Most of them are still generally denominated in dollars. Furthermore, its dollar price is extremely volatile, which imposes limitations on its performance as a measure of value or price setting of commodities. The economy would be in chaos if the standard of price itself would fluctuate by more than 10% in a few minutes due to speculative acts or because some influential persons send a twitter message. Prone to extreme volatility, cryptocurrency as a speculative financial asset is contradictory with its alleged monetary function.

As Store of Value

The unit price of Bitcoin soared to over USD 50K at early 2021, which made it a much sought-after asset in financial market. Some even optimistically predicate that it would go up to a million dollar.[24] Viewed from its investment potential, cryptocurrency appears to be a good medium of hoarding value. However, apart from being a speculative fad with the promise of potential application in the future, the price of private cryptocurrency is to a large extent spurred by the general assets inflation fuelled by the Quantitative Easing policy led by the USA in recent years. Furthermore, given its shortcomings as described above, the odds of its value crumbling to zero could not be excluded if one day a technologically more sophisticate product emerges as a substitute. In a word, private cryptocurrency entails no intrinsic value at all apart from people's good expectation. Despite its shinning technological appearance, its value might not be better secured than a tulip bulb in 1637 in the Dutch Republic.

As Standard of Deferred Payment

The fourth function of money is related with the creation of credit. Despite the existence of derivatives related to cryptocurrencies, and contrary to what happens with credit money, we observe that instead of absorbing credit functions and allowing the secondary creation of credit money to serve as a mainstay for the credit system, which is essential for the accumulation of capital, cryptocurrencies suppress such functions and such creation. Moreover, the limits imposed on the issuance of cryptocurrencies through "mining" prevent such issuance from meeting the needs of capital circulation. Equally relevant is the fact that private cryptocurrencies set out to supplant not only the Central Banks' monetary issuing function, but also to suppress their role as a lender of last resort, ignoring the fact that monetary centralisation and the regulatory and countercyclical role of monetary authorities emerged historically as a response to the imbalances and crises inherent to anarchic modern production.

Some recent initiatives have aimed to resolve some of the problems raised. Corda, for example, an international open source blockchain platform which seeks the State's obsolescence, sets out to reduce costs and facilitate access to the technologies necessary for the creation of cryptocurrencies, as well as carrying out all sorts of transactions through smart contracts and other mechanisms.[25]

In short, we may postulate that the development of cryptocurrency is confronted with a trilemma. This is to say that private cryptocurrency in its present form cannot have all these three qualities at the same time: decentralisation (anonymity), low transaction cost, and reliability. Bitcoin for example falls short of having low transaction cost when one considers the staggering amount of energy it has consumed globally. In any case, the preceding analysis shows that, far from being money, or a simple form of currency, cryptocurrencies are nothing more than a financial asset, through which capital circulates in search of fictitious gains, in purely speculative movements.[26]

Digital Fiat Currency as Other Major Competitor: Stablecoin and CBDC

Despite failing to become money in the full sense, decentralised cryptocurrencies will seemingly continue to exist as sought-after investment assets, at least for a certain period against this historical background, unless they are made illegal or banned by State authorities. Meanwhile, other alternatives or competitors are emerging. Currently, we see two key players alongside decentralised cryptocurrencies: Stablecoins and Central Bank Digital Currency, which can be categorised together as: digital fiat currencies (Table 6.1).

Table 6.1 Different types of digital currency

	Totally decentralised, unregulated	*Partially decentralised, regulated*
Private	Bitcoin, etc.	Permissioned Stablecoins
Public	–	Central Bank Digital Currency

Stablecoin: An Extension of Fiat Money
In mid-2019 IT megacorporation Facebook announced the Libra cryptocurrency[27] initiative and immediately attracted the world's attention. Their aim was to create, "a global and simple payment system and financial infrastructure that empowers billions of people". In response to the strong reaction by central banks in several countries Facebook modified the project in 2020 (Libra 20). Instead of creating a single transnational cryptocurrency, the Libra will be pegged or guaranteed by representative currencies—forming the LibraUSD, the LibraEUR, etc. These sorts of cryptocurrencies are known as stablecoin. In other words, Facebook compromised by giving up the idea of creating a new world money. Instead, Libra 2.0, redubbed as Diem, will function as a world-wide payment platform of existing fiat money, mainly the dollar. The details of Diem, expected to launch in 2021, are not yet fully known. However, the US monetary authority has already set the rules of the game. On January 2021, the United State Office of the Comptroller of the Currency (USOCC) addressed, "the legal permissibility of certain payment-related activities that involve the use of new technologies, including the use of independent node verification networks (INVNs or networks) and stablecoins, to engage in and facilitate payment activities. National banks and Federal savings associations [...] may use new technologies, including INVNs and related stablecoins, to perform bank-permissible functions" (USOCC, 2021).

In an early interpretive letter on September 2020 (USOCC, 2020), the OCC has clearly outlined the operational model of, "Stablecoin backed on a 1:1 basis by a single fiat currency where the bank verifies at least daily that reserve account balances are always equal to or greater than the number of the issuer's outstanding stablecoins".[28] In a word, unlike the regulation-free decentralised cryptocurrencies, the stablecoins permissioned by the US authority will be heavily regulated. They are going to serve as the digital extension (INVN platforms) of fiat currency, by default the dollar. The permissioned stablecoins or payment platform will use INVNs technologies different to the current distributed ledger system. For example, they still need clearing and monitoring agents. Unlike the simultaneous completion of transaction and verification, the transaction may be rolled back in case of legal or other problems although the data itself is rewriteable. Their anonymity is not going to be absolute and strings, for monitoring purposes, can be inserted into the blockchains.

100% backed by the dollar, the INVNs systems legalised in the USA may facilitate a smooth transition of dollar hegemony into the era of digital currency. And even after the US Fed comes up with its own CBDC, the dollar-pegged stablecoins or INVNs may continue to function as a powerful arm of dollar hegemony.

State Cryptocurrency: The Late Comer But the Power Player?

Despite warnings issued by multilateral agencies and monetary authorities in several countries regarding the volatility of cryptocurrency markets, which in some countries has culminated in the banning of these markets, the experience of private cryptocurrencies and in particular the technology of blockchains and of ***distributed ledger technologies*** (DLT)[29] were quickly identified by Central Banks as an object of study. Not least because the prospect of the growing strength of private decentralised cryptocurrencies aroused strong concerns related to their detachment from domestic regulatory systems, potential increases in financial instability at the national and global level, and the reduction in the scope and effectiveness of monetary policies, among others.

Some Central Banks, including in Sweden and China, have already launched their state cryptocurrencies on an experimental basis, called Central Bank Digital Currencies (CBDC). According to a study published by the Bank of International Settlements (BIS), the number of monetary authorities who indicate that they are planning to create their digital currencies in the short and medium term is increasing.[30] Nevertheless, questions remain; whether the anonymity guaranteed by private cryptocurrencies and by some forms of fictitious money will be reproduced in the case of CBDCs; whether these will be transacted through bank accounts or will be based merely on signs (tokens); and the extent to which decentralised registration and validation technologies, such as blockchains or DLTs, will be employed, if at all; whether CBDCs will be used only in "wholesale" situations (in interbank payments, for example), or also in retail; whether and to what extent they will compete with private payment systems[31]; whether their prices will be constant in nominal terms, or whether they will be indexed to some aggregate price index or whether they will be remunerated through an interest rate determined by the monetary authorities, also remain undefined. Technically, at least, several combinations are possible: centralised or decentralised control of CBDCs accounts, whose access presupposes user identification, as well as centralised or decentralised control of CBDCs in the form of tokens, whose use does not require identification authorisation (Auer & Böhme, 2020).

In any case, CBDCs apparently do not share many of the limitations of private cryptocurrencies, which make it impossible for them to sustain the fundamental determinations of money, and whose generalisation would impose decisive obstacles to the process of capital accumulation. So, they do not present too restrictive a limit on their issuance, do not constrain the credit system and the secondary production of money, and do not prohibit the basic functions of Central Banks. In fact, one can glimpse just the opposite. In addition, it appears that the implementation of state cryptocurrencies based on bank accounts—linked to Central Banks or other authorised banking institutions—would reduce money circulation costs (which would not be the case in a token-based system, as it would employ a form of registration and verification like that of private cryptocurrencies). On the other hand, given the broad ownership of smartphones, there would be the potential for the generalisation of portfolios or even digital accounts, reaching parts of the population that remain outside the banking system. In addition, these portfolios or digital accounts could be used to provide credit, fiscal stimuli, and income transfer policies, and to introduce interest rate policies for CBDC balances, as well as fees on their operations, in theory expanding the reach and effectiveness of monetary authorities.

E-renminbi

To make this analysis concrete, it is interesting to look at a pioneering Chinese initiative, planning for which started in 2014, based on the large-scale structure of digital payments produced by the "big techs" Alibaba, Tencent, and Baidu. In April 2020, the Central Bank of China (CBC) announced the start of tests of a CBDC, called a Digital Currency Electronic Payment (DCEP), in the cities of Shenzhen, Suzhou, Chengdu, and Xiongan. In August, the CBC announced that the tests would be extended to other major cities and stated the objective of ensuring the system's full operability by the Winter Olympics in Beijing, scheduled for the end of 2022. The total volume of business with DCEPs reached 1.1 billion yuan or USD 162.0 million in 3.3 million transactions. To this end, more than 113,300 personal digital portfolios and 8,800 corporate digital portfolios were opened in the pilot programmes (Bray & Tudor-Ackroyd, 2020). To speed up testing, DCEPs are being distributed by lot, in 50,000 "envelopes" containing 200 yuan each, a total of one million yuan, to residents of Shenzhen, who will be able to spend them in 3,389 stores located in the neighbourhood of Luohu, between the 12th and 18th October 2020. In addition, the Shenzhen government awarded 5,000 health workers with DCEPs during the pandemic, as a bonus (Zhou & Borak, 2020).

China's CBDC is a two-tier system, which refutes the worry that it would lead to the disintermediation and even obsolescence of commercial banks. The primary issuance of DCEPs is carried out by the Central Bank, which centralises all operations, the opposite of the decentralised concept of bitcoin, and this replicates the usual form of monetary policy. The DCEP will be available in commercial banks that can offer their customers an exchange of the traditional renminbi for the new digital e-renminbi, and loans, maintaining the functioning of the credit system through the secondary creation of the new currency. For its operation, the first link in the chain is the banks; the Industrial and Commercial Bank of China, Agricultural Bank of China, Bank of China, and Construction Bank of China, as well as the entire banking system. The government has a majority stake in the first four and they are the four largest banks in the world according to asset valuation (Herrera & Long, 2019: 100). Technically, the system was created through a platform based on DLTs, in which operations must be validated or confirmed in the Central Bank system that monitors the entire financial movement of the economy. For their part, banks can establish customer relationships in different ways, one of which is the use of blockchain, and end users have access to applications on their cell phones without the need to be connected to a network, in the same way that physical wallets are used with physical notes and coins. The Blockchain-based Service Network (BSN),[32] was created with the participation of or contribution from the giant Chinese telecommunications companies, to develop cheaper and more accessible environments, which have become networks, for the use of institutions and companies of any size. Finally, the entire system was, and is, being built through the development of technologies that link decentralised and point-to-point blockchains with DLTs that concentrate and finalise operations at the Central Bank.

It should be noted, however, that although this network is being developed at an accelerated pace and is being tested in several Chinese cities, its complexity and its substantial impacts have attracted traditional Chinese gradualism, and the same goes for the e-renminbi, especially because, according to Yifan He, CEO of Red Date Technology, a company that is at the forefront of BSN's development, the, "DCEP will only have a visible impact on the local economy once business-to-business and business-to-individual transactions are implemented. But this implementation will involve many changes, such as tax and bank settlements. I don't think we will see that being done in a short period" (apud Cointelegraph, 2020).

The immediate relationship between depositors in the banking system and users, companies, and consumers, is linked to other giants of the Chinese credit system, Alibaba, Tencent and Baidu, and other fintechs. Alipay, a payment application from the giant corporation Alibaba and Ant Group,[33] and Wechat, a Tencent application that, in addition to exchanging messages like WhatsApp, has many other functions, including a payment system, have about a billion users each. In 2019, the two main Alibaba and Tencent systems were already ensuring that about 80% of China's final commercial transactions are carried out via mobile devices in a market that moves USD 49 trillion, almost 50 times greater than of the USA, which moves only USD 99 billion (Tudor-Ackroyd, 2020).[34] American companies Starbucks, McDonald's and Subway are also participating in pilot projects. So, not only most of the population, but the entire transport system, shopping centres, shops, supermarkets, bars, restaurants, taxis, etc. are already fully adapted to transactions via mobile devices. From this point of view, the transition from the renminbi to the e-renminbi can be carried out almost seamlessly.

Sheng Songcheng, an ex-officer of Chinese central bank, believes that CBDC has advantages in four aspects by facilitating: (1) More effective regulation against money-laundering, tax-evasion, and improper capital flow etc.; (2) More accurate monetary indicators; (3) Better evaluation of systematic financial risk; (4) More effective conductive mechanism of monetary policy.

The Central Bank of China has, therefore, a huge advantage in the process of replacing the old currency and even paper money, as the procedures for purchases and sales and transfers of funds will be almost the same as those already used. However, it is not only the name of the traditional currency that changed under the new digital currency: what has changed is the whole apparatus of the technological platforms underlying the e-renminbi, which guarantees China a more favourable position in the monetary system and international credit.

State Cryptocurrencies and World Money

Marx considers, theoretically, that, as world money, money loses its domestic functions and must return to its original form of commodity, as a precious metal. In his words, "when money leaves the domestic sphere of circulation it loses the local functions it has acquired there, as the standard of prices, coin, and small change, and as a symbol of value, and falls back into its original form as precious metal in the shape of bullion" (Marx, 1990: 240). However, it is on the world market that this commodity takes on a, "social form of realisation of human labour in the abstract. Its mode of existence becomes adequate to its concept" (Marx, 1990: 240). In more concrete terms, we can consider that "World money serves as the universal means of payment, as the universal means of purchase, and as the absolute social materialisation of wealth as such (universal wealth)" (Marx, 1990: 241).

As described in the first section, the dollar has been the undisputed world money since the end of the World War II. The emergence of digital currency then poses the question of whether the dollar hegemony would be significantly challenged, not to mention being replaced, in the foreseeable future by a sovereignty digital currency or non-sovereignty super global digital payment networks.

The conflict of interests that arises with a sovereignty currency functioning as the world money has long been well recognised. As early as in the 1960s, less than two decades since the establishment of Bretton Woods regime, Robert Triffin has addressed the conflict between the short-term domestic economic interests of a country whose currency is taken as global reserve currency with long-term international objectives, later known as the Triffin Dilemma. The problem of the overspill effect of US monetary policy has intensified since 2008 when the Fed adopted a series of Quantitative Easing. The worry just got when the USA again adopted unlimited QE as well as large-scale relief program during the Covid-19 depression in 2020 and 2021.

On 23 August 2019, the Governor of the Bank of England Mark Carney, in view of the idea of a new payments infrastructure based on an international stablecoin fully backed by reserve assets in a basket of currencies and provided by public sector, raised the question of whether a new Synthetic Hegemonic Currency would dampen the domineering influence of the US dollar on global trade.[35] His speech echoes after 75 years with his countryman Keynes' Bancor proposed in 1944 during the Bretton Woods conference. Maybe it is not a coincidence because the world is in a similar historical moment as in 1944 when the establishment of a new global monetary order became imminent.

Admittedly, the replacement of the current fiduciary dollar by a digital currency as world money would be an extremely complex process because, in addition to the major technical issues, it involves the primary issue of contesting the USA as the dominant world power. In analysis, the US hegemony has been underpinned by five pillars: (1) Military power; (2) Economic power; (3) Ideological or Soft power; (4) Institutional power; and (5) Technological power. Undisputedly, the USA still holds the supremacy. However, the US hegemony does show signs of decline in different aspects since the 2008 Wall Street Crisis along with its military setbacks in the Middle East and finally the havoc during the Trump administration. A comprehensible analysis of the US hegemony facing challenge is beyond the scope of this essay. Suffice to say that the rise of digital currency is concerned with all the hegemonic pillars and even the military aspect.[36]

The USA remains the largest economy in the world.[37] However, the staggering public debts of the States and the mounting Federal budget deficits have cast shadow on the foundation of the dollar, especially after the unlimited Quantitative Easing and relief program of the USA under the impact of the Covid-19 pandemic in 2020 and 2021. So said, the challenge of a new sovereignty digital currency would mean substituting the dollar for a new currency with its international functions of measuring value, price standards, means of circulation and reserve of value, which have been consolidated over seven decades.

As a measure of value and price standards and their conversion into international market prices, the prices of the most traded commodities are determined on the main commodity exchanges, particularly that of Chicago. This determination is made in dollars and each country converts these prices into its national currencies at current exchange rates. All international transactions, both in international trade and in capital movements, international commerce, loans, and direct and portfolio investments are denominated in dollars. Debt and property securities, as well as international agreements and contracts are also denominated in the same currency. Most international trade and capital movement is conducted in dollars, but China has sought to escape this constraint through bilateral agreements, particularly with Russia and some other countries. So, replacing the dollar with a new digital currency implies a long process requiring numerous agreements and negotiations to convert all international prices, bonds, and debt contracts to the new currency.

The means of international circulation, a role that had been played by gold, which functioned as the world money and was fundamental as a means of paying deficits in the balance of payments, became the virtual dollar. According to the latest Triennial Central Bank Survey of Foreign Exchange and the BIS Over-the-counter Derivatives Markets, launched in December 2019, the dollar is involved in 88% of foreign exchange transactions in international markets, followed by the euro in 32% of transactions (Norfield, 2020).

In a word, the USA still has a stranglehold on the international financial institution with the dollar as the sole world money. Most international payments and transfers utilise the dollar through the SWIFT international payment system, in which the USA carries a weight and degree of control that no other country processes. The USA wields this institutional power at will. Through this system, the USA can establish restrictions, taxes, and blockades, as in the cases of Cuba, Venezuela, North Korea, and Iran. In recent years, the use of this system has been intensified in a coercive way by the United States, retaliating against economic practices that it considers problematic or adverse to the US interests. This intensification naturally alarms China since the USA has identified the second largest economy as its biggest competitor and rival against the backdrop of ongoing saga of Trade War and Technology War. The possibility of financial war if not currency war then becomes a sword of Damocles over China. In preparation for the scenario of financial sanction as well as search for greater independence from the dollar payment system, China established its Cross-Border Interbank Payment System (CIPS) in October 2015. In January 2021, China set up with SWIFT, the Belgium-based global system for financial messaging and cross-border payments, a joint venture in Beijing. The SWIFT owns a 55% stake while Chinese institutions hold the remaining 45%.[38]

The involvement of Chinese central bank's Digital Currency Research Institute as a shareholder reveals China's strategic consideration with this new joint venture. The Europe-based SWIFT is supposed to be a neutral international financial cooperation. However, over the years it has been submissive to US geo-political manoeuvre. Facing the rise of digital currency, SWIFT itself is challenged with its technical obsolescence which makes cross-border transactions through its platform slow and costly compared to the new platform. It is obliged to prepare itself for a new technological infrastructure for cross-border settlement of digital currency in near future, otherwise it might be weeded out of the game.

China's exploration in the internalisation of e-RMB does not stop there. In February 2021, China teams with the monetary authorities of Thailand, United Arab Emirates, and Hong Kong to launch the m-CDBC Bridge project to test central bank digital currencies in cross-border payments. A report says, "it aims to develop a proof-of-concept prototype that uses the distributed ledger technology to process in real time cross-border transactions that involve multiple currencies".[39]

Perhaps the most crucial aspect of the system, in contemporary capitalism, is the function of the world money as a store of value or hoarding. During the period of the gold standard, with all its problems and vicissitudes, nation states had to accumulate reserves in gold or silver to conclude international transactions with the final payment of trade balance balances, which were later added to the movement of capital. According to available data published by the IMF, at the end of June 2020, the accumulated international reserve of the largest economies was USD 15.6 trillion.[40] Of this total, 72.09% is allocated in US dollars to which can be added 4.78% in dollars not yet allocated 14.61% in euros, 4.14% in yen 1.37% in Canadian dollars 1.22% in Australian dollars and 1.79% in other currencies. This shows the absolute power of the dollar as world money in its value reserve function, which is mostly allocated to US treasury bonds, one form of fictitious capital.[41] In view of these numbers and those of the Japanese and Chinese reserves presented above, it is worth noting that "hoarding" no longer occurs in any currency, but there is an accumulation of capital in the form of interest-bearing capital and in particular forms of fictitious capital, such as US public debt.

Once again, it explains the "exorbitant privilege" through which the issue of the dollar as world money provides the USA with the ability to receive financing from all the economies of the world. For this reason, all countries must export and import direct and portfolio investments and loans in dollars and buy those dollars by issuing national currency or domestic debt securities to return them to the United States by purchasing US Treasury bonds.

Towards a Digital Currency War? Digital Regionalisation and Competition

The fact that the dollar hegemony is unlikely to be significantly challenged soon does not imply that the Americans are light-hearted about the raging digital currency competition. On 19 November 2019, the Harvard Kennedy School conducted a live simulation of a White House National Security Council meeting during a major national security crisis with former senior administration officials and thought leaders with the eye-catching title: "Digital Currency Wars: A National Security Crisis Simulation".[42]

It may be too sensational to speak of a digital currency war now, but we are witnessing the emergence of digital regionalisation and digital currency competition. Three Princeton researchers have suggested the idea of a, "Digital Currency Area" (DCA) defined as, "a network where payments and transactions are made digitally by using a currency that is specific to this network".[43] By "specific", they mean the network operates a payment platform that can only be used internally, between its participants and/or uses its own unit of account. Their insight is however limited by a narrow economic rationality. They suggest that DCA, just like optimal currency area, emerges for a fundamental reason: "to minimise transactions costs and, more generally, frictions in exchange". This apolitical perspective ignores the fact that DCAs are held together as much by geopolitical affiliation as by digital interconnectedness. The competition among digital currencies is not simply a competition among bundles of information services provided by each network, as suggested.

Facing this competition, the USA will aim to consolidate its hegemony through the digitalisation of the dollar, both by launching its own CBDC[44] and promoting privately run dollar-pegged permissioned stablecoins and cross-border payment platforms. It is also a practical consideration, as the astronomical expansion of the US money base caused by QEs needs to find outlets, otherwise the foundation of the dollar might be eventually shaken. In this sense, the digitalisation of the dollar is an endeavour to create the first truly *world money*. When we say the dollar is the world money after the WWII, it means the dollar is the major currency of reserve and international settlement. It is not yet the world money in the fullest sense. The digital dollar with its independent nodes cross-border payment platform could, however, become the first real world money in history. Of course, this ambition may be curbed by the digital regionalisation of other rivals as described above.

Consequently, a worrying aspect is the crowding-out effect of the digitalisation of dominant currencies equipped with cross-border payment platforms. Small economies with relatively weak currencies and technologies may see their sovereign currencies being crowded out by powerful cross-border payment systems pegged to foreign hard currencies. This may lead to the erosion of their economic and financial sovereignty.

To summarise, the crumbling of the dollar hegemony and its replacement by a new one seems unlikely to happen soon, but the emergence of digital regionalisation is going to reshape the global financial and monetary order. The world is justified in worrying that it may not proceed smoothly or without conflicts.

Gold: A Final Thought

Despite the consolidation of the dollar as world money, for various reasons countries continue to hold gold bars as part of their reserves. As Friedman and Keynes stated, even after the end of the gold-dollar standard, monetary authorities continue to maintain stocks of gold, gather the result of mining, and bury it in their coffers. Friedman maintains that, "[…] the resources spent to extract the gold from the earth, transport it to distant lands, use it in minting coins and bury them in bank vaults were almost certainly higher than the value of the new gold" (Friedman, 1994: 49). Keynes writes that, "[…] the war had the effect of collecting gold in the caverns of central banks […]" (Keynes, 2009: 102). Gold remains one of the great fetishes, and a desperate attempt by capital to have some reference point or outlet for its contradictions.

In June 2020, the gold stock registered by central banks, including the IMF, BIS, and the European Central Bank, reached 35,045 tonnes, estimated at USD 1,992 billion. This stock has changed little in recent decades, from 33.2 thousand tonnes in December 2000, falling to 30.8 tonnes in 2010 and rising to 34.7 tonnes in December 2019. In October 2020, the Central Banks of countries that held the largest gold stocks were the United States (8.1t), Germany (3.4t), Italy (2.5t), France (2.4t), Russia (2.3t), China (1.9t), and Switzerland (1.04t), in addition to the IMF (2.8t). This statistical information shows the objective impossibility of any nation attempting to return to the gold standard, as some have proposed for the Chinese economy. None of these world's largest economies have the objective possibility of creating a CBDC backed by its gold reserves, in an attempt to occupy the position currently held by the USA as the country issuing the world money, except under very restricted conditions or in very limited markets.

Brazil Amid Disputes Over Global Hegemony

According to the study by Boar et al. (2020), the Central Bank of Brazil (BCB) was one of the first to declare its intention to create a state digital currency, although with no official forecast date for its launch. At the end of 2020, the BCB did however launch PIX, an instant payment system, which incorporates a system of withdrawing money from registered merchants. To facilitate this, the Reserves Transfer System (RTS) was created, responsible for the gross settlement, in real time, of fund transfers between its participants (which forms the Brazilian Payment System, BPS). It is still in the process of implementation, and its operation is restricted to domestic markets. The objective of PIX, according to the BCB (2020), is to reduce the use of paper money; increase competition between payment service providers; expand access to the banking system; lower the costs of transactions (financial institutions must pay BRL 0.01 for every ten transactions, transactions between individuals will be free); and allow them to be fully mapped by monetary authorities (which increases the capacity for state control and surveillance over payment transactions). PIX will also make it possible to "customise" the system, based on the transaction data of each user, to allow all types of transactions and transfers, with limits established in each user's "profile" 24 hours a day, 7 days per week, and it will dispense with physical contacts, since payments can be made through use of keys or nicknames for account identification (cell phone number, CPF, CNPJ, e-mail etc.) and by Quick Response Codes (QR Codes), from a smartphone.[45]

Still regarding the BCB, the Complementary Law Project 19 of 2019, which grants the BCB formal autonomy and further subordinates monetary authority to the dictates of big capital, is in the process of being sanctioned by President Bolsonaro. Also close to approval is Bill 5,387, of

2019, which radicalises the liberalisation of the foreign exchange market and capital movements and which expands the use of foreign currency in the national territory. It permits the opening of bank accounts in dollars, which will, to some extent, start a process of the dollarisation of the Brazilian economy and increase the power exercised over it by the USA. These legislative changes are related not only to the economic policies of the current federal administration, but also the Brazilian economy's position in the world market.[46]

In the early 1980s, after decades of maintaining one of the highest growth rates on the planet, Brazil had consolidated a reasonably diversified industrial estate, but it had an Achilles' heel: a profound dependence on technologies and international flows of capital. Simultaneously, while the so-called microelectronic revolution was taking place in central capitalist countries, amid a reorganisation of the international division of labour marked by the transnationalisation and financialisation of production, the Brazilian economy was overwhelmed by the debt crisis triggered by the Volcker interest rate shock, entering what became known as the "lost decade".[47] This was a decisive moment in the subordination of Brazil to neoliberal economic policies, with their imperative for commercial and financial liberalisation, their "fiscal austerity" policies, privatisation, securitisation of debts, removal of labour rights and universal redistributive social policies, tax concessions favouring financial investments, legislative changes favouring creditors, and so on. From this point onward, the Brazilian economy returned to specialising in the production and export of commodities, and became a "platform for financial appreciation", as designated by Paulani (2012).

Against a backdrop of strong economic regression, in recent years a foreign policy characterised by automatic alignment with the United States has been consolidated, culminating in a vassal relationship between the Bolsonaro administration and the Donald Trump administration (Fiori, 2020). In addition to colourful episodes, such as Bolsonaro's gesture of saluting the American flag on his visit to Florida, which he repeated during the visit of John Bolton, Trump's security adviser to Brazil, at the very beginning of his term Bolsonaro announced a series of unilateral concessions, such as making available the Alcântara Aerospace Launching Base (MA) and the removal of its status as a developing country within the World Trade Organisation (Gonçalves & Teixeira, 2020). Efforts were also made to advance commercial agreements by incorporating Brazil into the US Trusted Trader programme. Regarding national infrastructure, investments by the US International Development Finance Corporation (the result of the merger between the Overseas Private Investment Corporation and the Development Credit Authority of the United States Agency for International Development—USAID) stand out, as well as the incorporation of Brazil into the Growth in the Americas Initiative, operated by the US Secretary of State. In the military ambit, the Research, Development, Test, and Evaluation Projects Agreement (RDT&E) was signed, in addition to the Master Information Exchange Agreement (MIEA), signed in 2017, under the Michel Temer government. In all these initiatives, the Brazilian position was subordinate, with much more being granted than received.

While reaffirming its alignment with the United States, and rehashing the rhetoric of the Cold War, the Bolsonaro administration has sought to mark its opposition to China. For example, faced with the outbreak of the Covid-19 pandemic, and reiterating the provocations of Donald Trump, Jair Bolsonaro, Chancellor Ernesto Araújo, former Minister of Education Benjamin Weintraub, and Federal Deputy Eduardo Bolsonaro bellowed about the "Chinese virus", and on several occasions launched attacks against an alleged international communist plan, with China as one of its fundamental pillars (Ibañez, 2020). The Chancellor hurried to denounce the worldwide spread of what he called the "communavirus".[48] In addition to successive diplomatic provocations and aggression towards China, the Bolsonaro administration promoted the halting of an infrastructure investment fund, agreed in 2017, which would be almost entirely financed by Chinese capital, raised barriers to Chinese participation in the Angra 3[49] project, and acted sharply to reject Chinese 5G technology.[50]

Despite the ideological rhetoric of the Bolsonaro administration, the Brazilian economy is increasingly dependent on China, as shown in the analysis of foreign trade and foreign direct investment in Brazil. In 1999, the European Union was Brazil's main trading partner, receiving 29.7% of total exports and supplying 25.6% of total imports. That same year, the United States was the destination for 24.8% of exports and supplied 24.9% of Brazilian imports. China, for perspective, received 2.5% of total exports and provided 2.8% of total imports. By 2009, China had become Brazil's main trading partner, and data from February 2021 show that it is the largest destination for Brazilian exports, totalling 29.91%, with an emphasis on iron ore, oil, crude oil, soy, beef, and cellulose, followed by the USA with 10.54%. The same data showed that China supplied 22.03% of Brazilian imports, followed by the USA, with 13.64%.[51]

One of the pillars of the Bolsonaro government's economic policy—the expansion of areas dedicated to agricultural and mineral production, especially in the Amazon region—has been to the detriment of environmental preservation areas and indigenous and quilombola lands, and aims, ultimately and above all, to meet Chinese demand. It should be said that it is in this context that the dismantling of state structures for environmental inspection and conservation has taken place, that deforestation and fires have intensified in the Amazon and the Pantanal, that a regime of terror against indigenous populations has been established, and that large-scale land grabbing has been legitimised (Young & Matheus, 2020).

Furthermore, according to data from the Ministry of Economy (2020), between the beginning of 2003 and the third quarter of 2019, foreign direct investments in Brazil came mostly from the USA, totalling almost USD 83 billion, 32% of the total. For the same period, China invested just over USD 80.5 billion, approximately 31% of the total. It should be noted that Chinese investments have increased significantly since 2010. Furthermore, while the United States has invested mainly in the industrial sector, Chinese investments, once heavily concentrated in the agricultural, oil and, mining sectors, have diversified, now covering the transport, telecommunications, financial services, industrial, and especially the electricity sectors, which now receives 45% of the total of these resources. It must be borne in mind that more than 85% of foreign direct investments in Brazil, in this period in, comprise merger and acquisition operations (brownfield investments), and not the expansion of productive capacity (greenfield investments).

Finally, despite having explicitly stated that under no circumstances would he buy Coronavac, a vaccine produced in China, and in view of the disastrous management of the health crisis, which means that Brazil has joint leadership in the total number of deaths from Covid-19, Bolsonaro has mobilised the diplomatic apparatus to negotiate a supply of the vaccine from China. These considerations indicate that opposition to China is much more a rhetorical device to mobilise the Bolsonarista political base, than a connected set of actions.

Regardless, given the increasing loss of its international economic and political relevance, and the cynical and widespread acceptance of its subordinate and dependent position in the world market, everything indicates that Brazil will play a largely passive and secondary role within the growing disputes between the United States and China, reiterating its condition as a space for productive and financial exploitation with a neo-colonial edge (Sampaio, 2007). In this sense, the monetary initiatives of the Central Bank of Brazil, whether in search of a digital currency or digital means of payment, serve to deepen this pattern of subordinate insertion.

New Frontier: Digital Hegemony and Digital Governability

Apart from the economic and financial aspects, the development of technologies related with digital currency may steer the society into uncharted areas that we should give some brief final considerations here. As mentioned, technology is an important pillar of hegemony upon which military power rests on. And for the first time in nearly a hundred years, the USA does not have absolute supremacy on the frontier of advanced technologies. It explains the anxiety and reactions the American elites have over the rivals they identified. China is in fact not the first one. During the 1980–1990s, the USA had launched technology war against Japan in the same vein. However, the saga of the technological race between the USA and China may be contextualised in a new historicity in which a new mode of hegemony is emerging. We may call it digital hegemony. It is a new mode of hegemony based on big data and global information networks at the cutting edge of digital and informational technologies. Digital currency will no doubt play an essential part in the formation of digital hegemony because money at the last analysis represents social relations as Marx has insightfully remained us.

Therefore, unsurprisingly, this technological competition is ideologically charged. A consistent accusation against all technological advancement China has made by the USA is the so-called development of digital authoritarianism,[52] whether it is 5G, AI, quantum computing or digital currency, although the US government has long been the biggest and most powerful agent of information surveillance around the world. It has been a tradition for the USA to demonise its rivals. But the ideological dimension of the technologies related with digital currency is particularly relevant because information technology has become the constitutive fabric of a new sort of sociality which may be called the digital governability.

Technology is never neutral. It can only be understood in concrete social relationship. Likewise, money is never simply a neutral medium of economic exchange. It embodies the alienation of social existence within power relationship. The fetishism of digital currency is especially complex and essential as it is intricately connected with big data. That is the reason why the IT giant Facebook's ambition in digital currency draws so much concern as the megacorporation has one of the biggest big data banks of customers at its disposal. The rise of social media as a new form of social interconnectivity also obliges us to have serious reflection. In contrast to the optimism some people held a few decades ago when information society first emerged, decentralised social media with unregulated circulation of information turns out not to facilitate a horizontal, transparent, and democratic society as some has imagined. What we witness are instead phenomena such as disinformation, echo chamber, stratosphere, populist mobilisation through emotions and politics of discrimination and hatred, etc. Decentralised social media in effect renders the foundation of democracy, namely communicative rationality, and ethics impossible. The case of psychological engineering through social media, such as the infamous role of Cambridge Analytics in Brexit and 2016 US presidential election also alarms us about the adverse and detrimental effects of social media on democracy. The marriage of social media with digital currency implies dark sides that we should be and cautious and critical of.

The impact of Blockchain technology on social formation can be profound and extensive. Some classify the present distributed ledger system of decentralised currency exemplified by bitcoin as Blockchain 1.0. The application of its related technologies such as smart contracts in financial sector can be known as Blockchain 2.0. Many are envisioning its extension into other social aspects such as legal affairs, education, medical care, logistics, big data, and Internet of Things, which is Blockchain 3.0.

We should not be blinded by enthusiastic optimism. Nevertheless, it is not enough for critical intellectuals to simply cry for a technological dystopia taking shape. Social relationships are human creation. Technology can only be understood in social practice. Social struggle also involves technological practice. Against the neo-liberal ideology of building an atomised society in which nobody trusts anybody, progressive social movement can apply a new form of blockchain technology to fabricate social trust and facilitate community-building as well as self-governance. Some social initiatives in China and other parts of the world are envisioning this possibility, which deserve our attention and further study.

Final Considerations

For now, those embarking on the study of state cryptocurrencies find themselves immersed in a sea of vagueness, as their implementation processes are still at an early stage. Any predictions made are, therefore, purely speculative. If state cryptocurrencies are confirmed as a means of circulation with lower cost, greater scope and efficiency, and as a technology that facilitates the supply of credit, it is evident that their consolidation on a large scale is merely a matter of time. Even if this is the case, their immediate economic impacts will tend to be limited. After all, it has now become sufficiently evident that the vicissitudes of the international monetary and credit system are expressions of the contradictions inherent in the current dynamics of capital accumulation. The search for a "monetary" solution to the dilemmas of contemporary capitalism is thus quixotic. As Marx notes in his polemic against the Proudhonists and the work bonus panacea in the *Grundrisse*,

> Various forms of money may correspond better to social production in various stages; one form may remedy evils against which another is powerless; but none of them, as long as they remain forms of money, and as long as money remains an essential relation of production, is capable of overcoming the contradictions inherent in the money relation and can instead only hope to reproduce these contradictions in one or another form. (Marx, 1993: 123)

If state cryptocurrencies do not contribute substantially to solving the problem of the over-accumulation of capital, or launch the extraction of surplus value, or overcome the barriers imposed by the increasingly organic composition of capital, or attack the spiral of state debt and private, etc., then the relevance of this innovation seems to lie elsewhere. State cryptocurrencies appear to create an obstacle to the reduction of the effectiveness of domestic monetary policies in the face of the issue of private cryptocurrencies by large economic conglomerates, as is the case of Facebook's Libra. It is likely that one of the reasons for the Chinese engagement in the consolidation of its state cryptocurrency is to strengthen the Chinese position in global digital commerce, and, together with BSN, to improve inter and intra-industrial integration and communication. More generally, the race for this innovation demonstrates its strategic importance within the global technological struggle, which tends to guarantee competitive advantages to the pioneer countries. This seems to be decisive within the hegemonic disputes within the inter-state system.

In the short term, despite Chinese pioneerism in this field, the dollar remains without rivals. There is nothing on the horizon that points to the resolution of the increasingly acute contradictions inherent to the international monetary and financial system. Neither the e-renminbi, nor a possible e-dollar, will change this situation substantially in near future. On the contrary, maybe the overcoming of American hegemony and the displacement of the dollar from the position of world money will not come from Chinese strengthening and the reorganisation of the inter-state system, but from an economic, social, and environmental cataclysm of unprecedented proportions. It seems that the global system is not susceptible to reform. Perhaps the only chance remaining is to emancipate ourselves from the work of Sisyphus and from the accumulation of capital by destroying its foundations—fetishism and objectification, labour and abstract wealth, private property, the state, class divisions, militarism, etc.—by organising the processes of the material and spiritual reproduction of life so that it is based on solidarity, equality, free association, conscious planning, and a relationship that forbids any kind of predation between people, and between people and nature.

Notes

1. In 2019, Governor of the Bank of England, Mark Carney, declared that a new form of global digital currency could be the, "answer to the destabilising dominance of the dollar in the current world monetary system" (cf. https://www.fx-markets.com/technology/4440846/carney-digital-currency-could-help-fix-global-monetary-system).
2. American participation in world industrial production went from 23% in 1870 to 36% in 1913, while British participation fell from 32 to 14% and German participation increased from 13 to 16%. In the same period, real GDP growth in the USA was 478%, against 124% in Britain and 242% in Germany (Mazzucchelli, 2009: 179), and in 1900 the US GDP had surpassed the combined total of British and German GDP. By this time, intense migratory flows had produced a demographic boom, the population of the United States jumped from 39 to 97 million inhabitants.
3. On the functioning of the gold-exchange standard and its differences from the gold standard, which prevailed before the First World War, cf. Einchengreen (2007, ch. 2), and Gontijo (2011). On the Bretton Woods

system and its collapse, cf. Einchengreen (2007, ch. 4), and Belluzzo (1995).

4. For an analysis of the impacts of WWII on the main allied countries, Cf. Mazzucchelli (2009, ch. 10).
5. On post WWII American economic performance, Cf. Mazzucchelli (2014, ch. 2).
6. Such markets emerged in the early 1950s, at first because of Soviet bloc countries needed to preserve dollar balances deposited in European banks to carry out commercial transactions with Western countries. The seeds of the growth of these markets at the end of the 1950s were the large capital flows from American corporations, who, faced with poor conditions for productively investing their surpluses, the fiscal barriers to repatriating them, and strict American banking legislation, ended up depositing them mainly in the City of London. In view of the constant decline of Sterling, British banks started to carry out their operations in dollars, initially making use of the accounts of American multinationals. Furthermore, with the creation of the European Common Market, euro-dollar markets have become a means of offsetting the persistent deficit and surplus positions of some countries (cf. Lima, 1985).
7. Cf. https://data.imf.org/regular.aspx?key=41175.
8. PBoC. Template on International Reserves and Foreign Currency Liquidity. http://www.pbc.gov.cn/diaochatongjisi/116219/116319/3959050/3959052/index.html. Accessed on 10/12/2020.
9. US. Major Foreign Holders of U.S. Treasury Securities. Fonte: https://www.treasury.gov/resource-center/data-chart-center/tic/Pages/ticsec2.aspx. Acesso em 10/10/2020.
10. Cf. https://data.imf.org/?sk=7A51304B-6426-40C0-83DD-CA473CA1FD52.
11. Cf. https://www.census.gov/foreign-trade/balance/.
12. Cf. https://www.federalreserve.gov/releases/h10/summary/.
13. Convém destacar que os Estados Unidos possuem também os maiores mercados de ativos financeiros tais como títulos, ações, contratos futuros e de opções, ao passo que a Inglaterra possui o maior mercado de swaps baseados em taxas de juros e de moeda estrangeira.
14. Cf. https://data.imf.org/?sk=7A51304B-6426-40C0-83DD-CA473CA1FD52.
15. Cf. https://www.economist.com/special-report/2020/05/07/as-china-goes-global-its-banks-are-coming-out-too.
16. Cf. https://www.moneytimes.com.br/goldman-sachs-e-morgan-stanley-recebem-aprovacao-para-elevar-participacao-na-china/.
17. Danny Bradbury reports that, "written testimony presented to the U.S. Senate Committee on Energy and Natural Resources in August 2018 claims that bitcoin mining accounts for about 1% of the world's

energy consumption" (https://www.thebalance.com/how-much-power-does-the-bitcoin-network-use-391280). In February 2021, an analysis by Cambridge University estimated that bitcoin mining consumed more electricity annually that the whole of Argentina. If bitcoin was a country, it would be in the top 30 energy consumers worldwide (https://www.bbc.com/news/technology-56012952).

18. For an analysis of private cryptocurrencies and their fetishistic character, cf. Nakatani and Mello (2019). For a more encompassing view, cf. Parana (2020).
19. In early October 2020, Bitcoin's average blockchain size rose above 300 Mb and the average confirmation time fell from in 30 days to around 80 minutes (cf. https://www.blockchain.com/charts/blocks-size. Accessed on 08/10/2020).
20. Its advocates believe that cryptocurrencies have four advantages as means of value exchange. (1) They are non-rewritable or nonreplicable and therefore reliable without the worry of double payment; (2) They are decentralised without the need of authorised and centralised agent; (3) They implies low transaction cost; (4) They are programmable and therefore adaptable to specific applications.
21. According to an estimate, the bitcoin mining energy consumption in early 2020 has amounted to the equivalent of 156 million horses (1.3 million horses per GW) or 49,440 wind turbines (412 turbines per GW) generating power at peak production per second. See Danny Bradbury, "How much power it takes to create a bitcoin", The Balance, updated 22 April 2020 (https://www.thebalance.com/how-much-power-does-the-bitcoin-network-use-391280.
22. A blockchain has multiple uses, so hundreds of large companies and banks are using the platform for other uses.
23. Regarding the security and anonymity offered by using cryptocurrencies, numerous frauds resulting from cyber-attacks have been registered, and it is a market that serves as a screen and an instrument for money laundering for illegal activities. However, these aspects are of little relevance to the argument presented here.
24. One of the reasons why cryptocurrencies attract financial groups has been the contraction of revenues from FICC by investment banks in recent years. Cryptocurrencies therefore have become the new frontier of financial investment.
25. It is worth reading a significant passage of his *white paper*: "The end state vision is one where real-world entities manage legally enforceable contracts, and transfer value without technological constraints or loss of privacy. In contrast to 'unpermissioned' blockchain platforms, the Corda platform is intended to manage real-world transactions between identifiable parties, with privacy and legal certainty. In contrast to other

'permissioned' blockchain platforms, the Corda Platform is intended to allow multiple groups of participants (and associated applications) to co-exist and interoperate across the same open network. The network's governance model is explicitly designed to reflect the common interests of the diverse user-base of the platform" (Brown, 2018: 3).

26. "In the end it is up to us to see, as a natural development of this logical path, its alleged monetary nature, this demonstrates why this cryptocurrency is not, and cannot be, money, in the full sense of the term" (Parana, 2020: 145).
27. See its official website (https://libra.org/) and their *white paper* (Libra, 2020).
28. "This letter addresses the authority of a national bank to hold deposits that serve as reserves for certain "stablecoins". Generally, a stablecoin is a type of cryptocurrency designed to have a stable value as compared with other types of cryptocurrency, which frequently experience significant volatility. One type of stablecoin is backed by an asset such as a fiat currency. Reports suggest stablecoins have various applications, including the potential to enhance payments on a broad scale, and are increasingly in demand. As described further below, stablecoin issuers may desire to place assets in a reserve account with a national bank to provide assurance that the issuer has sufficient assets backing the stablecoin in situations where there is a hosted wallet. For the reasons discussed below, we conclude that a national bank may hold such stablecoin "reserves" as a service to bank customers. We are not presently addressing the authority to support stablecoin transactions involving un-hosted wallets. In addition, this letter only addresses the use of stablecoin backed on a 1:1 basis by a single fiat currency where the bank verifies at least daily that reserve account balances are always equal to or greater than the number of the issuer's outstanding stablecoins. A bank providing services in support of a stablecoin project must comply with all applicable laws and regulations and ensure that it has instituted appropriate controls and conducted sufficient due diligence commensurate with the risks associated with maintaining a relationship with a stablecoin issuer. The due diligence process should facilitate an understanding of the risks of cryptocurrency and include a review for compliance with applicable laws and regulations, including those related to the Bank Secrecy Act (BSA) and anti-money laundering. In this regard, the review should include, but not be limited to, customer due diligence requirements under the BSA6 and the customer identification requirements under section 326 of the USA Patriot Act. A national bank or FSA must also identify and verify the beneficial owners of legal entity customers opening accounts. A national bank or FSA must also comply with applicable federal securities laws" (USOCC, 2020).

29. DLT is a more general technology with fewer restrictions than a blockchain, which can therefore be considered a particular form of it.
30. "Our survey shows that central banks are undertaking extensive work on central bank digital currencies. Globally, emerging market economies are moving from conceptual research to intensive practical development, driven by stronger motivations than those of advanced economy central banks. Central banks representing a fifth of the world's population say they are likely to issue the first CBDCs in the next few years" (Boar et al., 2020: 1).
31. At least potentially, "by creating their own digital currencies, governments may be able to bypass the conventional banking system and tax, and take deposits from, and make payments to citizens at the touch of a button" (*The Economist*, 2020).
32. Blockchain-based Service Network in mid-2019 the Chinese government announced the Blockchain-based Service Network (BSN) as "a cross-cloud, cross-portal, cross-framework global infrastructure network used to deploy and operate all types of blockchain applications" (2020: 1), that is, the result of a complex mix of big data technologies, cloud computing, blockchain, smart contracts, among others, forming an international network widely accessible to users, who would then have at their disposal the technological tools necessary to develop their applications and, consequently, "accelerating the development and universal adaptation of blockchain technology" (BSN, 2020: 1). One of BSN's purposes is to meet the, "urgent need within the industry to create a public infrastructure network that is commonly recognised by all organisations" (BSN, 2020: 4). Cf. the BSN *white paper* at https://www.bsnbase.com/p/main/index.
33. According to reporting by *The Economist* in October 2020, Ant Group (formerly Ant Financial) mediated in 2019 payments of USD 16 trillion. In addition to this service, the company also offered its clients the ability to invest in more than 6,000 stocks, acquire health insurance and take loans. The planned IPO of Ant Group at early 2021 was supposed to be the largest in history in absolute volumes, and, in terms of market capitalisation, its value would have been equivalent to that of JP Morgan Chase, the largest bank in the world (*The Economist*, 2020). However to the surprise of the global market, the IPO was called off a few days before its scheduled launch because the Chinese authority was concerned with the potential risk it might bring into China's financial system. Its business model was basically the facilitation of individual small loans on its internet platform and then the package of these loans into Assets Backed Securities to be sold to investors tier by tier, a model which exactly was cause of the 2007 Subprime Crisis in the USA.

34. Furthermore, it is also a worldwide trend that protagonism in this area are taken on by non-conventional companies, after all "conventional banks now account for only 72% of the stock market value of the global banking and payments industry, down from 96% in 2010" (*The Economist*, 2020).
35. https://www.bankofengland.co.uk/-/media/boe/files/speech/2019/the-growing-challenges-for-monetary-policy-speech-by-mark-carney.pdf.
36. The US Department of Defense is conducting research to deploy blockchain solution for securing sensitive research and development (R&D) data.
37. In 2021, China's nominal GDP has amounted to over 80% of US GDP, the second nation in history after Japan in the 1990s.
38. China National Clearing Center 34%, CIPS 5%, the People's Bank of China Digital Currency Research Institute 3% and the Payment & Clearing Association of China 3%
39. Cf. https://technode.com/2021/02/24/china-test-digital-currency-transactions-with-thailand-uae/.
40. IMF. International Data. Official reserves assets and other foreign currency assets. https://data.imf.org/?sk=E6A5F467-C14B-4AA8-9F6D-5A09EC4E62A4. Accessed on 10/10/2020.
41. In the case of Brazil, international reserves were USD 356.88 billion in December 2019, with "86.77% in US dollars, 7.35% in euros 2.11% in sterling 1.73% in yen, 0.94% in gold and 1.1% in other currencies" (BCB, 2020: 17). Investments were, "93.03% in government bonds; 1.78% in agency securities; 1.63% in deposits with central banks and supranational organisations; 1.04% in stock index Exchange Traded Funds" (BCB, 2020: 18), and the rest in other investments. Most of that 93.03% is invested in US Treasury bonds.
42. https://iop.harvard.edu/forum/digital-currency-wars-national-security-crisis-simulation.
43. Markus K Brunnermeier, Harold James and Jean-Pierre Landau, "Digital Currency Areas", 3 July 2019 (https://voxeu.org/article/digital-currency-areas).
44. The Fed, jointly with the Massachusetts Institute of Technology (MIT) and other institutions, is engaged in studies and experiments related to the creation of its own CBDC, according to the announcements in February and August 2020 by Lael Brainard, of the Federal Reserve Board of Governors. Cf. https://www.federalreserve.gov/newsevents/speech/brainard20200205a.htm and https://www.federalreserve.gov/newsevents/speech/brainard20200813a.htm.
45. Cf. https://www.bcb.gov.br/estabilidadefinanceira/pix.
46. Cf. Chapters 4, 5 and, most importantly 7 of this book.
47. To give perspective, Brazilian GDP went from an average rate of increase of 8.7% in the 1970s to 1.6% in the 1980s 2.6% in the 1990s, 3.6%

in the 2000s and 0.29% in the 2010s (cf. https://www.ibge.gov.br/estatisticas/economicas/contas-nacionais/9300-contas-nacionais-trimestrais.html?=&t=series-historicas&utm_source=landing&utm_medium=explica&utm_campaign=pib#evolucao-taxa).
48. Cf. https://oglobo.globo.com/mundo/covid-19-ernesto-araujo-denuncia-comunavirus-ataca-oms-24387155.
49. Cf. https://www1.folha.uol.com.br/mercado/2020/08/brasil-cria-travas-que-dificultam-investimentos-chines-no-pais.shtml.
50. Cf. https://www1.folha.uol.com.br/cotidiano/2020/10/nao-acredito-que-vacina-chinesa-transmita-seguranca-pela-sua-origem-diz-bolsonaro.shtml.
51. Cf. https://balanca.economia.gov.br/balanca/pg_principal_bc/principais_resultados.html.
52. For example, see Yaya J. Fanusie and Emily Jin, China's Digital Currency: Adding Financial Data to Digital Authoritarianism (https://www.cnas.org/publications/reports/chinas-digital-currency).

References

Auer, R., & Böhme, R. (2020, March). The technology of retail central bank digital currency. *BIS Quarterly Review*.

Barreiros, D. (2019). *Projeções sobre o Futuro da Guerra: Tecnologias disruptivas e mudanças paradigmáticas (2020–2060)* (IE-UFRJ DISCUSSION PAPER, TD 025).

Banco Central do Brasil. (2020). *Relatório de Gestão das Reservas Internacionais* (Vol. 12). https://www.bcb.gov.br/estabilidadefinanceira/relgestaoreservas. Acesso em 10 October 2020.

Belluzzo, L. G. (1995). O declínio de Bretton Woods e a emergência dos mercados "globalizados." *Economia e Sociedade, 4*(4–5), 11–20.

Boar, C., Holden, H., & Wadsworth, A. (2020, January) *Impending arrival—A sequel to the survey on central bank digital currency* (BIS Papers No 107).

Bray, C., & Tudor-Ackroyd, A. (2020, October 5). People's Bank of China's digital currency already used for pilot transactions worth 1.1 billion yuan. *South China Morning Post*. Available at: https://www.scmp.com/business/banking-finance/article/3104281/peoples-bank-chinas-digital-currency-already-used-pilot. Accessed on 8 October 2020.

Brown, R. G. (2018). *The Corda platform: An introduction*. Available at: https://www.corda.net/content/corda-platform-whitepaper.pdf.

BSN. (2020). *Development association* (Introductory White Paper). Available at: http://www.liandufin.top/incubator/file/Blockchain-based%20Service%20Network%20(BSN)%20Introductory%20White%20Paper.pdf.

Cintra, M. A. M., & Pinto, E. C. (2017) China em transformação: transição e estratégias de desenvolvimento. *Revista de Economia Política, 37* 2(147), 381–400.

Cointelegraph. (2020). *China's Digital Yuan CBDC is close, but many details remain unknown.* Available at: https://cointelegraph.com/news/chinas-digital-yuan-cbdc-is-close-but-many-details-remain-unknown.

Einchengreen, B. (2007). *A Globalização do Capital: uma história do sistema monetário internacional.* Editora 34.

Fiori, J. L. (2018). A síndrome de babel e a nova doutrina de segurança dos Estados Unidos. *Revista Tempo do Mundo, 4*(2).

Fiori, J. L. (2020). A lenta construção de um "Estado Vassalo". *Outras Palavras.* Disponível em: https://outraspalavras.net/direita-assanhada/a-lenta-construcao-de-um-estado-vassalo/.

Fiori, J. L., & Nozaki, W. (2020). Escalada militar na pandemia. *A Terra é Redonda.* Available at: https://aterraeredonda.com.br/escalada-militar-na-pandemia/.

Friedman, M. (1994). *Episódios da história monetária.* Record.

Gonçalves, W., & Teixeira, T. (2020). Considerações sobre a política externa brasileira no governo Bolsonaro e as relações Brasil-EUA. *Sul Global, 1*(1), 192–211.

Gontijo, C. (2011). *Os mecanismos de funcionamento do "padrão-ouro": uma visão crítica.* UFMG/CEDEPLAR (Texto para Discussão n° 435).

Herrera, R., & Long, Z. (2019). *La Chine est-elle capitaliste?* Editions Critiques.

Ibañez. (2020). Geopolítica e diplomacia em tempos de Covid-19: Brasil e China no limiar de um contencioso. *Espaço e Economia, 18.* Available at: http://journals.openedition.org/espacoeconomia/13257.

Keynes, J. M. (2009). *Sur la monnaie et l'économie.* Payot.

Libra Association Members. (2020). *An introduction to Libra.* Disponível em: https://libra.org/en-US/wp-content/uploads/sites/23/2019/06/LibraWhitePaper_en_US.pdf.

Lima, M. L. P. (1985). *O euromercado e a expansão do capital financeiro internacional* (Campinas, dissertação de mestrado, IE/Unicamp).

Mandel, E. (1982). *O capitalismo tardio.* Abril Cultural.

Marx, K. (1975). *Economic and philosophical manuscripts.* In*Collected works* (Vol. 3). Lawrence and Wishart.

Marx, K. (1990). *Capital: A critique of political economy* (Vol. 1). Penguin Books.

Marx, K. (1993). *Grundrisse: Foundations of the critique of political economy.* New York Penguin Books associada à New Left Review.

Mazzucchelli, F. (2009). *Os anos de chumbo: economia e política internacional nos entreguerras.* UNESP-FACAMP.

Mazzucchelli, F. (2014). *Os dias de sol.* Facamp.

Ministério da Economia. (2020). *Boletim de Investimentos Estrangeiros*, n. 3. Disponível em: http://www.economia.gov.br/central-de-conteudos/publicacoes/boletim-deinvestimentos-

Nakatani, P., & Mello, G. M. C. M. (2019). Crypto-currencies: From the fetishism of gold to Hayek. In G. M. C. M. Mello & M. S. Sabadini (Eds.), *Financial speculation and fictitious profits*. Springer International Publishing.

Norfield, T. (2020). China & US power. *Economics of Imperialism* (Author's blog). Available at: https://economicsofimperialism.blogspot.com/2020/07/china-us-power.html.

Parana, E. (2020). *Bitcoin: a utopia tecnocrática do dinheiro apolítico*. Autonomia Literária.

Paulani, L. M. (2012). A inserção da economia brasileira no cenário mundial: uma reflexão sobre a situação atual à luz da história. *Boletim de Economia e Política Internacional* - DINTE/IPEA, nº 10.

Prado, E. F. S. (2020). Entre a ficção e o fetiche. *Economia e Complexidade* (Author's blog). Available at: https://eleuterioprado.files.wordpress.com/2020/07/entre-a-ficcao-e-o-fetiche-novo-2.pdf.

Sampaio JR., & Plínio de Arrida. (2007). Globalização e reversão neocolonial: o impasse brasileiro. In *Filosofía y teorías políticas entre la crítica y la utopía*. CLACSO.

Tavares, M. C. (1997). A retomada da hegemonia norte-americana. In M. C. Tavares & J. L. Fiori (orgs). *Poder e dinheiro: uma economia política da globalização*. Vozes.

The Economist. (2020) *Ant Group and fintech come of age*. Available at: https://www.economist.com/leaders/2020/10/08/ant-group-and-fintech-come-of-age.

Tudor-Ackroyd, A. (2020, September 5). What will China's central bank digital currency mean for Alipay and WeChat Pay? *South China Morning Post*. Accessed on 8 October 2020.

USOCC. (2020). "OCC Chief Counsel's Interpretation on National Bank and Federal Savings Association Authority to Hold Stablecoin Reserves". *Interpretive Letter*, n.1172, October.

USOCC. (2021, January). OCC Chief Counsel's interpretation on national bank and federal savings association authority to use independent node verification networks and stablecoins for payment activities. *Interpretive Letter, 1174*.

Young, C. E. F., & Mathias, C. F. M. (Eds.). (2020). *Covid-19, meio ambiente e políticas públicas*. Hucitec.

Zhou, C., & Borak, M. (2020, October 9). China's Shenzhen giving away millions in sovereign digital yuan to test technology and boost consumption. *South China Morning Post*. Accessed on 9 October 2020.

CHAPTER 7

Brazil Amid the Structural Crisis of Capital

Helder Gomes

Introduction

This chapter confronts the interpretation that, at the beginning of the third decade of the twenty-first century, Brazil is going through an exceptionally historic moment. The argument is that in the first 15 years of the twenty-first century, Brazil should have developed a virtuous cycle, with evident economic and social prosperity, and should have overcome the difficulties experienced in the immediately preceding period. To contradict this perspective is to realise that the experience of the first two decades of the twenty-first century has reaffirmed structural records that now appear to be the result of the saturation of the model of systematic integration of Brazil into the imperialist order. The criticism here presupposes two elements: (a) the effects of an inorganic process of decolonisation in the formation of a subordinate nation state, and its most striking inheritance in present-day Brazil; (b) the internal reactions to the exacerbation of the crisis of the expanded reproduction of capital, at a global level, which makes increasingly explicit, the limits to achieving the weary ideal of *Brazil —power of the future*.

H. Gomes (✉)
SCM, Vitória, Brazil

G. M. de C. Mello and H. P. Braga (eds.), *Wealth and Poverty in Contemporary Brazilian Capitalism*, Marx, Engels, and Marxisms,
https://doi.org/10.1007/978-3-030-82298-9_7

From Gilberto Mathias and Pierre Salama (1983), we take the perspective that the nation states that inherited the Old Colonial System were created inorganically under strong exogenous pressure. As capitalism consolidated itself as an organised global mode of production through the nineteenth century, it was possible to establish independent nations with guaranteed ties of international subordination based on the new market relationships of unequal development, which would determine quite different trajectories, distinguishing the economic-social formations of emerging capital countries from those that arose organically from the historical experiences of integrated industrialisation.

As the objective is to highlight the historical manifestations of these more general processes, we also revisit the warnings from the classics of Brazilian Social Thought, especially regarding the importance of understanding the meaning of the inheritances of our colonial past and how they reveal themselves in the contemporary world, with special appreciation for the contributions of Caio Prado Júnior (1966), Florestan Fernandes (2006), and Ruy Mauro Marini (2000).

Criticism of interpretations of the global economic crisis is based on various studies by Paulo Nakatani and Reinaldo Carcanholo, particularly those that resulted in the formulation of the category of *fictitious profits* (Melo & Sabadini, 2019), through which we learned to reflect on how far we have yet to travel in the process of permanent sublation (*Aufhebung*), characteristic of the dialectic of the Critique of Political Economy.

To achieve this, the text is organised into three parts. An initial outline presents the importance of understanding organised capitalism at a global level, as a mode of production in an advanced stage of evolution, including in its scope, a prerequisite understanding of the singularities of Brazil's transition in the industrialisation process of the great imperialist powers. The text then turns to the first concrete steps in the formation of Brazil as a subordinate State and their consequences, up until its capture in the speculation trap during the world economic crisis that began in the 1970s. In the final part, the most recent efforts to read just the Brazilian economy are set out, as a legacy of the *Real Plan*, and its most damaging manifestations: the ever deeper denationalisation of its internal productive capacity and the consequent loss of the last traces of sovereignty regarding investment decisions; and the lack of macroeconomic control stemming from its unique forms of public and private debt.

Production Organised at the Global Level

References to the formation of the Brazilian nation have been common because of a unique process of primitive capital accumulation. Such perspectives reflect the specific way in which wage labour markets were formed following the abolition of slavery, through a long period of *passive revolution*, which saw heavy state participation in industrial production. Such conceptions appear to derive from studies of the classic experiences of the evolution of capitalism in European countries, the United States, and Japan in the nineteenth century, when these nations, each in their turn, advanced their respective processes of industrialisation.

We, however, follow the proposition that the formation of new nation states that emerged in the transition from the Old Colonial System to the imperialist stage, occurred quite differently (Mathias & Salama, 1983). In the former colonies, which had only just been formally emancipated, nascent industrial production was always linked to the need to overcome obstacles to the accumulation of capital for the great capitalist powers, in a process of consolidation. Mandel (1982), for example, shows us that the transition from slavery to free labour, in countries like Brazil, satisfied a need to reduce technological gaps, manifested in the great differences in labour productivity, since these made it difficult to reduce the costs of basic inputs and food produced in the former colonies and destined for the countries that housed the factories for producing machines, equipment and the means of consumption and possessing a greater degree of innovation. In other words, compulsory labour was an obstacle to productivity gains in the reproduction of capital in two ways: it made the supply of inputs more expensive, in relation to the value of industrial production; and it hindered the production of relative added value in Europe and other large centres, due to the rigidity in the value of food and other means of consumption destined for the waged classes.

Therefore, it is worth revisiting some founding elements related to the movement of capital in general, which can help to synthetically identify the roots of these distinctions. It is necessary to revisit the concept of industrialisation (Oliveira, 2003), understood as the integrated control of the manufacture of the means of subsistence and durable products for human consumption, as well as the industrial production of inputs, machines, and equipment. From this point of view, a complete industrialisation process means commanding the integration of the means of consumption and means of production, which were consolidated during the formation of the imperialist powers, guaranteeing them the monopoly in technology, production, and lines of credit.

In this way, by the end of the nineteenth century, some solutions seem to have been found to the great dilemma of centralised accumulation at the international level. The *big* capital based in Europe, the United States, and Japan, rigorously monitored the capital export process, controlling the connections between new overseas investments, the transfer of technical and scientific knowledge and the lines of credit. Guaranteeing the hierarchical command of the imperialist race would mean integrating, and simultaneously restricting, the access of new nations (ex-colonies) to the global industrialisation process, a process put in place with the formation of large cartels and trusts and with the political, legal, and military support of the respective nation states.

The imperialist race resulted from the consolidation of two distinct waves of late industrialisation (Oliveira, 2003). First, the United States, Germany, and France, and then Russia, Japan, and Italy, each at their own pace and based on different motivations, promoted surplus industrial production, integrating their respective production capacities. So, the new world powers, that would compete with Victorian England, emerged, ending the competitive era and establishing international protectionism, in a similar process to that which resulted in the domination of oligopolistic capital. A new phase of the command of production was born in the former colonies and in the neo-colonial border areas, to avoid increasing industrial inputs and the consequent reduction of the advantages resulting from the productivity gains achieved in the highly technological production lines of the time. This control over the expansion of industrial production and over the extraction of surpluses overseas, ushered in a new phase of exporting capital by the great powers and not just by the British.

Technological innovations (steel, electricity, combustion engines) brought an end to the era of iron and steam, creating greater autonomy for owners of the means of production, as the separation between manual labour and intellectual labour was developed (Oliveira, 2003). The production of technological knowledge became exclusive to professional teams (engineering, chemistry, management, etc.) and industrial secrecy became a new weapon in the centralisation of capital, whose spatial reflexes produced a new period of uneven development between nations. At that time in the rise of backward capitalist economies, banks were transformed from intermediaries into promoters and controllers of a trust-based industrial expansion. Production, commerce, and the credit system began to be organised globally by holding companies with numerous subsidiaries distributed around the globe, creating a new hierarchy of dominance and subordination.

The *Exportation of Capital* gained supremacy as a means for extracting and centralising surpluses. The ability to command an immense volume of capital, based on the control of ordinary shares in the hierarchical chain of companies, created a spatial tangle of investment and production decisions, in a context of structural separation between ownership, capital and the management of the ventures associated with it. So, the expanded reproduction of the capitalist mode of production gained a more total form of unequal development, creating a hierarchy of control over the partial integration of property and the management of productive and commercial complexes, centralised by the imperialist powers that hosted the controlling companies.

In this process of creating new forms of command over the international division of labour, the generalisation of production relationships proper to an advanced stage of capitalist evolution remained the prerogative of the great imperialist powers. Emerging nations, whose past was founded on colonial obedience to the *metropolitan exclusive* economies, were reserved for merging a gradual, fragmented, and incomplete expansion of industrial production, with quite violent forms of accumulation.

This perspective seems to clarify the limits imposed on industrial production in the ex-colonies that were the last to be emancipated. At the turn of the twentieth century, the creation of the main record of the process of Brazil's integration into the international division of labour would begin: the specialisation of the production of industrial bases to meet a significant portion of the global demand for primary materials, meaning that formal political independence would not mean full national sovereignty over major domestic investment decisions.

As in the economic field, new nation states were also appearing inorganically in most of the former colonies. In the nineteenth century, superstructural relations in newly emancipated territories were moulded to the demands of the new international economic order, dispensing with the need for classic bourgeois revolutions, because in the context of global oligopolisation, the formation of economically and politically strong bourgeoisies in emerging nations was not desirable.

At the time, power relations under the rule of the great bourgeoisie were practically resolved and consolidated at a global level. The popular uprisings in Europe in the 1840s greatly favoured bourgeois power and imposed a major defeat on the direction that the nobility had set in motion from the beginning of the nineteenth century. Bourgeois political domination began to be centralised in the great powers that formed, linking direct control of production and the extraction of surpluses in these emerging nations. Both production relationships and the international division of labour were altered, maintaining centralised command of the global process of accumulation, which was reflected in the process of subordinating the political interests of the new national elites that were formed in the decolonisation process.

In the process of these former colonies becoming formally independent, this was the means that centralised capital accumulation found to guarantee what was fundamental to it: economic, social, and political conditions favouring the transfer of wealth, in favour of the organised capital of the great imperialist powers.

The Subordinate State and Its Particularities in Brazil

The specifics of the political organisation in nations emancipated from the Old Colonial System in the nineteenth century must be understood, therefore, as a fundamental element of the imperialist period. The historical particularities of the formation of each new nation generally, and their specific function as guarantors of the industrial extraction of surpluses and their continuous transfer, demanded that these new nation states express themselves concretely as rigidly authoritarian political regimes (Mathias & Salama, 1983).

This authoritarian rigidity stemmed from the need to guarantee the mediation of disputes between the strata emerging within the national elites for the appropriation of the remaining surpluses.

To the extent that most of the wealth produced in the former colonies would continue to be transferred to the great imperialist powers, the portions retained from this surplus began to be competitively fought for, a surplus whose character mixed advanced mechanisms, typical of integrated market relations worldwide, with the maintenance of the predominant financial instruments of the colonial period. Furthermore, authoritarianism is required as a way of guaranteeing compensation and attracting foreign investments, based on a strict regime of exploitation of the workforce (Marini, 2000).

This trajectory becomes more and more explicit in the case of Brazil as the legacies of its subordinate position in the process of global imperialist industrialisation are revealed. The Brazilian economy moulded itself very slowly to the more general contradictions that emerged with the end of the Old Colonial System. This was because the social relations of production linked to agriculture and mineral extraction remained strong elements marking the national sociability, even when one allows for the introduction of innovations in the industrial processing of strategic raw materials.

External pressures to increase labour productivity, which eventually resulted in the abolition of the slave regime, were not sufficient to immediately forge typical capitalist production relations within Brazil. On the contrary, the inheritances of the old colonial pact, which involved a metropolitan exclusive in commercial and usurious transactions, prevented both integrated internal accumulation and the formation of a wage labour market in general. In the immediate aftermath of abolition, for example, the previously enslaved population was forced to form a marginalised lumpenproletariat, while incentivising European immigration created new relations of production. However, the new working regimes, centred on immigrants, were linked to the compensation of the expenses of long ocean voyages, which reproduced archaic forms of work and postponed the generalisation of waged labour (Martins, 1986).

Because of the inter-regional diversity that exists in Brazil, this was not a linear process. The power relations that arose from this inorganic process of adapting domestic production to the demands of imperialist accumulation ended up reproducing, for a significant time, political control exercised by regional oligarchies. It can be said that, in general, far from organically forming a typically bourgeois power, political command was exercised, in fact, from the barony of coffee, at the end of the short imperial stage, and, later in most of the country, by the marked "Coronelismo" of the First Republic (1889–1930). External influence on these oligarchic relations was operated by merchant commissioners from import and export houses, and by executives of foreign banks who, in the transition to industrialised production of coffee, some foods, textiles and minerals, delineated both the potential and the limits of this initial productive diversification (Rego & Marques, 2003).

This inorganic nature would also not be undone during the transition to heavy industry in Brazil in the middle of the twentieth century. The absence of an internal bourgeoisie with the capacity to centralise capital, made the Brazilian State responsible for both the structuring and organisation of labour markets, but as its main direct investor, especially in the formation of *joint ventures* with foreign capital (Evans, 1980). Only in this way was it possible to break down some of the barriers to industrial diversification, although it remained restricted to some specific sectors (steel, energy, transport, and communication), which complemented the initial production of inputs and some processed foodstuffs, within the framework of hierarchical global integration.

The transfer of value to the great imperialist powers was, therefore, maintained through direct foreign participation in fundamental investments and in the supply of credit. As a result, forms of external control over the production regime, technology transfer, and forms of financing developed, imposing a productive specialisation in strategic and cheaper industrial inputs, geared towards exports (Marini, 2000).

Another aspect of this new model of a subordinate State was the control and regulation of accumulation by Brazilian oligarchies, including the maintenance of archaic forms of production relationships. In this respect, it was necessary to preserve the landownership structure, concentrating land as an effective way of preventing access by a good part of the popular strata to the means of directly producing their living conditions, forming an industrial reserve army and a lumpenproletariat of a magnitude appropriate to a capitalist regime which had violent relationships of accumulation within its reproduction.

So, the subordinate state of Brazil was born, functioning legally, politically, and ideologically to guarantee two movements proper to its subordinate position: the net and continuous transfer of wealth to the great imperialist powers and the maintenance of a regime of hybrid internal capital accumulation, mixing innovative commercial forms with the most primitive expropriation procedures, both in the countryside and in the city (Marini, 2000).

It is as such that the major political, economic, and social changes in Brazil must be understood. Rather than radical revolutionary ruptures, these movements emerged as moments in the reproduction of the inorganic process of forming a subordinate State, just as the internationalisation of capital demanded. In this way, the dispersed, contradictory, dominant interests tried to reconcile the brutality of agribusiness, inherited from former *barons* and *colonels*, with the inorganic propulsion of urbanisation and industrial production, necessary for the integration of the nation into the imperialist hierarchy which made investment decisions and appropriated surpluses.

One of the political novelties in the transition to heavy industry was the retaking of power, centralised in the Federal Executive, and the replacement of the more liberal approach of the First Republic with a more interventionist approach. With the creation of the Ministry of Labour, Industry and Commerce (Ministério do Trabalho, Indústria e Comércio, MTIC), the Executive Branch began to concentrate the power to formulate laws and to impose instruments to control capital-labour relations. Simultaneously, it started to invest directly in heavy industry and to encourage private investments in production and trade, it also tried to encourage harmony between the classes, creating spaces for the integration of their interests within the state apparatus (Draibe, 1985). An example of this was the tutelary regulation for the procedures of Union association (Decree Law n° 1,042, of 1939), which unified the rules for the organisation of the official labour and employer representation entities, whose recognition by the MTIC is dependent on the formal adherence of its leaders to the established regulations, centred on the resolution of disagreements, and including adherence to the prohibition against participating in political-party activism.

It is necessary to be clear that these policies for resolving antagonistic interestswere implemented during the resurgence of an authoritarian political regime typical of the subordinate Brazilian state. The instruments for co-opting working families and their political representation were only instituted after violent repression of union mobilisation and strike actions. With the consolidation of the so-called Estado Novo (1937–1946), the political rights of leaders were revoked and the most organised and militant and anyone who challenged the brutal established order was tortured and killed.

The softening of this regime based on force would only occur after the end of World War II. Once again, the geopolitical reorganisation required changes to the internal political and economic arrangements, which also created opportunities for the integration of the Brazilian economy into the international scene, which was now under the explicit command of the United States of America and which imposed a new pattern of production and consumption, demanding a degree of industrial diversification in Brazil. This movement resulted in the intensification of state planning, aimed at a new leap forward in the economic integration of the nation through strong public investment in transport, energy and telecommunications infrastructure, the promotion of private production, and the creation of the National Bank for Economic Development (BNDE) in the 1950s.

The imperialist expansion strategies of the post-war period included the development of links in the production chains for durable consumer goods in countries like Brazil. The technological advances resulting from the war effort began to dynamise the centralised production of the means of production and further expanding the production of durable consumer goods on a global scale (Teixeira, 1993). This production required the continuous growth of large consumer markets for automobiles and household appliances. As a result, far more advanced technological production of the means of consumption was added to the internal production capacity.

It is interesting to note that with these new forms of integration the international distinctions between the processes of change in the political regimes responsible for the management of the new *golden age* would become clear. Once the authoritarian regimes which emerged in the interwar period were defeated, various experiences of democratisation emerged across the globe. In Europe, for example, the geopolitical situation caused by the threat posed by the Soviet Union and the need to incorporate significant numbers of ex-combatants into production and consumption meant, in capitalist nations, the expansion of the political participation of the working classes. Tax and labour concessions for business and the intensification of compensatory public policies, generated a period marked by the creation of the *Welfare State*.

Changes in the autocratic regimes in Latin America were quite different. In Brazil, efforts to adapt to the new international order also created pressure for greater popular participation in the economy, promoted, for example, in the official propaganda of the Kubitschek government: *to grow 50 years in 5* (Skidmore, 2010). However, after a brief period of political liberation, the reality of international subordination soon hit home, which explains the restrictions placed on developing a *welfare* regime. The first half of the 1960s saw yet another faltering of popular struggles, which were repressed with even more violence. This period also saw the intensification of the restriction of political rights, forced exile and the torture and murder of militants (Brazil: Nunca mais, 2021).

The 1964 military coup put Brazil on a new path internationally, at a time when the world was involved in yet another major economic crisis. With the reconstruction of European nations, signs of exhaustion were emerging following the *great wave* of high rates of economic growth experienced in the post-war period. From the early 1960s, there had been indications that Germany, France, and Japan would soon begin to challenge the USA's power over regulating international markets. Faced with such threats to its supreme domination, the United States began to form alliances on several fronts, paying special attention to the countries of the American continent following the Cuban Revolution of 1959. In the early 1960s, the American government was already celebrating the continental *Alliance for Progress* agreement with Latin American governments, which was regulated by the *United States Agency for International Development* (USAID). Cooperation agreements comprised not only the transfer of technology for the diversification of production capacity, but also US standards for public services, especially those aimed at educational and ideological dissemination, which later expanded to the military training of repressive political organisations.

From the perspective of economic performance, however, there were several significant movements. With the economic and fiscal reforms implemented following the military coup of 1964, the Brazilian economy plunged into a period of recession until 1968. Among these initiatives, the policies of cutting spending and issuing public bonds at generous interest rates stand out, justified as a measure for cooling inflationary pressure.

The global picture of disputes changed dramatically in the late 1960s. There were signs of yet another serious economic crisis of capital overproduction. As a result, the great imperialist powers opposed to the established order, started to increase their gold stocks, which meant promoting direct attacks on the dollar as a world currency, which undermined the terms of the *Bretton Woods* agreements (Anderson, 2015). Such movements had an objective consequence on flows of capital, opening new paths in the search for alternative means of accumulation.

The recessionary crisis in the Brazilian economy had delivered an economic environment with high levels of unemployment and a substantial portion of its installed industrial capacity idle. Furthermore, changes in the command of military governments began to mark a new moment for macroeconomic policy, with the introduction of new movements of capital at the international level. State investments in infrastructure, in direct industrial production and in the training of the workforce were high, as were tax incentives and direct lines of credit, at subsidised interest rates, aimed at promoting private investments. In addition, new ways of protecting production were established internally and direct consumer credit was expanded, based on financial disbursement and incentives from the Sistema Financeiro de Habitação (Financial System for Housing) (Belluzzo & Coutinho, 1982). After this period of recession, industrial production started to grow, utilising the idle production capacity. This was a first step on the path of heavy private investments, mainly from multinational conglomerates, who were seeking alternatives during the crisis that was occurring worldwide.

In fact, this internal movement was a national reaction of the implications of the beginning of a serious international economic crisis. The most dynamic markets in world capitalism were witnessing a sharp fall in economic growth rates and, in the following years, economic recession was widespread among the great powers. This was the moment in which the Brazilian economy was captured, under the guise of the *Economic Miracle*, in a new and more vicious foreign debt trap, caused by speculative accumulation (Cruz, 1984), which came to dominate all other functional forms of capital.

With the economy fuelled by a new cycle of foreign investments, growth based on the use of idle capacity was no longer possible. Average annual growth rates were around 11%, between 1967 and 1973, considered high in comparison to the other periods, both before and after (Belluzzo & Coutinho, 1982). The process of industrial development remained, however, incomplete. It was motivated by the production of consumer durables and did not, therefore, develop a fully diversified production capacity. This kept the economy dependent on the import of machinery, equipment, and a variety of other inputs.

Of all this movement, the most perverse impact on the following decades was, without doubt, its *capture* by the new movements of international speculative capital. Under the alleged need to attract foreign investment, the institutional apparatus was set up to encourage private companies based in Brazil, both national and multinational subsidiaries, to raise funds in the Euromarket and other places as the main instrument of economic development, as recommended by the economic team of the military government. This not-so-explicit arrangement was based on the building of a significant volume of foreign exchange reserves, which would serve as a guarantee for the administration of the loans themselves and, also, for the flow of imports required, in the face of the great international shocks underway at that time (Cruz, 1984). So, it is possible to observe that this external indebtedness was of a subordinate, not sovereign, nature and has been driven, since then, by essentially speculative motivations.

From 1972 onwards, however, the Brazilian economy would experience a period of decreased growth rates accompanied by slight inflationary pressure. At the international level, the pace of productive activities encountered its critical point in the first oil shock (1973), a time when the global economic crisis would become apparent, manifested in the reduction of international credit and trade flows, and an increase in basic rates, interest rates, and *spreads*.

The Brazilian government, however, sought to create an atmosphere of tranquillity and took the initiative to resume investments. In 1974, the final National Development Plan (II PND) was launched, based on the presumptive idea that Brazil would be an *island of tranquillity in a rough sea* (Cruz, 1984). The Brazilian State undertook a series of investments in large industrial plants and expanded the range of subsidised lines of credit to attract external partners, intended to guarantee technology transfer. The formal objectives of the II PND made its intentions clear, as it was focused on the transformation of various industrial inputs, on the substitution of imported durable consumer goods with domestically produced ones, on the reduction of energy dependence on imported oil through support for ethanol production (Proálcool), and on increasing exports and steering state investments in basic inputs to regions away from the Rio-São Paulo hub. The hoped for internal industrial deconcentration occurred, however, only in specific activities, revealing that technology-based activities, that were hardly the most daring, would tend to follow the same path as the large investments of the so-called *dirty industries* (mineral extraction, steel, cellulose, agrofuels, etc.) in the most industrially backward regions.

The Unfinished Democratic Transition and the Escalation of Crises

The 1980s were marked by the resumption of the myth of *sovereign Brazil* and ideas about the possibility of fully achieving democratic freedoms. So much so that the decade ended with the real prospect of delivering on the approved formal process that would culminate with the announcement of a new Federal Constitution in 1988, as if it were somehow possible to build a Welfare State in the largest country in Latin America just as the countries of the cradle of *Welfare* were showing signs of coming to the end of the so-called *golden years*.

The Brazilian economy suffered economic stagnation, following a period of outright recession, from the turn of the decade until 1983. It was a troubled time, marked by increases in international interest rates and the need to transfer liquid resources abroad, resulting from the rolling foreign debt trap. Internationally, there were major changes in the geopolitical field, the Soviet Union was undergoing further disruption and the Ronald Regan government was seeking to demonstrate its superiority to the capitalist world.

The economic crisis had brought serious consequences for the world economy. At the turn of the 1980s, the low capacity to honour debtor countries' external commitments threatened international credit markets, which were restricted by official requests for a moratorium. The fiscal crisis began to deeply mark most capitalist economies, forcing remedial measures to defend the continuity of the accumulation process, such as privatisations and the cutting of government services. Trapped in this speculative trap, controlling the deficit in public accounts proved to be an impossible task.

Meanwhile, the dispute over control of international transactions had resulted in a series of trade conventions that broke with traditional bilateral agreements. The attempt to form large commercial blocs, delimiting the agreed regions, was one of the fundamental marks of international diplomacy from the early 1980s onwards. Part of that framework was a real change in the technological base, following a long process of productive restructuring, imposing changes on the organisation of competition structures.

To guarantee governability, government officials from debtor countries sought credibility for their respective national currencies through conventional measures of monetary stabilisation. Brazil was no exception, as it had increased public, external, and internal indebtedness, the administration of which began to consume tax resources, making government investments unfeasible. The transfer of dollars abroad, in the form of interest, reached an average of more than USD 10 billion annually, which depleted foreign exchange reserves and forced unplanned defaults. Expectations were at their most pessimistic, the 1980s had an average annual growth rate below 3.0%, while inflation rates broke records every month. Attempts to control this started to topple the public policies of the civilian governments that had succeeded the military regime.

In early 1986, the first measures of the *Cruzado Plan* for inflationary control were announced with the freezing of product prices and wages. After elections that year, controls were loosened and inflation started to increase again, forcing the issue of several other IMF packages. Failing to fight inflation and under union pressure, the government adopted mechanisms for automatic wage readjustments through monthly indices until the end of its mandate in 1990. The forced moratorium, at the end of the first civilian government, demanded a readjustment based on the negotiations of the *Brady Plan* for the securitisation of debt securities, creating an apparent backlash.

At the global level, foreign debt was becoming a chronic problem for most countries. At the periphery, agreements to change the debt profile were unable to guarantee the fulfilment of the commitments of debtor economies, with negative effects on the attempts to control inflation. So, the US government and multilateral financing organisations decided to devise new models of monetary stabilisation, with even more daring measures. In the Latin American economies, new efforts were made to adapt to a macroeconomic policy based on the pegging of the respective national currencies to the dollar, associated with greater liberation of trade, the deregulation of monetary flows, increased inflows of external origin and the privatisation of companies and public services, recommendations that became known as the *Washington Consensus*.

According to this new model, monetary stability would result from the intervention of the respective central banks to avoid fluctuations in exchange rates and by maintaining a relative differential between domestic interest rates and those of international credit markets. The additional dollars required to maintain a satisfactory volume of foreign exchange reserves would thereby be attracted, which would guarantee the parity of the local currency against the US dollar.

Due to political upheavals during its democratisation process, the Brazilian economy was one of the last to try these new models of monetary stabilisation. The internal conditions were not so secure, so much so that the first directly elected President of the post-military Republic was removed under accusations of extensive corruption. However, before their final removal, several monetary stabilisation measures were attempted and there was intense commercial liberalisation, with the removal of several customs and tax obligations, aiming to force an increase in the competitiveness of domestic production by eliminating *protectionist barriers*. These efforts sought to align with the guidelines of the new inter-American pact, outlined in the *Initiatives for the Americas* plan, under the guidance of the George Bush government, by which the United States sought to maintain control over trade conventions and to promote political stability on the continent.

This situation would lead to a provisional government that managed the situation until the preparation of the *Real Plan*. In August 1993, there was a predicted change in the monetary standard, when the old currency was replaced by the Cruzeiro Real. Inflation rates at that time were around 35% per month and, without effective control, by early 1994 it had exceeded 40% per month. On 1st March 1994, a Provisional Measure created the Reference Unit of Value (RUV), setting conversion rules for wages and leaving the conversion of other prices free. According to this, the price system would gradually adapt to the new index until, on July 1st of that year, it would definitively convert to the new monetary standard: the Real.

At that time, the proposal to control inflation was not linked to a price freeze. The new model would be based instead on the creation of a new indexed currency (the RUV) and on the promotion of hyperinflation in the old currency (Carcanholo, 2005). In this way, it would be free to adjust prices, in Cruzeiro Real, as well as the date of its conversion to the RUV, within a pre-established period (until the end of June 1994). Salaries in general and public sector salaries were, however, compulsorily converted to RUV according to the annual base date for collective bargaining for each labour category. In fact, the so-called *inflationary tax* ended up being definitively incorporated into wages as the criterion used, because the wage levels used to calculate the average, i.e. those in effect on the days of actual payments and not those contracted, brought internal inflationary erosion of up to 40% every month.

As of 1st July 1994, wages would be adjusted annually using the base date of each category by an indicator created especially for this purpose, the Real Consumer Price Index (IPCr). However, from 1995 onwards, another Provisional Measure totally deindexed salary readjustment and even prohibited the establishment of indexation norms in collective labour agreements and conventions. This meant a radical change in the relationship between wages and prices in general, with losses for salaried families.

The plan also included exchange rate parity between the Real and the US dollar 1 to 1, which could fluctuate within a restricted range. The bet would be similar to that of the 1970s: in the absence of significant favourable balances in the Balance of Payments Current Account, maintaining a differential between domestic interest rates and those on the international loan markets would maintain a flow of resources that would guarantee a high volume of foreign exchange reserves, sufficient to avoid pressures for sudden increases of the exchange rate.

The immediate results of the *Real Plan* were a drastic and continuous reduction in rates of inflation and an acceleration in domestic production provided by the easing of consumer credit. However, anchoring the exchange rate and opening trade required attracting dollars to form a reserve and to cover the expense of imports, via foreign direct investment and external debt, which would become domestic debt. The maintenance of high interest rates internally, contrary to the argument for the need to control inflation, created, and continued to create, a differential in relation to the rates charged internationally on loans in dollars. This difference in interest rates served to stimulate companies based in Brazil, both domestic and foreign, to take external loans to lend to the Central Bank of Brazil, which started to operate with the highest interest rates in the world. This was one of the primary mechanisms for converting external debt into domestic debt.

In turn, the privatisation of companies and public services would work both ways within the proposed model: attracting foreign investment by selling state assets and, at the same time, partially financing expenses that would grow considerably with the explosion of public debt.

Furthermore, under pressure from large exporting companies, mostly associated with foreign capital, who had complained about the fictitious overvaluation of the exchange rate, several mechanisms were implemented to support exports. Among these was the financing of suppliers of inputs, machines, and equipment to exporters; facilities for closing foreign exchange operations; the financing of foreign importers of some Brazilian products and immunity of exports from the application of a fundamental tax under the responsibility of the state governments: The Tax on the Circulation of Goods and Services (ICMS), Federal Law No. 87/96, the so-called *Kandir Law*. Such incentives were not, however, sufficient to cover imports, a situation demonstrated by a continuous Balance of Trade deficit.

Faced with a drastic rise in debt levels, the official discussion publicly emphasised the persistence of the primary imbalance in budgets as one of the obstacles to inflationary control. As a result, those wishing to continue the economic policy initiated with the *Real Plan* foresaw the need for wide-ranging tax and social security reform and a drastic cut in public spending, mainly by containing staff salaries at all three federal levels (Federal, State, and Municipal). Other problems identified by the economic teams for budgetary execution, under several successive governments, was the alleged excess of resources allocated to some expenses, including constitutional transfers to states and municipalities. So, the Fiscal Stabilisation Fund (FSF) was created, later called the Unlinking of Union Resources (UUR), under which portions of some expenses constitutionally linked to the financing of essential services and the relevant transfers would now be retained in the Union, with a view to making the budget more flexible.

The largest officially awaited impact on public accounts would be from the implementation of a comprehensive reform of the Brazilian State. The diagnosis supporting the propositions advocated by the federal government was expressed by Pereira (1995: 270): "As we have already seen extensively in this book, the fundamental cause of this economic crisis was the crisis of the State. [...] Crisis that is defined as a fiscal crisis, as a crisis in the State's mode of intervention, as a crisis in the bureaucratic way in which the State is managed". From this perspective, the reform would serve, "[...] in the short term, to facilitate fiscal adjustment, particularly in states and municipalities, where there is a clear problem of excess staff; in the medium term, make public administration more efficient and modern, turning it to serve citizens" (Pereira, 1995: 282). The fiscal adjustment would thus be "[...] carried out mainly with the dismissal of employees [...], with the clear definition of the remuneration ceiling [...] and with changes in the retirement system" (Pereira, 1995: 282).

Several fronts began to guide the actions and the discussions of the federal government, expressing an explicitly liberal position. Minister Bresser Pereira tried to deflect this liberal connotation, stating that the proposal would be, "[...] the Social-Liberal State, which continues to be responsible for the provision of social rights, but which gradually ceases to directly exercise the functions of education, health, and social assistance and hire public non-state organisations to carry them out" (Pereira, 1995: 270). In practice, an extensive programme for privatising public companies was implemented, continuing the programmes of the

Collor government. After the sale of shares in several companies in the energy sector and the Vale do Rio Doce Cia mining company, expectations turned to the privatisation of telecommunications companies. In this way, the government sought to establish, "[...] a regulatory and resource transferring State, which guarantees the non-repayable financing of activities that the market is unable to carry out." (Pereira, 1995: 285)

The proposals and the implementation of effective measures for their achievement were not, however, limited to the federal administration. State governments, especially, had to immediately adapt to the new paradigm for privatisations and radical cuts in public spending. Mired in an unprecedented fiscal crisis, governors generally did not hesitate to adhere to and subordinate themselves to the new management logic, in exchange for the renegotiation of their respective internal and external public debts, based on contracts with federal government financing agencies (BNDES, etc.).

The abrupt increase in public debt was a clear demonstration that the privatisation policy did not obtain the results forecast as its justification. Quite the contrary, insofar as the loss of state assets was linked to a clear process of denationalisation, the debt trap would soon prove to be even more perverse, as can be seen below.

At the beginning of 1998, the exchange rate situation was very vulnerable. The solution found for managing the pressure to devalue the Real, was to again ask for help from the International Monetary Fund (IMF), creating, with an additional injection of loans, the conditions for maintaining a certain degree of external credibility, even if this was short-lived. After the election period of that year, the situation worsened further, and the easing of the exchange rate parity began in January 1999.

From then on, economic policy would be packaged under the name of *selective flexibility*. In place of the rigid mechanisms of exchange rate parity, a floating exchange rate system was implemented, which, within the guidelines of the agreement with the IMF, was accompanied by a monetary and fiscal policy based on predicted annual targets for inflation and primary surplus. In this way, the famous macroeconomic tripod was formed, which would dictate the norms of the new policy and have applied to all governments since then, regardless of party and the doctrinal proclivities of their respective economic teams.

So, the new century was inaugurated with a new adaptation of the Brazilian economy to the demands of the deepening international depression. Economic adjustment to the recommendations of multilateral agencies (IMF, World Bank, etc.) included selective fiscal control and the maintenance of the gradual privatisation guidelines of the remaining state-owned companies and public services. In addition to initiatives aimed at expanding the State's proposed reforms, the first two decades of the new century were marked by the creation of new institutional frameworks, which sought to ensure the attraction of foreign investments based on the following instruments: flexibility in labour legislation and in policies relating to environmental protection and traditional communities; greater regression and permissiveness in tax policy; opening of new subsidised credit lines, especially aimed at financing private mergers and acquisitions; and new production strategies that followed the creation of mega-companies amid the deepening of the global economic crisis.

Early in the period, the approval of the Fiscal Responsibility Law (N°. 101/2000) saw the management of public debt commitments being favoured, to the detriment of other public expenditure. The new tax legislation governed public spending in the three spheres of government, imposing an intense austerity regime on regional and local administrations. In addition to drastic and widespread budgetary cuts, such impositions involved the privatisation of state banks, other companies, and essential public services.

There were several periods of increased flexibility in legislation and labour rules during the mandates of governments considered to be progressive. A large part of these institutional changes was delivered through changes in the internal procedures for the inspection of labour relations, and passed through the legal process without much fanfare when compared to the measures that required constitutional and legal changes. These legislative changes resulted in clashes with the union movements, but gradually the governors delivered, with reduced resistance, a broad reform of Brazilian social protection and the regulation of labour contracts (Filgueiras & Gonçalves, 2007). The change in the pension systems, for example, imposed an increase in the minimum retirement age and the required contribution time, creating a series of difficulties in analysing the requirements, making it increasingly clear that both in private contracts and the public sector the tendency would be to favour the generalisation of capitalisation and supplementary pension schemes, all centralised by the international banking network (Batich, 2010).

If the apology for the need to reform the social protection system was framed by the intensification of the fiscal crisis and, therefore, the inevitability of greater adjustment of public accounts, then the call for greater flexibility in the regulation of labour contracts was based on the need to attract foreign investments in the face of the growing global economic crisis: *we must reduce the cost to Brazil*.

It is interesting to note that much of the initial reform of the legal labour protection apparatus occurred at the height of progressive governments in Brazil. It was the moment of creation and expansion of a series of public measures to combat poverty, focused on the those living in absolute poverty. At the same time, so-called *hard won social rights* were removed from national legislation, creating a fragile relationship between public demands and the Chief Executive, who began to grant immediate assistance, according to their priority criteria and no longer having to comply with the regulations previously recognised as being *cast in stone*. The result of this accommodation of interests, in favour of capital in crisis, reveals much regarding the selection of government priorities at the time, which were increasingly focused on increasing the popularity of the government, as the criticism attests:

> [...] the flexibility and precariousness of work are perfectly combined with focused and flexible policies to combat poverty. Both governed by the same short-term logic, inconsequential immediacy, punctual and precarious interventions, which, in order not to oppose the 'neoliberal economic order' and the World Bank's determinations, are subordinate to the realm of volatility, without intervening in the causes structural problems of Brazilian society./ In the context of research on economics and sociology of work, the vast majority of results have shown that flexibility, in its different dimensions (deregulation, changes in labour legislation, different forms of contract, subcontracting and outsourcing, flexible hours work, flexible wages, multifunctionality or versatility, forms of management and organisation inspired by Toyotism), invariably imply unemployment and precarious work. (Filgueiras & Gonçalves, 2007: 171–172)

The appeal to reduce the so-called *Cost to Brazil* was also used as pressure for changes to the National Tax Code. The most successful period of achievements of the *Real Plan* goals, namely the deregulation of capital inflows and outflows justified by the need to attract investments and the creation of alternative forms of external financing, had resulted in *tax exemptions* in relation to Income Tax and the Social Contribution on Net Profit. It even created an artifice for considering the distribution of the profits of companies as *interest on their own capital*, and exempted the transfer abroad of profits and dividends earned internally by foreign companies, including the exemption the balances derived from speculation.

The reproduction of this model of exemptions has deepened with each government in recent decades. The regressive nature of the Brazilian tax structure has worsened, increasing the relative weight of indirect taxes, while the necessary monetary adjustments have not been made in exemptions from direct taxes on wages. In addition, government officials have expanded the range of exemptions from employers' obligations (Oliveira, 2019), especially those linked to the payments to employees.

However, these efforts to attract new investments have not been enough, and a broad offer of subsidised credit via official financing agencies and a drastic reduction in environmental protection standards has been added to the strategy of easing labour laws and tax exemptions. In their eagerness to create a broad programme of mergers and acquisitions, government officials did not hesitate to adapt to a new wave of productive specialisation, identifying the economic sectors that could be fostered under the prescription of competitive insertion, based on the building of the so-called axis of integration, creating export corridors for the operations of mega-companies that manufacture primary and semi-finished products, and which would become the champions of the nation (Oliveira, 2019).

The expansion of production capacity for ores (metal and energy), steel, food (soy, meat, fruit, etc.), cellulose, and agro fuels has meant overcoming several ecological and cultural barriers. Much of the territorial expansion of these activities has been in previously protected areas, areas for the preservation of biodiversity and the culture of traditional peoples (indigenous, quilombolas, riverside dwellers, among others). Direct clashes have increased since then, around the advancement of extraction, energy, steel, and agro-industrial production in the Amazon and the Cerrado, for example, and provide a record of how much the dominant domestic interest groups, subordinate to imperialist interests, have been willing to revisit more violent forms of capital accumulation in Brazil. With this, the subordinate Brazilian State has started to revisit the original traits of its, apparently outdated, tradition, not only promoting violence, but selectively moving away from the regulation of antagonisms. This has removed some of the fundamental instruments for protecting the interests of those directly affected by the renewed expansion of the frontiers of ecological and cultural destruction, as Eliane Brum (2014) attests.

Considerations, Illustrative of Brazilian Subordination

Since the beginning of the century, Brazil's external accounts have been showing unprecedented fluctuations. After attaining positive balances in the middle of the first decade, it began to experience serious problems as it was no longer able to compensate for the continuous negative balances in the Services Balance (international travel, transportation, equipment rental, information, royalties, etc.) and in the Income Balance (profits and dividends, interest, etc.), as can be seen in Fig. 7.1.

The situation worsened, even in years when the Brazilian Trade Balance had returned to significant positive balances, because of denationalisation and the intensive specialisation of the internal productive capacity over the last decades. The export basket was totally reversed in qualitative terms. At the beginning of the twenty-first century, basic products represented around 23% of total sales of goods abroad, by 2019 they began to have a much greater weight, with approximately 52.8% of the total exported (Alves, 2020).

It is not, however, just the Trade Balance that is the villain of the current deficit, as can be seen in Figs. 7.1 and 7.2. The negative balances in payments for equipment rental services and travel abroad fluctuated substantially, added to an increase in services involving computing and information, resulting from productive specialisation. The apparently smoother situation which began in 2015, is much more the result of the worsening of economic activity in general, than of a redirection of domestic economic policy.

In the Income account, we see the results of the process of denationalisation of production capacity after the privatisations of large companies and the success of the official policy of fostering mergers and acquisitions, insofar as the remittances of profits and dividends reached unprecedented levels, especially after 2004, in terms of the volume of dollars remitted annually abroad (Fig. 7.3).

In addition to the immediate macroeconomic impacts, denationalisation has meant transferring decision-making regarding the quantity and quality of investments to centres abroad, destroying any possibility of sovereign planning regarding Brazilian production capacity both then and in the future. Without more significant Trade Balances, further remittances of profits and dividends required attracting even greater amounts of dollars via loans. Due to the choices that government officials have

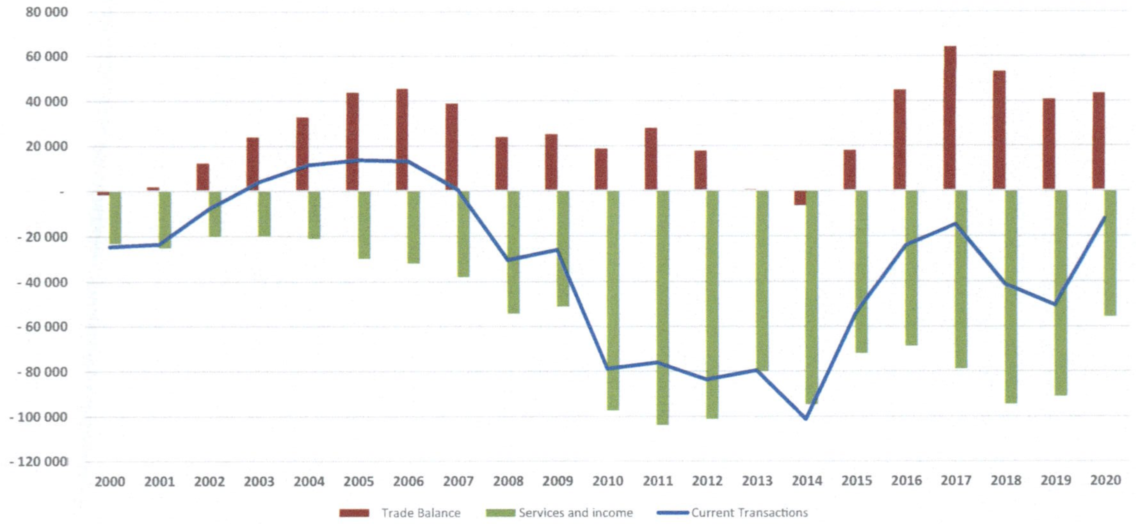

Fig. 7.1 Balance of the current transactions account—Brazil (In USD millions) (*Source* Central Bank of Brazil [2021]. Author's production)

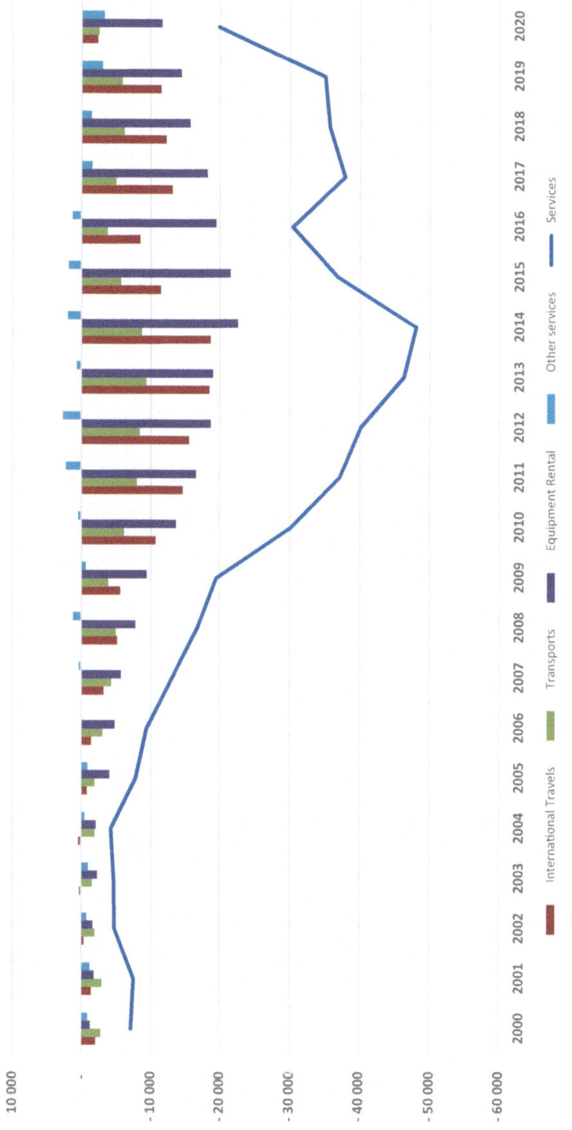

Fig. 7.2 Service account balance—Brazil (In USD millions) (*Source* Central Bank of Brazil [2021]. Author's production)

Fig. 7.3 Income account Balance—Brazil (In USD millions) (*Source* Central Bank of Brazil [2021]. Author's production)

taken since the *Real Plan*, the Brazilian economy has become more and more entangled in the external debt trap, continuously converted into internal debt, whose volumes are making it impossible to project any Brazilian sovereignty. Brazil had accumulated a stock of gross foreign debt of around USD 620 billion by mid-2020, an increase of approximately 170% from the volume of around USD 228 billion in 2001 (Banco Central Do Brasil, 2021). When considering the total volume of government bonds issued by the federal government, we see that, at the end of 1993, gross domestic debt had reached around R$ 4.99 billion. The adjustments in preparing for the *Real Plan* alone raised the total volume of securities issued to R$ 56 billion in July 1994, the month of the conversion to the new currency. Since the introduction of the Brazilian Real as the new monetary standard in Brazil, gross domestic debt has exploded, as can be seen in Table 7.1.

One of the instruments most used by the Central Bank of Brazil in its use of government bonds has been *compromised operations* (Oliveira, 2019). These operations take place daily and are the means by which the federal government remunerates banks' daily deposit balances. In this way, debt management creates diverse mechanisms for its own reproduction over time.

The fact that, until 2013, the Brazilian economy implemented the *Real Plan* model, while the government managed to generate positive balances in its annual fiscal balance, helps in understanding the current dilemmas. For a long time, the federal government reduced spending to generate this so-called Primary Surplus. With the reduction in growth rates, however, a broad tax exemption policy for private companies was implemented, thereby removing one of the main instruments for managing and rolling over debt: partial payments of previous commitments. Since

Table 7.1 Volume of Brazilian gross domestic debt securities issued (In R$ billions)

Date	*Domestic debt securities (in R$ billions)*
December 1994	65.00
December 2002	848.57
December 2009	1,947.76
December 2018	5,265.82
December 2020	6,483.30

Source Central Bank of Brazil (2021). Author's production

2014, even with all the budget cuts implemented, the primary deficit has persisted at high levels. This has led the authorities to propose desperate cuts in current investments and expenses, while trying to accelerate the privatisation of banks, infrastructure companies, postal services, growing portions of Petrobrás and its subsidiaries, and several essential services (Fig. 7.4).

In 2020, the total loss of control over macroeconomic policy became even more evident. The continuous deficits in the primary results of the central government since 2014, already declared as a tragedy, reached a level of complete despair at the inability to manage the financing of the welfare policies necessary to confront the economic conditions imposed by the Covid-19 pandemic. The difficulties in maintaining emergency aid to the poorest families, that operated precariously in 2020, justified by the explosion of the deficit in the primary results of the central government of around R$ 776 billion, demonstrates the complete bankruptcy of the management model set up since the beginning of the *Real plan*.

So, with the threat that the Brazilian economy will not be able to meet its external commitments, international risk rating agencies have demanded the maintenance of a large volume of foreign exchange reserves. At the beginning of 2021, the volume of reserves in Brazil was around USD 356 billion (Banco Central Do Brasil, 2021). As these international reserves are formed from greater indebtedness, external vulnerability has reached a level that makes a technical moratorium highly probable in relation to the short-term commitments. Furthermore, short-term dollar flows have totalled an average external liability of approximately USD 1.5 trillion in recent times, which further complicates the risk of strangulation.

It is in this way that we can better understand the intensification of national dilemmas over the last four years: as a clear manifestation of the despair of the Brazilian elite as it loses the ability to satisfy their historical mission within the imperialist order. In view of the evident indicators of the collapse of the main anchors of monetary stabilisation policies generated since the *Real Plan*, reliance has fallen on ever greater doses of selective fiscal austerity, alienation of what remained of state assets, tax exemption for business operations, dismantling the social protection of working families, legalisation allowing even more precarious forms of employment, and the deregulation of the main instruments of environmental protection. The intensification of these measures by the government of the time resulted in the impeachment of 2016, when

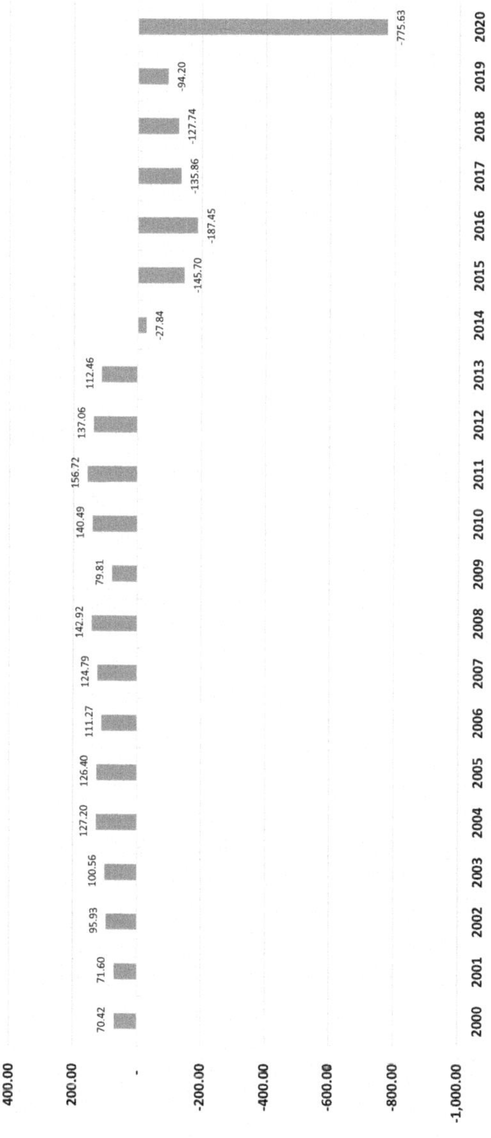

Fig. 7.4 Evolution of the Fiscal Surplus in Brazil (in R$ millions) (*Source* Brasil [2021]. Price in January 2021. IPCA. Author's production)

conservative forces joined with traditional opportunism in their eagerness to generate new opportunities for the appropriation of booty.

However, the union of forces built to remove the ability to maintain the process of successive progressive governments soon dissolved. The degree of political dislocation became more striking with this tragic change, and the absence of a solution like the one put in place between 1993 and 1994. As a result, the high level of political fragmentation of Brazilian elites prevented them from keeping the political successions under their control and opened a vacuum that resulted in the election, in 2018, of a leader averse to any rationality. More than that, a head of state was elected whose speciality has been the use of irrationalism as a way of legitimising his barbarities, and which placed on the official agenda the creating of opportunities for even more intense forms of violent accumulation, based on the motto "I did not come to build, I came to destroy that thing" (sic) (Freitas, 2019).

In their desperation, at the beginning of the third decade of the twenty-first century, the Brazilian subordinate elites created the opportunity to experiment with the *realm of informality*. This is a moment of great tension, in which the elite are seeking to legitimise more violent forms of accumulation, even risking the permanent loss of the political ability to manage internal conflicts, while remaining the privileged guardians of one of the greatest strategic natural heritages of the planet.

Concluding in the early 1990s, looking at what seemed to be the end of the developmentalist dream started more than half a century ago, the economist Celso Furtado (1992) set out the now famous interpretation that Brazil resembled an interrupted construction. From the point of view of criticism of the myth of *Brazil-power*, however, it seems no exaggeration to say that the reforms initiated at that time could have been an opportunity to deconstruct an illusion. But the stakes have moved in another direction.

It now seems clear that, far from being a state of exception, the turn of the third decade of the twenty-first century in Brazil is explicitly a stage of exasperation due to its subordinate historical integration within the imperialist hierarchy. There is profound desperation in an era of real intensification of the contradictions of capital generally, but which has taken on an even more tragic flavour in this part of the world, where barbarism has reached the extreme of pouring military arms and paramilitaries into urban and rural slums, and into indigenous villages, aimed at the resistant roots of the Brazilian people. Meanwhile, the most privileged representatives of the nation's elites, referenced in *Forbes* and other publications, have no way to hide the failure of their subordinate function anymore, as they draw from their tax havens (OS 300 DE Luxembourg, 2021) the fruits of their mediocrity: the crumbs they have managed to retain, as a reward, from the current violent management of the tropical traits of the senility of capitalism.

References

Alves, J. E. D. (2020). *A balança comercial em 2019 e a especialização regressiva brasileira*. Ecodebate. Available at: https://www.ecodebate.com.br/2020/01/08/a-balanca-comercial-em-2019-e-a-especializacao-regressiva-brasileira-artigo-de-jose-eustaquio-diniz-alves/. Acessed 9 January 2021.

Anderson, P. (2015). *A política externa norte-americana e seus teóricos*. Boitempo.

Banco Central Do Brasil. (2021). *Tabelas Especiais*. Available at: https://www.bcb.gov.br/estatisticas/tabelasespeciais. Acessed 8 fev. 2021.

Batich, M. (2010). A Previdência Social sob a Mira dos Fundos de Pensão. In R. M. Marques & M. R. J. Ferreira (Eds.), *O Brasil sob a nova ordem: a economia brasileira contemporânea, uma análise dos governos Collor a Lula*. Saraiva.

Belluzzo, L. G. de Mello, & Coutinho, R. (Orgs.). (1982). *Desenvolvimento capitalista no Brasil: ensaios sobre a crise*. Brasiliense.

Brasil. (2021). *Secretaria do Tesouro Nacional. Séries Temporais*. Disponível em: https://www.tesourotransparente.gov.br/visualizacao/series-temporais-do-tesouro-nacional. Acesso: 28 fev. 2021.

Brasil: nunca mais. (2021). Disponível em: http://bnmdigital.mpf.mp.br/pt-br/. Acesso em 28 January 2021.

Brum, E. (2014). *Belo Monte: a anatomia de um etnocídio. El País*. Available at: https://brasil.elpais.com/brasil/2014/12/01/opinion/1417437633_930086.html. Acessed 15 January 2021.

Carcanholo, M. D. (2005). *A vulnerabilidade econômica do Brasil*. Ideias e Letras.

Cruz, P. D. (1984). *Dívida externa e política econômica: a experiência brasileira nos anos setenta*. BRASILIENSE.

Draibe, S. (1985). *Rumos e metamorfoses: Estado e industrialização no Brasil—1930/1960*. Paz e Terra.

Evans, Peter. (1980). *A tríplice aliança: As multinacionais, as estatais e o capital nacional no desenvolvimento dependente brasileiro*. ZAHAR.

Fernandes, Florestan. (2006). *A revolução burguesa no Brasil: Ensaio de interpretação sociológica* (5th ed.). Globo.

Filgueiras, L. A. M., & Goncalves, R. (2007). *A economia política do governo Lula*. Contraponto.

Freitas, J. de. (2019). *Duas obviedades: com fogo na Amazônia, Bolsonaro descumpre a Constituição e desrespeita tratados*. Folha de São Paulo. 25 ago. 2019. Available at: https://www1.folha.uol.com.br/colunas/janiodefreitas/2019/08/duas-obviedades.shtml. Acess: 28 fev. 2021.

Furtado, Celso. (1992). *A construção interrompida*. Paz e Terra.

Mandel, E. (1982). *O capitalismo tardio*. Abril Cultural. (Os Economistas).

Marini, R. M. (2000). *A dialética da dependência*Vozes. CLACSO.

Martins, J. de S. . (1986). *O cativeiro da terra* (3rd ed.). HUCITEC.

Mathias, G., & Salama, P. (1983). *O Estado superdesenvolvido: das metrópoles ao terceiro mundo*. BRASILIENSE.

Mello, G. M. de Cavalcanti, & Sabadini, M. de Souza (Eds.). (2019). *Financial speculation and fictitious profits: A Marxist analysis*. Palgrave Macmillan/Springer International.

Oliveira, C. A. B. de. (2003). *Processo de industrialização: do capitalismo originário ao atrasado*. Editora UNESP. UNICAMP.

Oliveira, F. A . (2019). *Governo Lula, Dilma e Temer: Do espetáculo do crescimento ao inferno da recessão e da estagnação (2003–2018)*. Letra Capital.

OS 300 De Luxemburgo. (2021). *Piauí*. Available at: https://piaui.folha.uol.com.br/OS-300-DE-LUXEMBURGO/#. Acess: 08 fev. 2021.

Pereira, L. C. B. (1995). *Crise econômica e reforma do Estado no Brasil: para uma nova interpretação da américa Latina*. Editora 34.

Prado Jr, C. (1966). *A revolução brasileira*. BRASILIENSE.

Rego, J. M., & Marques, R. M. (Orgs.). (2003). *Formação Econômica do Brasil*. Saraiva.

Skidmore, T. (2010). *De Getúlio à Castelo (1930–1964)*. Companhia das Letras.

Teixeira, Aloísio. (1993). *O movimento da industrialização nas economias capitalistas centrais no pós-guerra*. UFRJ/IEI.

CHAPTER 8

Final Words

Gustavo Moura de Cavalcanti Mello
and Henrique Pereira Braga

From our analyses, it is evident that the ongoing catastrophe in Brazil has been disastrous. By mid-March 2021, even allowing for underreporting, Brazil had lost more than 300,000 people to Covid-19. Even when faced with the imminent and unprecedented collapse of the national health system, the federal government continued its crusade against social isolation measures, defending fanciful "early treatments" and even ruling out the use of masks and mourning the victims.[1] Since the beginning of the pandemic, and encouraged by Jair Bolsonaro, crowds of supporters have periodically protested the "lockdown", based on a, sometimes tacit, sometimes explicit, defence of social Darwinism (Silva, 2020), and feeding the false disjunctive of, "economy versus life".

G. M. de C. Mello (✉) · H. P. Braga
Department of Economics, Federal University of Espírito Santo, Vitória, Brazil
e-mail: gustavo.m.mello@ufes.br

H. P. Braga
e-mail: henrique.p.braga@ufes.br

G. M. de C. Mello and H. P. Braga (eds.), *Wealth and Poverty in Contemporary Brazilian Capitalism*, Marx, Engels, and Marxisms,
https://doi.org/10.1007/978-3-030-82298-9_8

At a point when this calamitous situation was already well defined, the minister responsible for the Environment portfolio, in a meeting of Bolsonaro and his ministers, summarised the strategy: to take advantage of the context of the pandemic to "place the cattle"[2] above environmental legislation and open vast territories in the Cerrado and in the Amazon and Pantanal regions for the extraction and agricultural industries and for real estate speculation. Since then, this policy has been diligently implemented through the regularisation of illegal land-grabbing, the pardoning of environmental crimes, an offensive against environmental, indigenous, and quilombola reserves and the dismantling of inspection and environmental protection bodies.[3] The result has been a significant increase in the rates of deforestation and wildfires, and of rural conflicts, with killings of native populations (Pastoral Land Commission, 2021). This strategy has not been limited to the environmental sphere and has spread across a wide variety of state actions: from urban licensing to civilian arms policy[4]; from education policy[5] to sanitation policy (Marques et.al., 2021). It has affected monetary policy, with the formal autonomy of the Central Bank (Complementary Bill 19 2019) and through the liberalisation of the foreign exchange market, the expansion of the use of foreign currency in Brazil, and other related measures (Bill 5.387). This is not to mention privatisation policies (Cardoso Jr, 2020), the dismantling of "social" policies (Bravo et al., 2020), and the so-called "institutional reforms" (labour, social security, tax, administrative, etc.), that have deepened and accelerated the worsening of living conditions for Brazilian workers over recent years.

Despite the deliberate boycotting of strategies to combat the transmission of the virus, in the name of individual "freedom" and the "economy", from the perspective of capital accumulation the results were drastic: in 2020 Brazilian GDP fell 4.1% and GDP per capita fell 4.8%. At the beginning of 2021, more than 14 million workers were unemployed, others were discouraged, and more than 20% of the population were living below the poverty line. This seriousness of the situation was only lessened by state policies introduced by the National Congress, such as emergency financial aid to those who had lost their income due to the pandemic–belatedly approved, after much resistance from the federal government–and funding, subsidies, and tax incentives for entrepreneurs. It is worth mentioning in passing, that after the implementation of this emergency aid, the federal government was "surprised" by the existence of around 50 million "invisible" Brazilians–considered disposable–who did not meet at least one of the requirements necessary to access this aid (having a civil registry or a cell phone with internet and a bank account).[6]

As expected, the largest financial and non-financial companies were by far the main beneficiaries of such policies (as well as a binge on the stock markets). The net worth of the 400 largest publicly traded companies in Brazil rose over the course of 2020, while a large proportion of small and medium-sized companies dropped (Pinto, 2020). In addition, following a worldwide trend, the fortunes of Brazilian businesspeople on the world rich list, produced by Forbes, grew 54.82% in 2020, and the net worth of Brazilian billionaires who invest in health-related companies increased by 134.76% over the same period.[7]

As argued throughout the book, under a dynamic of capital accumulation marked by chronic over-accumulation and the prominence of its fictitious forms, the predatory tendencies of capital are sharpened. There is pressure on the working population through the intensification of work, increased working hours, the perfecting of mechanisms for the subsumption and control of work, the exacerbation of competition, and structural unemployment, all in a situation of a growing relative overpopulation. This was combined with the proliferation of the expropriation and exploitation of indigenous populations, or those not really subsumed to capital, and of the natural environment in general, reduced to being merely inputs or obstacles to capitalist expansion. Violence and material and existential poverty reveal themselves as the counterpoint of the capitalist "bonanza", with increasing material wealth produced by the impoverishment of workers.

In the protests against social isolation measures, car horns were blasted in front of hospitals alongside[8] lively choreographies involving cardboard coffins and other props.[9] There were calls for "military intervention now", and even the motto "work makes you free" was used (Guerreiro, 2021), once displayed on the gates of Auschwitz. In other words, "naked life" is affirmed here. Life is denied, because it has been reduced to being the support and substance of capital and, consequently, to mere potential abstract work. Ultimately, a life ready to be vampirised by the "automatic subject".

In these terms, the murderous and suicidal character of capital, the "contradiction in process", which threatens humanity and other living beings with its economic, military, and environmental holocausts, tends to produce destructive and even self-destructive individuals (Safatle, 2020). Politically, in Brazil, this tendency is at the root of the rise of extreme right-wing social forces and the election of Jair Bolsonaro, which translated the prospect of the collapse of capitalism into properly eschatological worldviews, and which supported the accelerationist practices mentioned above. It is worth remembering that currently, such practices are in line with the "new time in the world" (Arantes, 2014) but to see that, it is necessary to step back a little.

In understanding the relationship between the centre and periphery, the chasm between the modern and the backward–or between civilization and nature, between culture and barbarism–what conventional economic thinking identified in a dualistic way really formed a contradictory whole, within which, for example, the generalisation of wage labour in central capitalist countries has modern slavery as its counterpart (Alencastro, 2020; Williams, 2014). As well as the forming of nation-states and their "lines of friendship and enmity", the state of permanent exception in the peripheral countries had a counterpart (Kurz, 2005). Such processes were contemporary to the practices that characterised the period of the starting of the engines of capital reproduction in the context of "original accumulation"–torture, compulsory labour, murder, and the expropriation of land–that were then perpetuated in the peripheries of the "modern system for producing goods" (Kurz, 1993).

It should be noted that the arrow of time, or the "temporalisation of history" (Koseleck, 2003), was fired when capital emerged onto its stage–the world market–creating a unified but profoundly unequal global space, characterised by the simultaneity of the asynchronous, by the coexistence of immeasurable realities, and co-pertinently and hierarchically ordered (Tupinambá, 2020).

In recent decades, with the worsening of capitalist barbarism, the prospect of global "convergence" and the modernisation of the peripheries dissolved, and with this the ideology of progress was further weakened, with the almost total foreshortening the horizon of expectations. In this new era, two tendencies have prevailed: that of managing barbarism, in the sense of postponing the end of time (Anders, 2013), and that with an apocalyptic leaning,[10] which seeks to accelerate the end of the world. Both share the fatalism and the perception that, deep down, "there is no alternative".

In this critical context, combining advanced surveillance technology with elementary forms of direct violence and the use of brute force in countries such as Brazil, paradigmatic patterns of labour force exploitation and social control, marked by the military and militia management of social life and the dynamics of territorial confinement, seem to emerge, that are then added to the mass incarceration and the systematic genocide of the most impoverished sections of the population. So, the peripheral countries of the capitalist system seem to generate social dynamics that tend to spread, with the appropriate updates, to the countries at the centre, according to the propositions of Mbembe (2019), about the "world becoming black", or of Arantes (2004), on the Brazilianisation of the world.

By dealing with the different dimensions of this process, with an emphasis on social divides, the plundering character of capital reproduction in human and environmental terms, its impacts on the labour market, taking into account its patriarchal determinations, the dynamics of financialisation, the effects of geopolitical disputes, and the specificities of Brazil's economic formation and its recent evolution, the chapters of this book contribute, in our opinion, by characterising contemporary capitalism from the Brazilian perspective, which allows us, because of the specific form of Brazilian society's insertion into the world market, to point out the current trends of the capital society. From this point of view, in the light of the principal trends of global capital accumulation, the Brazilian reality becomes both intelligible and gains in intelligibility.

Notes

1. Cf., for example, https://www1.folha.uol.com.br/poder/2021/03/relembre-o-que-bolsonaro-ja-disse-sobre-a-pandemia-de-gripezinha-e-pais-de-maricas-a-frescura-e-mimimi.shtml and https://www1.folha.uol.com.br/equilibrioesaude/2021/03/para-atacar-isolamento-bolsonaro-faz-declaracoes-falsas-sobre-oms-atestados-de-obito-e-stf.shtml.
2. Cf. https://www.youtube.com/watch?v=TjndWfgiRQQ.
3. Cf. https://www.oeco.org.br/noticias/retrospectiva-da-boiada-qual-foi-a-maior-de-2020-e-qual-devemos-temer-em-2021/.
4. Cf. https://www.cnnbrasil.com.br/politica/2021/02/15/desde-inicio-do-governo-bolsonaro-mudou-31-vezes-a-politica-de-armas-no-brasil.
5. Cf. https://educacao.estadao.com.br/noticias/geral,passam-a-boiada-no-mec,70003654960.
6. Cf. https://globoplay.globo.com/v/8511033/.
7. Cf. https://forbes.com.br/forbes-money/2021/02/bilionarios-brasileiros-da-area-da-saude-sao-os-que-mais-ganharam-dinheiro-durante-a-pandemia/.

8. Cf. https://www.em.com.br/app/noticia/nacional/2021/03/14/interna_nacional,1246577/carreata-faz-buzinaco-em-hospital-superlotado-de-pacientes-com-covid-no-rs.shtml.
9. Cf.https://www.correiobraziliense.com.br/app/noticia/politica/2020/05/09/interna_politica,853123/bolsonaristas-dancam-com-caixao-e-negam-10-mil-mortes-mata-muito-men.shtml.
10. The removal of the horizon of expectation and the tendency towards the concretisation of the present which it engenders, bringing present and future closer together, create the perception of an acceleration, which was traditionally a sign of the "millennium". In the words of Lactâncio, "Then the year, the same and the day will be shortened; and 'this is the senescence and decrepitude of the world', according to Trismegisto. When these things happen, we must know that the moment has come when God will return to transform this world" (Koseleck, 2003, p. 49).

References

Anders, G. (2013). Teses para a Era Atômica. *Sopro*, n. 87. Disponível em: http://culturaebarbarie.org/sopro/outros/anders.html#.XyWskOdv_IU.

Arantes, P. (2004). A fratura brasileira do mundo. In *Zero à esquerda*. Conrad.

Arantes, P. (2014). O novo tempo do mundo: a experiência da história numa era das expectativas decrescentes. In P. Arantes (Eds.), *O novo tempo do mundo*. Boitempo.

Bravo, M. I. S., Matos, M. C., Freire, S. M. F., & (Org.). (2020). *Políticas sociais e ultra neoliberalismo*. Navegando Publicações.

Cardoso Jr., J. C. (2020). *Brasil Rumo à Catástrofe: desmonte do Estado e condições para superação da crise*. AFIPEA, Nota técnica n. 12.

Comissão Pastoral da Terra. (2021). *2020: o fim do mundo... como o conhecemos*. Disponível em: https://www.cptnacional.org.br/publicacoes-2/destaque/5467-2020-o-ano-do-fim-do-mundo-como-o-conhecemos.

De Alencastro, L. F. (2020). *O trato dos viventes: formação do Brasil no Atlântico Sul*. Companhia das Letras.

Guerreiro, I. A. (2021). Lockdown: o problema e o falso problema. *Passa Palavra*. Disponível em: https://passapalavra.info/2021/03/136800/.

Koseleck, R. (2003). *Aceleración, Prognosis y Secularización*. Pre-textos.

Kurz, R. (1993). *O colapso da modernização: da derrocada do socialismo de caserna à crise da economia mundial*. Paz & Terra.

Kurz, R. (2005). *Imperialismo de exclusão e estado de exceção*. Disponível em. http://www.obeco-online.org/rkurz415.pdf.

Marques, D. H. F., Cançado, C. J., & de campos Souza, P. (2021). *Reflexões sobre o novo marco regulatório do saneamento básico: possíveis impactos no planejamento de Minas Gerais*. FJP.

Mbembe, A. (2019). *Crítica da razão negra*. N-1 Edições.
Pinto, E. C. (2020). "O andar de cima não apoia o impeachment". Disponível em: https://www.youtube.com/watch?v=DPjBMPdbMMM.
Safatle. V. (2020) *Bem-vindo ao Estado suicidário*. N-1 Edições (Série Pandemia Crítica).
Silva, V. H. (2020). A hora do abate. *Passa Palavra*. Disponível em: https://passapalavra.info/2020/05/131744/.
Tupinambá, G. (2020). Um pensador na periferia da História. *Revista Porto Alegre*. Disponível em. http://revistaportoalegre.com/um-pensador-na-periferia-da-historia/.
Williams, E. (2014). *Capitalism and slavery*. UNC Press Books.

Index

G. M. de C. Mello and H. P. Braga (eds.), *Wealth and Poverty in Contemporary Brazilian Capitalism*, Marx, Engels, and Marxisms, https://doi.org/10.1007/978-3-030-82298-9

F

G

I

M

O

P

R

S

The manufacturer's authorised representative in the EU is Springer Nature Customer Service Centre GmbH, Europaplatz 3, 69115 Heidelberg, Germany. If you have any concerns regarding our products, please contact ProductSafety@springernature.com

Printed and bound by CPI Group (UK) Ltd, Croydon, CR0 4YY
30/09/2026
02225700-0003